RETIRING FROM MILITARY SERVICE

RETIRING FROM MILITARY SERVICE

A COMMONSENSE GUIDE

SECOND EDITION

K. C. Jacobsen

Naval Institute Press
Annapolis, Maryland

Library of Congress Cataloging-in-Publication Data

Jacobsen, K. C. (Kenneth C.)
     Retiring from military service : a commonsense guide / K.C.
Jacobsen. — 2nd ed.
          p.   cm.
     Includes bibliographical references and index.
     ISBN 1-55750-401-6 (acid-free paper)
     1. Retired military personnel—United States.   2. Retired military
personnel—Life skills guides. 3. Retired military personnel—
—Employment. I. Title.
UB357.J35 1994
362.86'0973—dc20   94-7805

     Printed in the United States of America on acid-free paper ∞

                    9 8 7 6 5 4 3 2

                         First printing

For Carol, Susan, Kristin, and Kasey,

who were there for the hard part.

CONTENTS

9

PREFACE
TO
THE SECOND EDITION

When the first edition of this book was conceived and written, transition from military to civilian life was an experience known by many but studied by few. Except for the help offered by people like Stan Hyman and organizations like The Retired Officers Association (TROA) and the Non Commissioned Officers Association (NCOA), retiring from the service was mostly a do-it-yourself process.

The massive force reductions of the '90s changed all that. In 1989 the phrase "military to civilian transition" began to appear in the *Congressional Record*, and before long both the Department of Defense (DOD) and the Department of Labor were gearing up new programs to assist people leaving the service. Today there's a transitions office in the Pentagon and there are transition-assistance offices at most military installations. Transition has become a big business.

As good as DOD programs are, they were designed to meet a particular need and can't offer all the assistance needed by the "full-term" retiree. There's a big difference between the life situation of a thirty-year-old E-5 and that of an O-6 or E-9 finishing a career. Service-transition programs can help both groups, but for the careerist they're only the beginning, a first step in a lifelong process of change and redirection.

The second edition of *Retiring from Military Service* will, I hope, continue to give a wider insight into this varied, exciting, and often confusing process. While recognizing the value of organized transition programs as an adjunct to the total retirement process, I also remain convinced that making that huge leap from the military to the civilian world is a major turning point in life, one that involves a lot more than figuring out what you are going to do for a living.

At the time the first edition was written there were many opportunities for retired military people to move into defense-related jobs. For some it almost made the gruesome chore of a job search unnecessary. That's not true anymore, and the need for more education or training is far more important than it once was. The "back to school" alternative now deserves much more serious thought than you might have given it in the past. For the retiree of the '90s, education and the ability to learn new skills will be almost a requirement.

American society and the American workplace are going through great changes in the last decade of the twentieth century. Some areas like medical care are still in flux. The traditional definitions of "work" and "retirement" are being questioned, and in the future we may see a radical transformation in how we view these activities. At the same time, other issues, like finding a new career and adjusting to civilian life, have not fundamentally changed. Common sense and the experience of your military career are still valuable assets. They always will be.

Surrounded by change, we constantly hear of the necessity for people and institutions to "reinvent themselves" (whatever that means). For someone nearing the end of a military career it may seem that this need for reinvention will require a major personal makeover, that the last twenty-plus years of our lives will have to be put on a shelf somewhere, beside the old jungle boots and the ratty flight jacket.

Don't believe that for a minute. Every public-opinion poll taken this decade has shown that the American people have more respect for the military services than they do for most other institutions in modern society. Despite the trauma of Vietnam and the endless stress of the Cold War, the American military establishment has emerged as one of the few organizations still capable of doing what it is supposed to. And people like you and me made it that way.

So don't expect this book to help you reinvent yourself. What it *will* suggest is that you take the professionalism and skill you have used for most of your adult life and apply them to the challenges of the world you are about to enter. You will have to work hard at transition, and yes, you will have to adapt to a changing society. But you will also find that the values and experience you've gained during your military career will help you every step of the way.

In 1989, when I was finishing the original manuscript of this book, I made a surprising discovery. Rereading the words I had written over the months, I began to realize that the process of writing the book had not only been a project to complete, it had also been the journal of a personal voyage. My own fears, successes and failures, frustrations, and occasional insights were all there on paper. The process I tried to describe was not just something that happened to other people, it was something that was happening to *me*.

Well, I survived it. I even took some of my own advice, and after eight years of civilian life. I'm not the guy in the sailor suit anymore. I will always cherish the values learned and the friends made during my twenty-six years in uniform—they have not failed me yet. And when I see a destroyer standing out to sea on a bright morning, there's still a little part of me out there with her. At the same time, I've also learned to respect the quiet valor of my civilian friends whose battles are not commemorated by any campaign ribbons but who nevertheless live their days with dignity and honor. They are not so different after all. The frontier we cross when we leave military life behind us does not lead to a strange and puzzling place. It leads to our very selves.

Newport News
December 1993

RETIRING FROM MILITARY SERVICE

1

A NEW LOOK
AT RETIRING

◆

If there is one word that exemplifies a love-hate relationship, it is *retirement*. Most of us pretend that we look forward to retiring, reluctant to admit that deep inside a tiny dread simmers, a little fear of the unknown, and maybe just a little of that ancient refusal to accept that somewhere, sometime, all the things basic to our everyday lives will come to an end. Leafing through one of the glossy little pamphlets that advertise retirement communities, we look at photos of bronzed, silver-haired men and sprightly women, dressed for some outdoor game. We want to believe that the game is golf or tennis, but in our hearts we know it's shuffleboard.

In our society the very word *retirement* conjures up pictures of people who are out of the mainstream of life. Even the dictionary seems to encourage this gloomy image. Definitions drip with words like *withdraw, go apart, no longer active,* and the ultimate insult—*to go to bed.* But the dictionary does not leave us completely without hope.

Way at the bottom of the list of definitions we see "Retirement: An orderly withdrawal of a military force, according to plan, without pressure from the enemy." Now that's more like it!

The biggest problem most military people have with the idea of retiring is very simple and understandable; we're just not ready for it . . . yet. Most of us leave active duty in our forties or fifties, right in the middle of the most productive period of our lives. Throughout our careers we have directed our energies toward preparing for the next promotion or a higher level of responsibility. Now suddenly there are no more heights to reach and (we think) no place to go. One day you are a person with a place, a well-defined position in life, and everything that goes with it, and the next you are a retiree. Somehow the future has crept up and blindsided you.

Surprise! It doesn't have to be like that. Whether you realize it or not, your situation as a retiring military careerist is unique in the job world, and, even more important, it presents you with some opportunities that your civilian contemporaries would kill for. In midlife, at a time when many people are beginning to discover that the light at the end of their career tunnel is a neon sign that reads "dead end," you are being handed the keys to a brand-new life and more freedom of choice than you have had since you were a kid.

This is a book about that opportunity and what it can mean to you. It is not an administrative check-off list or a do-it-yourself psychoanalysis kit. Instead, it is a straightforward look at the process of moving from one life to another, a bridge between the familiar territory that has been home for so many years and a new place that at first may seem a little foggy and maybe even dangerous.

This book came into being because my own experience and that of a lot of old friends and shipmates convinced me that there was something lacking in almost everything we had read or heard about retirement. The books, the seminars, and the checklists were all there, and in bewildering profusion, but there was nothing that captured the very personal nature of the experience and put it in the perspective it deserves. The books and seminars on career transition came at me in a solid phalanx of blue pinstripe, scolding and nagging about networking and résumés, while the "experts" on second careers sneered at my career achievements and showed me clever devices that I could use to disguise my military experience as some bland civilian job. I began to get the unpleasant sensation that perhaps my future lay in the direction of being a full-time horrible example, doomed, like some twentieth-century Flying Dutchman, to wander forever, tattered résumés in hand, gravy stains on my red tie, in the corridors of unknown corporations.

And then the light dawned. One morning as I sat at my typewriter composing yet another saccharine cover letter to accompany my evasive résumé for a job I didn't really want with a company I knew nothing about, I began laughing. The situation was so absurd and yet so serious. It was then that I started to think about why it was that I could laugh instead of opening a vein or signing up for a college course in depression. I realized that all the funny, frightening, and dangerous experiences of twenty-six years in the navy were not wasted. They had prepared me for just this moment. The sense of humor and the ability to take almost any surprise in stride without losing one's perspective were valuable assets for retirement that I had been ignoring.

The adaptability learned through years of experience at becoming an instant expert on any matter with ACTION stamped on it and writing authoritative point papers on topics I could barely spell was something that I should be using to my advantage instead of warping my mind trying to think like a civilian. And I didn't have to hate myself while I was doing it. Rather than trying to force whatever small amount of insight and wisdom I had into a new and uncomfortable mold, why not concentrate on using it to translate this new set of civilian operational requirements into something I could handle on more familiar terms?

This book is an attempt at that translation. It looks at retiring as a complete process, from the time the decision is made through a period ending about a year after the retirement date. I have drawn freely on my own experience and that of many other friends and shipmates who have gone before me. In evaluating subjects like résumés, interviewing, and other standard job search matters, I do not propose any radical departures from accepted conventions; my purpose is not to pay homage to these icons in new ways but to look at them with the slightly raised eyebrow (and occasional snicker) they deserve.

There is something different about conversations with friends on a Sunday night. In those closing hours of the weekend, when the start of a new week is only hours away, there seems to be more of an atmosphere of introspection in what people talk about, a need to have questions answered and to encounter Monday with the hope of fresh starts and new possibilities. It is on Sunday nights that the big question about retiring often comes up. And when the discussion begins to wind down and the latest rumors, horror stories, and anecdotes have been exhausted, almost any recent retiree who is present can expect the inevitable challenge: "Well, what's it *really* like?"

The purpose of this book is to offer some answers to that question.

HOW TO READ THIS BOOK

The nine chapters in this book are organized chronologically, beginning with the decision to retire and ending with a retrospective on the process from the viewpoint of later life. The sequence in which retirement milestones occur will be roughly similar for everyone, but the time between various phases will depend on individual situations. You may wish to begin a job search months or even years before your actual retirement date. Choices about where to live after retirement may have been made long ago and future career paths already selected. You may be years from retirement when you read this book, you may already be retired, or you may be smack in the middle of the preretirement process.

For the greatest benefit, read the entire book regardless of where you are on the retirement road. Almost no one remembers to do everything right, and most decisions and choices can be made at different times than are suggested. Except for some of the key preretirement actions, there is no timetable but your own and no downchecks for late arrival at an imaginary milestone. The better organized among us will complete a skills inventory (Chapter 3) and choose a career field long before they are out of uniform; others will want to get out into the world, sniff the air, and then decide what to do. The crucial thing is to know what you are doing no matter when you end up doing it.

The last three chapters deal mostly with life after career, job, and location decisions have been made. This phase can begin months or years after retirement, but it is rooted in the actions we take before leaving the service. To a great extent, what happens in later life will depend on what you do in the period immediately before and after departure from active duty. So if a look into the future lights any lights or rings any alarms, now is a good time to act.

The book has been written primarily for officers and senior enlisted people of all services.* Procedures, nomenclature, and other details may differ among the various branches, but we all share the experience of retiring from active duty. Challenges, problems, and opportunity have much more to do with human nature than with service affiliation. Our concern with the issues facing us during the passage from military to civilian life is a universal feeling regardless of uniform or rank.

THE DECISION

The first decision that must be made about retiring, and maybe the hardest one, is to do it. It may come at you in any number of ways, from the completely planned approach dictated by an agenda you set a long time ago, to the realization that comes when you look out the window one day and realize that your biological clock is trying to tell you something. Or maybe it happens on that morning when you are preparing to brief yet another new boss and suddenly realize that you are beginning to feel as stale as the three-year-old coffee stains on your briefing notes. The old enthusiasm, the drive to make a good impression, just isn't there anymore, and you begin to think it may be time for a change. The last time you talked to the assignment people about a new job there was a lot of forced joviality and some embarrassingly long silences on both ends of the line, and at the end of the conversation you realized that all the options that were suggested were jobs that you used to

---

*This book was written for both men and women but for consistency of style the personal pronoun *he* has been used in most instances.

call preretirement billets. There's nothing wrong with it except that it is a horizontal move. Your career can continue if you wish, right up to the thirty-year point and perhaps even beyond, but from now on there will probably be fewer and fewer new things to fill your day and, more often, the nagging feeling that you have done it all before.

Admittedly, those worries don't apply to everyone. You can gain much genuine job satisfaction from finally being allowed to do the kind of work you know well without having to worry about what will be next on the career ladder. In fact, the chance to do a job without having to look over your shoulder for the selection board can be a liberating experience and a great way to freshen up your outlook.

It's also possible that your retirement may be mandated by military force reductions, medical reasons, or other factors beyond your control. If this happens, the very first step in your transition process should be to accept the situation. Like it or not, the decision has been made for you. It's final. Nothing you can do will change that. Refusing to accept the unpleasant reality or becoming permanently angry and resentful about it can sap your energy and distort your outlook. You'll be starting the most important race of your life with your shoelaces tied together.

Regardless of whether your retirement is a result of your conscious planning, a directive from above, or your willingness to drift along until it becomes impossible to evade a decision, the time comes to start the machinery in motion. It may not be the best time, it may not come the way you expected, but there it is. Ready or not, you're off.

Start by letting your family in on the secret. It's probably no surprise to them anyway, but you might find out that they are just as nervous about the subject as you are. Until now, the retirement plans that have been discussed over so many cups of after-dinner coffee seemed less than real.

From now on they will be very important, so before you think of making an irrevocable decision, be sure that everyone in the family has been heard from. If you are single, tell your dog. Your pet will appreciate it and you will get the chance to form the words "I am retiring" in front of an uncritical and sympathetic audience.

The need for family participation in a retirement decision may seem obvious to most people, but it is amazing how easily a misunderstanding can begin if it isn't done right. Your spouse has probably seen you storm into the house a dozen times, swearing that you are going to put your letter in tomorrow, and this time you mean it, seriously. Spouses become so inured to this ritual that when you mention the real thing you are in the same position as the boy who cried wolf.

A full, no-holds-barred discussion with all members of your family is an absolute necessity. They may have an agenda that you don't know very much about and it could include things that won't fit in with your plans. But if the planning for your future is done in a way that includes your family's desires, you will find that in those difficult moments that are bound to come during the next year or so, support will be available when you need it.

Transition to a completely new life can be just as big a challenge to your family as it is to you. Over the years you have probably grumbled more than a little about attending awards ceremonies and changes of command, moving every few years to a new home, or being called away in the middle of the night to handle some mysterious crisis. Families complain about these things, too, and secretly long for a magic land of stability where everything is simple and each day is like an episode of "Father Knows Best." But they don't always mean it. The excitement of a military life is something that family members get hooked on, just as you did. The teenage daughter who tried to handcuff herself to the porch railing rather than leave her old high school may find herself feeling a little less special when she realizes that from now on she will be a permanent resident for the first time, just like all the other kids. The friends that your spouse has made over the years and the special closeness your family has shared in those times when you were in harm's way have given them an outlook on the world that is as much a part of their lives as that old commissioning pennant is of yours. Don't underestimate the power of those emotions.

PRACTICAL MATTERS

One of the best ways to get accustomed to the reality of the step you are about to take is to get into the nuts-and-bolts side of the business. Chances are that the first thing you will find out is that your useful knowledge of the mechanics of retirement is on a par with what you knew about sex at the age of twelve. The information is incomplete, inaccurate, and garbled, and you haven't had the chance to use it anyway. Over the years hundreds of pieces of information on retirement have passed through your hands, barely slowing down on their way to the "out" basket or the circular file. There was always time to look at that stuff later. Well, later has just arrived, and it is time to begin.

Open your campaign by learning everything you can about the service and DOD programs available to you. In the last few years, military-to-civilian transition has become a much more organized procedure than it used to be. Programs like DOD's "Operation Transition" and the organizations that support it have taken a lot of the guesswork out of retirement. Although primarily designed for people who are leaving the service early because of force reductions, military transition assistance offers a lot of help to

everyone who is retiring. Sign up for everything. It won't
hurt a bit, and even better, it's free.

Get hold of one of the service handbooks on the subject,
like the navy's *Guide for Retired Personnel and their Families* or
the army's *Handbook on Retirement Services*. Read the book
from cover to cover, even the parts that don't seem to apply
to you, because some very useful information will probably
be hidden away in unlikely places. Frankly, some of this
stuff will be deadly dull and, at first reading, almost incomprehensible. The discussion of the Survivors' Benefit Plan
(SBP), for example, will probably come across as something
written by a sadistic accountant. *Read it anyway.* The decisions that you make about SBP can have a powerful impact
on your family's future and will be virtually irreversible
once you have retired. Look closely at the section on veterans' benefits because as time goes on they will begin to
overlap, and in some cases replace, your retirement benefits, and some programs will have time limits and expiration
dates.

At this early stage very few immediate decisions will need
to be made, but you will find a lot of food for thought and
discussion with your family. Survivors' benefits should be
one of these early discussion topics. Everyone has heard at
one time or another that the amount of money that will be
deducted from each retirement check for SBP could be better spent on an insurance program and provide better benefits for your survivors. In the abstract, this may be true, but
human nature, yours and mine for example, has a way of
defeating the ideal. Try this test. Do you remember when,
early in your career, you were the first in line to sign up for
a savings bond drive to set a good example for your men?
Did you keep those bonds to maturity or did you cash them
the first chance you had (as some of us did) when the cash
got a little tight? Be honest. Before you make the final SBP

election in the months before retirement, find out how much it will cost you for comparable insurance coverage. And remember, SBP is subtracted from retirement pay *before* your taxable income is figured. Other types of insurance will not give you that tax break.

Decisions on matters like SBP, like many of the other issues you will be facing in the months ahead, will require a lot more serious thought than you might have imagined. While on active duty we tend to assume that the system will take care of us without much effort on our part. New forms appear from time to time, the numbers on paychecks change, but as long as things seem to be normal we trust the system to make it all come out even in the long run. But in the world of retirement all this will change. Once you sign for that new gray ID card and turn in the green one, you will become your own paymaster and personnel officer, and if you don't get it right now, all you can do then is stand in front of the mirror and chew yourself out. (Be sure you close the bathroom door when you do this or people will start giving you funny looks.)

MEDICAL PLANNING

The movie about Admiral "Bull" Halsey's career made a running joke about the admiral's reluctance to take his immunization shots or have anything to do with doctors. This attitude, ingrained in some of us who remain untouched by the health and fitness craze, is usually characterized by an avoidance of anything medical under all but the most desperate circumstances. As a result, we are often less than conscientious about scheduling periodic physical exams and have only the vaguest idea about what information is in our health records. Although this doesn't cause much of a problem when we are on active duty, it can be disastrous later on in life. One of the sad truths about medical benefits for retirees is that they are not quite what you have been used to. For openers, the medical records you have been ignoring all these years will disappear into an archive somewhere. Getting your hands on them after that happens will be a lot of fun. No one will remind you to take a periodic physical or force you to get a flu shot. In short, your health will be entirely in your own hands.

Don't expect the same treatment you have been receiving at medical facilities either. Active duty people and their dependents will take preference (as they should), and in many cases overcrowded, understaffed clinics will not be able to take care of retired people at all. This is where CHAMPUS comes in along with Veterans Administration (VA) benefits and a few other goodies and not-so-goodies that you might not know much about.

Health care is in a state of change that will probably continue through most of the '90s. As a new national health-care policy emerges, it is quite possible that some aspects of retiree heath care will change; at the very least you can expect some benefits to be reorganized or given different names. The trend is toward a system that is more closely tied to nonmilitary health-care contractors, to use an approach similar to the private sector's health maintenance organizations (HMOs).

As a rule of thumb you can expect that using postretirement health care will require you to know more about the subject than you do now, and in most cases to pay more for the benefit than you do now. Because of this uncertainty, it is worth at least considering the possibility of enrolling in one of the "CHAMPUS Supplement" health-insurance programs offered by various service-related organizations.

This may sound like a gloomy picture of the future, but it is the real world, and with a little forethought and preparation you can arrange your medical affairs to minimize nasty surprises for you and your family if you begin working on the problem well before you retire. Here are a few things to consider.

Read *The CHAMPUS Handbook* and make sure that everyone in your family is signed up for DEERS. Don't assume anything until you are sure that you have seen all the documentation, have personally verified it, and have made copies of everything you can think of. Squaring away problems in this area, even minor ones, gets a lot harder after you are out of the service.

If you have not had an annual physical within the last six months or so, arrange to get one right after you make the decision to retire. This will give you a fresh datum to use for the retirement physical, which should be done as close as possible to your retirement date. If at all possible, persuade the medical people to do a complete workup on you, including an electrocardiogram, blood tests for cholesterol, and anything else that you and they can get away with.

See the dentist. Yes, now, you coward. It won't hurt any less when a civilian dentist works on you a year from now, but it will cost a shocking amount of money. And depending on how badly you have neglected yourself, the work could take some time. Be sure to tell the dental officer that you will be retiring within the year. He will probably understand the problem and lay out a schedule of appointments for you. He knows what kind of care you will get after retirement.

Read through your medical and dental records and don't hesitate to ask about anything you can't understand. After all, this is *your* body inside those covers. It might be nice to know what the professionals have to say about it.

WHERE WILL YOU LIVE?

For some people this will be an easy decision, but for others it will be too hard to worry about right now. A surprising number of us don't have strong feelings on this subject until we begin planning for our new lives, and then we end up reaching a decision by default. That is not necessarily bad. After all, you have suspected for years that that was the way the assignment officer made decisions, so why change now? But for those who would like the opportunity to have some control over where they live, there are a number of things to consider before making a decision. The scariest thing is the fear that wherever you choose, this is where you are going to have to live for the rest of your life. This thought alone can be depressing, bringing to mind vivid pictures of you sitting on the front porch of a house at some nameless crossroads, staring into the sunset and dreaming of all the places you will never see again.

This idea, of course, is nonsense. Nevertheless, the prospect of being somewhere *forever* has been known to throw perfectly reasonable people into mindless panic and indecision. Don't worry about it. Civilians move, too, and unless you really plan on retiring to the rocking chair and doing the old folks thing, so will you. And you don't have to decide right away. The government allows one full year after retirement to make the last move at its expense, and it can be to any place you choose, including overseas. The period can even be extended beyond a year for people who decide to go back to school. So if you are still undecided about where to live, relax. There is more time than you think.

Assuming that you are one of the majority who have not already made a firm decision about your future home, there are a number of factors that should be evaluated when you do start examining the alternatives. Most of these will affect everyone in the household. Discussing the options is a good place to begin getting the whole family involved in planning for the coming years. Here are some of the considerations that should guide your thinking.

Family Plans

In the past, your children have learned to accept changing schools every few years as a part of the military life, and chances are they have adapted fairly well to these dislocations. Now, though, the decision to move is more open-ended and personal. It is only reasonable to expect that they will want a voice in the decision. They know you can't blame the service this time, so listen to what they have to say.

If your spouse has a job or a career that will be influenced, swallow your pride and recognize its importance. For a while after you retire, this person could be supporting you.

Military Facilities

Depending on the priorities in your life, proximity to military facilities might be less important than you think. Commissaries and exchanges do save you money, and it is nice to have that uniformed security blanket close at hand, but living close to a base can also have disadvantages. The cost of living in an area heavy on military installations is not going to go down once you retire, but the things that made life affordable, like cost-of-living allowances, will no longer be there. The trend in medical benefits is toward more CHAMPUS or health-insurance coverage for the retired community, and living near a military hospital is not necessarily an advantage.

If you settle overseas, you will find that your normal ID card privileges are virtually nonexistent in many areas and that your retirement will change your status with the host government. Living abroad after retirement involves other special conditions that vary considerably. In some places, simply receiving your paycheck can be a major headache.

Before making a commitment to living overseas, do some research with the State Department, your service, and the nation's embassy.

Climate

Although we don't like to admit it, the United States is a nation of climatic extremes. It gets colder here than in England and hotter than in Spain—all in one place and sometimes all in one month. The most common comment about the weather, regardless of what part of the country you happen to be in, is "If you don't like the weather today, wait around." Climate is a very personal thing. In the middle of a howling April blizzard, New Englanders will tell you how much they love the change of seasons, and people broiling in the Arizona desert will wax poetic over the lovely sunsets.

The climate of a place can affect your life in many ways. The so-called Sun Belt has a disproportionate number of older retired residents competing for fewer low-paying jobs and rapidly escalating housing costs.

Quality of Life

This is the most subjective and elusive factor. It is determined by a combination of other attributes and depends on individual interests and priorities. A great local symphony orchestra will have little appeal to a country music fan. Small towns have low crime rates, but they are also very, very quiet, and large metropolitan areas are almost always expensive.

Cost of living can affect the quality of life in a number of ways. There's not much advantage to living in a place that offers great recreation, entertainment, and educational opportunities if a sky-high cost of living keeps you too broke to do anything but watch TV. Areas with very modest living costs also have their problems. Low taxes usually mean poor public services, bad roads, and marginal schools. Low living costs can also be an indicator of a dying community or one that is, for various reasons, an undesirable place to live. Local politics, customs, and attitudes may also define quality of life for you and your family. It's hard to put down roots in an area where you will be a permanent "outsider" or if local attitudes make you uncomfortable.

One way to get a sense of what a community is like is to subscribe to its newspaper for a while. Reading a daily or weekly paper for a few months will tell you more about issues, problems, values, and the local economy than you'll ever get from the chamber of commerce.

Trade-offs

The best way to evaluate the trade-offs among the various parts of the country is to do some research at the library. Richard Boyer's *Places Rated Almanac* and Thomas F. Bowman's *Finding Your Best Place to Live in America,* for example, cover every area in the country and include statistics on everything from average rainfall to state taxes.* Most of these books include a self-administered test to assist in prioritizing your requirements. Larger libraries also maintain files of city and state maps, industrial directories, and a collection of books on specific areas.

Jobs

After you have carefully done the research, consulted with your family, and weighed all possible pros and cons,

---

*Research in this area can provide some surprises, pleasant and otherwise. Some places tax retirement pay and some don't. Others have state and local income taxes; a few states have no income tax at all. A few localities tax everything you can imagine and prohibit everything else.

your decision as to where to settle may be determined more by future employment than anything else.

In evaluating the job potential for any area, it's important to look not only at the present but also at the future of both the career field and the location. Heavy manufacturing and defense-related businesses are declining nationwide; communities that still depend on these industries for jobs may be living on borrowed time.

PSYCHOLOGICAL FACTORS

Everything you do during the process of retiring and planning for the future will have some psychological impact on you and your family. The transition you are about to make is one of the most significant in adult life, right up there with marriage, divorce, and death. Even those people who make a show of taking the whole business in stride are profoundly affected by the experience. In fact, the attitude that it's no big thing may be the most dangerous of all because it contains elements of what psychologists refer to as denial, which is the same condition that keeps alcoholics from getting help and makes jilted suitors chase their old flames for years. Denial can be become a serious handicap to making a constructive transition to civilian life. In its most extreme forms it can lead people to stubbornly refuse to recognize their situation and delay retirement planning and decisions until the last possible moment and then, out of anger and resentment, make some remarkably poor judgments.

It is generally recognized by psychologists that major changes in life trigger a series of emotional reactions, all of which are perfectly normal parts of our mechanism for dealing with the world. Getting bogged down in these reactions can cause a great deal of trouble and pain if we are not prepared to accept things as they are, move forward, and get on with our lives.

Since the emotional experience of retirement will affect us all to some extent during the passage from active duty to civilian life, it is worth looking into, not as do-it-yourself therapy, but in a commonsense way that recognizes the issue and helps you to understand some of the predictable effects the experience of retiring is likely to have. This is important both to you and to your family because in their own way they will be going through the same experiences you are.

What this business is all about is loss, grief, and letting go. If that sounds a little heavyweight, try thinking about how you felt when you first left home for school or the service. For most of us it was an upsetting experience for a while. Whether we admitted it or not, we were scared, lonely, and occasionally overwhelmed by waves of doubt and an indefinable longing for the familiar. We may even have felt a little guilty about leaving others behind or angry because we were being forced to change and were unable to turn back. But time and the promise of the future eventually led us to let go of the past, accept the inevitability of change, and enjoy the new conditions life.

Although we may be reluctant to admit it, the experience of retiring is very similar to that first great passage in life. The feeling of loss, fear of the unknown, and a longing to wish the whole thing would go away are all part of the same complex of emotions that must be worked through whenever any loss or change comes into our lives. The problems only come up when we fail to recognize that our reactions to the situation are normal or when we get stuck in denial, fear, or anger. When that happens, our judgment is affected and emotional problems can arise that complicate the situation even more, beginning a vicious circle that can result in disaster. This is why a planned, well-thought-out approach to retiring is so important. Many people have had the same emotions you are experiencing. If you realize this and plan for the transition with a positive, relaxed attitude, it can make the difference between a miserable, traumatic couple of years and an experience that is challenging, stimulating, and fun. As Samuel Butler expressed it, "All our lives long, every day and every hour, we are engaged in the process of accommodating our changed and unchanged selves to changed and unchanged surroundings; living, in fact, is nothing else than this process of accommodation. When we fail in it a little we are stupid, when we fail flagrantly we are mad, when we suspend it temporarily we sleep, when we give up the attempt altogether, we die."

ONE MORE THOUGHT

At this point it is time to take a deep breath and pause to ask yourself one final question before charging into action. That question is, Do you *really* want to retire now? There are a lot of good arguments for staying around as long as you can, and unless you are facing statutory retirement because of age or time in service, this is the time to search your soul and be sure you are making the right decision for the right reasons. Your decision ought to be viewed as a positive action toward a new goal and a step toward the future. It should not be a way of acting out a temper tantrum or a resentment. If your thinking is negative, you run the risk of poisoning the atmosphere of the future, and that is not the best way to start a new life.

2

THE PHASES OF RETIRING

♦

Once your decision to retire has been confirmed and you have started digging into the practical matters mentioned in the preceding chapter, it will become apparent that most of the action required to get the process moving will fit into a logical order. The sequence begins when you put pen to paper and compose the retirement letter and comes to a climax on the day it actually happens, when you walk away from your retirement ceremony with a carefully folded flag under your arm, a slightly dazed expression on your face, and an odd feeling in your throat. There is a lot to do between those two points, not only on the official side but also in your personal affairs. This period is like a slowly accelerating train gliding out of the station with an almost unnoticeable motion but slowly building up speed until the station is out of sight and you are on your way.

Retirement preparations are much like the workup for a major command inspection. At first there will be a long list of things to do and it seems as though there is plenty of time to do them. Lulled by that innocent self-deception, you will find it easy to let things slide for a few weeks, then a few months, only to awaken one day to the horrible realization that time is slipping away at an alarming rate and nothing has been done. We all know what happens then— panic, crisis, recrimination, and, yes, maybe a little bit of cheating and sloppy work in those last few frenzied days before the big inspection.

A crisis approach won't work for retirement any more than it ever did for an inspection, and this time you may have to live with the consequences of failure for the rest of your life. You will not get a second try at it even if you fail miserably. The message, then, is to plan for the operation with the same wisdom and good sense that got you all those outstanding inspection grades once you learned about the importance of advance planning. That means that you will need a timetable and a set of realistic milestones to ensure that everything gets done on schedule. Depending on your background and your own natural inclinations, this schedule can be as simple or as elaborate as you wish. Some people make flow charts detailed enough to make the average amphibious operation look like a trip to the Seven-Eleven. Others, and I suspect most of us, will be satisfied with something more modest. The important thing is to have a plan with some milestones to help make the process as orderly and painless as possible.

For convenience, preretirement planning can be broken down into four separate phases. Each one is shorter than the last, and the pucker factor gets progressively higher as time goes on, culminating in the last day, when, ready or not, it's all over and you become a retiree. To get from now to then, you will have to go through all four phases described in the following pages. And no cheating.

THE BEGINNING

If you haven't already written your retirement letter, now is the time to get it on paper. Almost everyone has written a few of these mentally, usually the result of one of those days when everything went wrong and a new career as a sheep dipper began to look more and more attractive. Don't use that letter.* Maybe a few years from now all those things that were frustrating, infuriating, or terrifying when they happened will be fodder for great war stories with all the other retired people. For now though, keep your secret and let it mellow. If something is *really* bothering you, write a book about it after you retire. Those vituperative letters seldom accomplish anything but cause the writer embarrassment, inconvenience, or worse, and no one needs that.

The letter itself should be brief, straightforward, and businesslike to reduce the risk of confusion or a screwup by one of the many clerks, administrators, and others who will handle it as it goes its merry way. Your requested retirement date should be realistic and your plans flexible enough to accommodate minor changes if they become necessary. In other words, don't pay for Superbowl tickets a year in advance based on a projected retirement date. Remember, too, that retirement pay will be calculated to the nearest even month so there is nothing sacred about an exact anniversary of your service.

The letter must also include a statement that you understand "pre- and postretirement standards of conduct and employment activities." This has nothing to do with watching X-rated movies in the wardroom. It is important,

---

*Civilians who process retirement requests have been known to compare notes on the most outrageous letters to come across their desks. The winners get posted on the office bulletin board. How would *you* like to be the daily joke to a bunch of snickering civilians?

though, because it commits you to read and, if possible, get a briefing on all the laws that outline what retired people can and cannot legally do in the area of employment. This is all explained in DOD Directive 5500.7, Standards of Conduct. It is not very exciting reading, but put it on your list of things to do, preferably far enough in advance of your separation to give you time to clear up any questions that arise.

The final piece of required information is a statement of whether you intend to take separation leave or, as it is sometimes called, terminal leave. Although most people do take terminal leave believing that it is to their advantage, this is not always so. It is true that you can take thirty days of terminal leave before your actual retirement date, and if you have something specific planned, such as job interviews or starting immediately to work in a new job, it can be a good thing to do. But if your plans are not firm, you are likely to waste time hanging around the house and generally spinning your wheels. You are also using up leave that you could otherwise "sell back" and put in the bank. This is an important point to consider. That thirty days worth of leave can be the cushion that allows an extra month or two for job search and perhaps even the difference between hanging on a while longer for a better job or taking something that's not right for you just because funds are getting low. It's worth thinking about. If you have excess leave (more than sixty days) on your account, take the excess as terminal leave.

OTHER ADVANCE PLANNING

This is the time to check with the Veterans Administration to ensure that your records are up-to-date and correct. The VA is a large organization and has been known to move slowly. A complex problem could take six months to a year to sort out, and if you expect to be using any benefits shortly after retirement it will be comforting to know that everything is in place and tidied up well in advance. If you have used part of your educational benefits in the past and are thinking of additional schooling in a different discipline, you will have to file a form requesting a change in educational objective. The VA will take from two to six months to process this request. So get started now, when time and patience are still in abundant supply. A month or so after you have retired, the VA will send you an information package that will include the status of your educational benefits as well as a certificate of eligibility for home loans. A check of your status now will ensure that these statements are accurate and up-to-date.

Planning for your new home (if you expect to be moving) is a good way to get your family involved early in the transition process. Write letters to chambers of commerce and government agencies to begin building a library of information. Better yet, get the rest of the family to do the homework for you. This will be useful even if you are moving back to somewhere you have lived before. The gypsy outlook that most of us get over the years can result in an amazing degree of ignorance about some of our temporary homes. As a civilian that perspective will be entirely different.

Learning about different communities can be worthwhile even if you don't plan to move after retirement. It can put you in touch with potential job opportunities and lay the foundations for good future contacts. This is especially true of community organizations. Before too long, you and your family will be permanent residents, and community issues will become a bigger part of your lives. You may even want to begin to learn about local politics. It can't hurt, and who knows, there may be a future in it for you.

Health planning should be done now and appointments lined up, especially if any extensive therapy or dental work is expected. At most military installations, appointments for special requirements must be set up well in advance. You have a lot more clout with medical people now than you will after retirement and more time now than in the last few months of active duty when the train will be moving much faster. If you have a service-connected disability or believe that you might have one, get the paper moving as soon as possible. This is definitely not an "Oh, by the way" issue to be postponed until the doctor is telling you to say "Ah" during the retirement physical. Having an early "baseline" physical as suggested in Chapter 1 is the best way to establish a current health history for future use. If you haven't set up medical and dental appointments yet, don't waste any more time.

Unusual or chronic health problems of family members should also receive attention now. Your family members will be given their health records after you retire so any special treatment or medication should be carefully documented and verified, preferably by a family practice physician or someone who is familiar with the case history. This record verification is especially important if you will be moving after retirement.

Career planning comes next on the agenda. This task should be approached in two phases. First, decide what to do for a living; second, figure out how to get someone to pay you to do it. Those are the bare bones of the issue. Of course, it is not that simple. If it were, many high-priced people in the placement and career business would be out of work. Those two questions are unavoidable, though, and until you start working on answers to them, your plans for the future will be unfocused and fuzzy, no matter what else you do right. The next three chapters will examine this subject in detail. The action they suggest should begin now. This is the time to discard the folklore and war stories about second careers that you have been hearing from your friends all these years. Like sex, career planning ought to be learned through education and research, not by picking up a garbled version from the other kids.

Plans for continuing education, even if they are still tentative, will also require a long lead time. Start as soon as possible. Browse through college catalogs (most libraries keep a file), and begin putting together transcripts, grade records, and other paperwork you'll need. Some qualification examinations like the Graduate Record Examination (GRE) are scheduled only at certain times of the year, so give some thought to taking these tests early in the retirement process.

Once you have developed a program of action and an approach to these early planning matters, you are likely to make the pleasant discovery that many of them are not as big a problem as you expected. At the same time, you will come across other areas that will require more effort and advance planning than you would ever have imagined. That's why it is so important to get started thinking and planning early. The little hiccups that seem to be a minor annoyance now will precipitate sheer panic if they come back a week before retirement. Action involving military records, benefits, and medical needs should be assigned highest priority from now until the day of retirement. Job hunting can be postponed if necessary but admin and medical requirements *must* be completed while you are still in uniform.

THE LAST SIX MONTHS

These months are the most critical period in your retirement preparations. Everything postponed or overlooked now will loom progressively more serious as the days pass and your procrastination cushion slowly deflates. It is not unusual to get the feeling that there are more difficult decisions to make than you had ever thought of. At some point you may even become convinced that the situation is getting hopelessly away from you. Take heart. There's nothing wrong with that feeling. No matter how well organized you are, not everything is going to happen exactly the way you expect it to. That is the first lesson in coping with the last six months.

At work, your status will begin to change in subtle and almost imperceptible ways. Once the service confirms your retirement and assigns a separation date, the situation is similar in some ways to every other time you have been transferred, but in other ways it is completely different. The people around you will start speculating about a new boss or associate, long-term projects will be planned with your replacement in mind, and if you are in the Pentagon your friends will start looking for someone new for the car pool. You will be doing new and unfamiliar things and now, with that piece of paper in your hand making the decision official, your attitude and behavior will change a little. If you are still wrestling with denial and haven't begun to accept that a change in your life is inevitable, the situation will bother you more and more; this can carry over into your work in the form of irritability, grouchiness, and an increasingly unrealistic attitude. It is at about this point that some people develop a sudden sense of urgency about everything they are doing or the crazy idea that nothing must be unfinished when they leave. Forget it. If you start getting wound up about such things, by the time you get down to the last thirty days you will be a raving maniac. Instead, start becoming accustomed to the idea that things will go on very nicely without you. Your big priority, one that is getting bigger every day, is to get on with the business of the rest of your life.

At the six-month point you will need to make some decisions. Job and location decisions may not yet be resolved and in fact may not be permanently settled on the day you retire. As long as you are making progress in these areas and are comfortable with the overall plan you have made, don't worry about it. Concentrate instead on the administrative and financial milestones. They can't be postponed and will begin backing up on you soon.

Transition Assistance

Although the military force reductions of the '90s are bringing uncertainties to many career military people, they have also created new benefits for those leaving the service. DOD transition programs, which didn't even exist a few years ago, now offer state-of-the-art job counseling and assistance that include everything from résumé preparation to an international electronic job bank. Each of the services administers the program through transition offices at all major military installations.

Military transition assistance does not claim to be all things for all people. By necessity it is broad-based to meet the needs of junior enlisteds to senior officers. The program is more "generic" than senior career NCOs and officers might desire but nevertheless offers services that are too good to pass up, no matter what your rank.

About six months before your retirement date you will be introduced to your service transition program via the Defense Outplacement Referral System (DORS). You can expect to get a package that includes a DORS individual application form and information on counseling and seminars. At the same time your service should begin reviewing your personnel record to identify the special skills, training, or experience that you can offer a prospective employer. The DORS system will then take the information from your application and assist you in creating a "mini-résumé" that will be fed into the computer-based transition bulletin board, which is made available to employers throughout the nation.

If you haven't received this information at the five- or six-month point, don't sit on your dignity, waiting for it. Contact the local transition office and get hooked into the system. Pay particular attention to the DORS application form, especially the section on personal information. This part of the form is where you get to advertise yourself as an individual. It's your personal billboard, but it's limited to about fourteen typed lines of information, so make it good.

Chapter 5 of this book gives more details on how to describe yourself to a prospective employer. In addition, you should observe the following list of do's and don'ts when working on the personal-information section of the DORS form:

- *Do* highlight awards and other recognition of individual achievement and personal qualities.
- *Do* include skills and achievement outside service experience. This experience might include career-related hobbies, community service, and outside education.
- *Do* include special or unique combinations of skills and experience. Someone out there may be looking for just your special blend.
- *Don't* fill the section with a dull list of assignments or wordy job descriptions.
- *Don't* use technical language or unusual military terminology.
- *Don't* waste precious space by describing skills and experience not related to the kind of job you want.
- *Don't* pat yourself on the back. Let your record of achievement speak for you.

The transition-assistance people at your base may also be able to arrange for other counseling services and will schedule you for a transition-assistance seminar sometime before your retirement date. While you are doing this preliminary work you may also want to ask about aptitude and vocational testing. If the transition site can't provide it, they probably will know someone who can.

Financial Appraisal

Appraise your financial situation to get some idea of the constraints if you face a long job search. This is also a good time to sit down with a financial adviser and get some recommendations on how to reorder your affairs. Review wills and if necessary make new ones to accommodate any expected changes in status after retirement. Assignment of beneficiaries of Servicemen's Group Life Insurance (SGLI), SBP, commercial insurance, and your will should all agree. Conflict between these documents could cause problems for your heirs.

NCOA, TROA, and other organizations serving the military community offer very good booklets on financial planning for retirement. Most of these publications include some form of step-by-step financial appraisal. Although it will take some time and research to complete one of these appraisals, do it now. Pay particular attention to determining the difference between your active duty and your post-retirement income and expenses. These figures are important because they will be a major factor in most other decisions you have to make in the coming months. Doing a complete financial appraisal early on will also give you more time to get your economic house in order.

Veterans Group Life Insurance (VGLI). On retirement, your SGLI policy can be converted to VGLI with coverage up to a maximum of $200,000. The policy will be in effect for five years after your retirement date, at which time you will have the option of converting to individual insurance with a commercial carrier. The "conversion notice" you receive about six months before VGLI coverage expires gives you the right to convert VGLI to insurance with any of about two hundred companies contracted with the Department of Veterans Affairs, without taking a physical. But there's a catch to it. Five years from now, when you start contacting insurance companies, you will find they are not at all enthusiastic about "automatic conversion," and although they will honor the contract they will do it at a considerably higher rate than they offer for other comparable policies.

Why worry about this now? Because when your VGLI expires, you will be five years older, in a higher premium group, and stuck with an expiring policy. To avoid this situation, consider buying an individual policy now, when you are in a low-premium group. Get one for a small amount, but be sure it has a provision that allows you to increase coverage in the future without a physical or other restriction. In the long run it will save you money.

SBP. Your elections should be finalized during this time. You might find that the financial appraisal or your second career situation will cause you to rethink some of your leave plans. If you are still undecided about SBP options, contact a reputable financial planner and set up a meeting to get a quote on coverage comparable to SBP benefits. The Institute of Certified Financial Planners sets minimum standards in its field and certifies its members, but standards vary among the states. Almost all financial planners make some of their money selling insurance, so don't be surprised if the planner urges that option on you. Be gracious, get all the data broken down and on paper, and think about your options for a few weeks. SBP election is a decision you can't change.

Credit cards and loans. Add up your average monthly payments on credit cards and loans, including those paid by allotment. While you are earning full active duty pay and allowances, the total may not worry you. As a percentage of a much smaller retirement check, it could cause hardship. Unless you have a postretirement job secured, retirement pay might be your only source of income for a while, and you will need all of it. Give serious thought to paying off loans and credit card charges to as low a balance as you can before leaving the service.

Taxes. If you know where you are going to live after retirement, make an estimate of state and local income, personal property, and other nuisance taxes. Ask the finance office to arrange for having state income taxes deducted from your retirement check. It will hurt a lot less than a big tax surprise at the end of the year. State and local taxes may influence your decision about where you want to live.

The third account. Automatic teller machines and electronic deposits speed up the money flow so much that there is barely time to wave as it goes by. Living with fast-moving money becomes a habit, and as long as the checks are covered and the bills are paid, we are happy. But after retirement the situation may be different. The assured part of our income will be smaller than in the past, and job search, relocation, and other unpredictable expenses can quickly eat up whatever savings cushion we have.

A good way to minimize the impact of unexpected retirement costs is to open a third account. Most people have a checking and a savings account at the same institution. This is convenient, sometimes too convenient if you don't keep a tight rein on expenditures. A third account at another bank, earmarked only for large, onetime transition outlays will give you better control of your money. Since it will be used less often than other accounts, you can benefit from the favorable interest rates most banks offer on limited check-writing arrangements. Set the account up as soon as possible after you make a retirement decision and deposit in it all your money from sold leave and as much as possible of your last active-duty paycheck. If you expect to move after retirement, plan to add returned utility or security deposits to the account. Then grit your teeth and don't use the money for anything except transition expenses.

Administrative Details

Correspondence with agencies like the VA should be well under way now. Other matters requiring a long lead time for processing or verification by a military personnel office will have to be started. It will be much easier and more convenient for you to take care of these things while you are in uniform than it will be after retirement.

Be sure to make arrangements sometime during the last three months for the standard preretirement briefings provided by your service. They are an invaluable way to fill in any blanks in your own planning and are usually run by experts who can answer any questions you may have. Needless to say, this is another milestone that should be scheduled early in the last three months to allow time to take care of any new requirements or problems that the briefings bring to light. You may also want to sign up for a follow-on program such as the Air Force Retirement Transition Program for later in the retirement process.

If possible, your spouse should attend these briefings with you. In addition to getting important information, he or she might have questions to raise that did not occur to you. Over the years your spouse has dealt more closely with CHAMPUS and other programs than you have and developed a more critical and pragmatic perspective than yours. In other words, your spouse will know enough to ask intelligent questions. You might not.

Make copies of every document you think might be useful later. Despite restrictions on the use of government copying machines, it is legal to copy a reasonable amount of information for your own records. Or you can get material copied commercially. Squirrel away old telephone directories from military installations and places like the Pentagon. As long as they are not restricted, there is nothing wrong with keeping such directories, but don't appropriate a new one. If you can get the administrative people to give you spare copies of directories on subjects that relate to retiring, benefits, or anything else you might need later, do it. When you are no longer on active duty it will be more difficult and time-consuming to get your hands on this information.

Visit the Educational Services or off-duty education office and request that a DD-295 (Application for Evaluation of Learning Experience during Military Service) be completed for you. This form lists all the schools and training courses you attended while in the service and assigns to each one a standard amount of academic credit at the high school or college level. The *Guide to Evaluation of Educational Experience in the Armed Forces* published by the American Council on Education is the source document for this information, and if you take the time to leaf through it, you will be pleasantly surprised to learn how much academic credit you have earned over the years. A completed DD-295 will be useful even if you are not planning to go back to school right away. The credit you are eligible for will look good on your résumé, and it can be documented.

Dig into your pocket and buy a copy of the *Retired Military Almanac*. It's available at most military exchanges and is worth the modest price. The almanac holds a wealth of information on benefits, VA information, and so forth, and is updated every year. And while you have your checkbook out, sign up for one of the military retiree organizations such as TROA, NCOA, or The Retired Enlisted Association (TREA). These organizations provide a wide range of services from CHAMPUS supplemental medical insurance to job placement. And the dues are tax deductible. Who could ask for more?

Your records may be transferred to the retirement section of the administrative support organization some time during the last three months. This is another milestone in your journey from the familiar places you have inhabited for some years to the new territory "out there." It is also a chance for you to work with the experts. Get to know these folks and don't hesitate to call on their experience. They process people like you through retirement every day and can head off problems before, it gets to be panic time. Don't be like one person I know of, who vented his anger and frustration on the people in the retirement section. They got even. After he retired and moved away, he discovered problems in his paperwork that kept him busy for six months.

Plan a retirement ceremony. For some reason, people develop a peculiar sense of false modesty when the time comes to do this. They hang their heads shyly and scuff their toes in the dust like Jimmy Stewart with the new schoolmarm, creating a general impression of syrupy self-effacement that doesn't fool anyone. A ceremony, an honest-to-goodness event with color guards, speeches, and a band, is what you should plan for, and nothing less. Retirement is an important day in your life and in the lives of your family and friends. It ought to be an experience to be remembered and cherished in the years to come. So don't get modest and do the "Aw, Shucks" thing. Plan a ceremony—the best one you are permitted.

If events seem to be accelerating more and more quickly as you come up to the thirty-day point, don't worry. Things *are* moving faster, just as they always did in the last month before a big deployment. And just like then, if you stay cool and get things done in an organized way, everything will come out even. (Well, almost everything. Nobody's perfect.)

THE LAST THIRTY DAYS

The clock is ticking faster now,* and you suddenly realize that this time next month you will be retired. If you are like most people you may be starting to feel the way you did waiting for the school bus on the first day of kindergarten. You know that this is something that everyone has to do, but that doesn't make you feel any better about it.

That last month can be a strange time, and we do some strange things. An example is a navy captain I know who worked until midnight on the day before his departure, just to make sure everything got done. Only he knows whether he did this out of an extraordinary sense of dedication or because of his own ego. The sad fact is that the guy was kidding himself. Regardless of what he may have believed, his exit from the scene did not bring the Department of Defense to a grinding halt, and neither will yours. So start letting go. It is nonsense to expect to conduct "business as usual" in the last month of your active service, and if you try it won't help you, your family, or the unfortunates who have to work with you.

There will be a temptation to pretend that nothing unusual is happening and an urge to persist in hanging on to

*If you are taking terminal leave, be sure to adjust planning for the last thirty days so everything comes out even.

your role until the last minute. As we face one of the most important passages in adult life, some of us carry on with the job until the last possible moment, driven to increase the pace in the last thirty days of a career, refusing to admit that no matter what, the work will be left unfinished. When this attitude takes over, long-neglected projects are pushed to a hasty completion and sent up the line still dripping wet, and all sorts of things are finished off that would probably be better left for someone else to worry about. There are mutterings and black looks from subordinates as they struggle to complete your jobs at the expense of more urgent tasks, and in the end everyone's life becomes a little more unpleasant.

Relax. The most important accomplishments of your career have already been done. You are not going to top them in the last thirty days. Your long-term usefulness began to decrease on the day you received the retirement orders. For this one month your most important mission is to make sure that everything that must be done is complete before the band starts playing on the day of your ceremony. The service realizes this, your associates accept it, and heaven knows your family does, whether you realize it or not.

Plan the first week after retirement. If you have been lucky enough to get a job lined up already, try to arrange a breathing space between retirement and the first day of work. This is another way of marking the transition from one phase of life to another. Look on this first week or so as a pause in the rhythm of events, a time for relaxed contemplation, and an opportunity to catch your breath before plunging into the mainstream again. It can be an especially pleasant time for you and your family to reward yourselves and pave the way for a smooth passage into the future.

The retirement physical should be scheduled as close as possible to the beginning of the last thirty days. This will allow all lab work and tests to be completed in enough time for you to sit down with a doctor and go over every page of your health records in as much detail as you think is necessary. If you seem to have any conditions that might involve a disability, be sure to get them explained and documented completely. After retirement you will have a year to bring disabilities to the attention of the VA, but if there is no pre-retirement documentation, this will be an uphill battle, no matter how valid the argument for your case may be. Don't forget to make copies of everything new that has been placed in medical and dental records. A month from now it will be too late.

Expect to do some last-minute running around. Even if the last six months or so have been planned with the precision of the Prussian General Staff, there will be many things to do in the last few weeks. Anticipate this and allow plenty of time. If most of your early preparations are complete, tying up loose ends should be easy, and it's good to get out of the office for a while when you are beginning to feel more and more useless every day. This is not a time to get impatient or exasperated. To paraphrase an old homily, "retire in haste, repent at leisure."

Read what you sign. In the last few weeks and days one or two sessions will probably be scheduled with the clerk or admin type who is the retirement specialist. What you will be told and the papers you will be given to sign are important; read them all. The DD 214 form (Certificate of Release or Discharge from Active Duty) is an especially important record. It even tells you so. Right at the top of the first page it reads, "THIS IS AN IMPORTANT RECORD." Now is your last chance to correct any mistakes in your service record that could come back to haunt you in later years, so pay attention to everything and don't hesitate to ask dumb questions. Remember, once you sign it, you're stuck with it.

Make your farewells. During these last days make the time to say good-bye individually to all the people you may not see again. Even if they have been invited to the retirement ceremony, a personal handshake and a few minutes of conversation will mean a lot to both you and them. Once again, this is a part of the leaving-taking process that is significant to you now and for the future.

THE DAY

It's here at last. In your wallet there will soon be a gray ID card with a picture of someone a little older and wiser than the kid who posed for that first official photo just a few years ago. Papers have been signed and the last active-duty paycheck has been figured. If you are a fanatic for detail, you have gotten a big "R" decal to put on the car's base sticker. Sometime during the day you will put on your uniform, look in the mirror, and realize with a shock that this is the last day you are going to do this. Ever.

Arrangements for receptions, dinners, or any other social event connected with this day are a matter of individual preference and can range from a quiet dinner with family to a full-bore gala with champagne and dancing girls (well, maybe not dancing girls, but you know what I mean). It is a onetime event so make up your mind to enjoy it. Anything still undone will have to stay that way. A flurry of last-minute worrying is not going to change anything and will only ruin a special occasion. Promise yourself that you will radiate calm and the properly serene manner of the old hand you are.

Your remarks at the ceremony can cover almost any subject you like, but this is not a good time to unburden your soul of secret grievances. If there is going to be a guest speaker, try to find out what the general tone and theme of the comments will be. If the speech is going to be a long one, you probably can't stop it, but be prepared. For your own remarks, you can take as much time as you want; the guests will have to sit there and listen to you no matter how long you talk. But brevity is the soul of wit.

So there you are. The sun is shining, the band is playing, and there in the front row is your family, feeling every bit as nervous, sad, and excited as you do. And before any of you realize what's happening, it's all over.

Enjoy. This is a milestone and for you a unique "Hail and Farewell." Even though the "Farewell" may seem to be the most obvious theme, it is also a time to look ahead and face the future with excitement and anticipation. But most of all, today is a part of the reward you have earned by giving a big part of yourself for many years of your life. For a day, just this one day, rest on your laurels and be proud.

THE FIRST DAY AS A CIVILIAN

As the years pass, you will remember the day you retired with fondness and nostalgia. But you might not think too much about the day after that, the first day of a new life that is going to be very different from what you have been accustomed to for most of your adult years. The realization that you are on the threshold of something entirely new can come in many ways. A friend of mine, a retired army colonel, said thoughtfully, "I suddenly realized that for the first time since I started kindergarten, there was no place I had to be today." That first day feeling can be one of release and anticipation or it can be a blend of fear and emptiness. Either way, this day will be a hint of the future.

You might think about taking a vacation. Most books on job search and career transition recommend against taking a holiday after leaving a position. They are assuming that the person has lost a job, is probably upset, and is facing an uncertain future. For someone in that situation a vacation is not a good idea because it can lead to worrying, agonizing over its cost, and making everyone miserable. At the end of it, one returns to a stack of bills, no job, and a haunting feeling of guilt.

For civilians who have been unexpectedly tossed onto the job market this theory makes sense. Experience has proved it to be valid. But your situation is different. When you are piped over the side and handed the flag, you are formally completing a process that began a long time ago when you first raised your hand and took the oath. It is the predictable and proper closing to a distinct phase in life, and a vacation with the family you have been dragging all over the world for the last few decades may not be a bad idea. They have earned it as much as you have.

If a vacation is not possible immediately after retirement, at least plan on doing something special and preferably frivolous on the first new day. What you do is not really important, but by all means don't hang around the house, because if you do the first day could go something like this:

You wake up. If the hour is early you curse the biological clock that insists on holding reveille at 0630; if you sleep late, a guilty little voice somewhere inside you says "My God, it's 1030. I'm going soft already."

You go to the kitchen and get a cup of coffee. With no schedule to meet and no place to go, you will be as useful as a fifth wheel. If it is a weekday everyone else will be getting ready to go somewhere and sooner or later you will find yourself either alone or getting in people's way as they go about the important business of running the household. (If you want to cause a real disaster, give your spouse the benefit of your great supervisory experience.) Whatever happens, the time will come when you are there with your coffee cup, looking at the clock, and feeling a tiny bit depressed.

Turn on the TV. Boy, are you in for a surprise. Daytime television programming is a phenomenon that defies rational description.* It is one of those dim alleys of life that, like spiritualism and collecting ceramic butterflies, is best left to others.

Soap operas are particularly dangerous. If you watch them long enough to begin understanding the plot, you are in big trouble and probably only a step away from haunting the laundromat in search of the whitest wash in town.

The end of the day approaches. This can be really bad if your spouse works because you will be wondering what you are supposed to do when he or she gets home. At the appointed hour, the working partner will sweep into the house, aglow and fresh from the great world of work, and sit down and kick off shoes. You will probably feel obligated to ask how the day went. You will be told and then will come the question you have been dreading all day: "And how was your first day of retirement?"

Well, how was it?

SUMMING UP

All the events you have read about in this chapter have happened to someone at some time. All the mistakes have already been make, and all the frustration and the emotional turmoil that can go with the process have been experienced by many who have gone before. We all survived. You will too. In a very short time, all the headaches over

---

*Studies have shown that daytime television will eventually turn your brain into something that resembles cottage cheese but is not useful.

paperwork of the last few months, the newness of everything, and the peculiar feeling that you should be wearing a uniform every day will fade into the distance. As time goes by, the memories will be of the exciting times, great friends, and a career that was satisfying and rewarding. Not too many people in the world can make that claim.

3

A NEW CAREER

♦

Somewhere inside us all, there is an urge to be someone else. Contented and fulfilled as we may be by our careers, most of us have at some time wished we could do something entirely new. For some, the idea of a different role is just another daydream that passes and is forgotten. For others, like the professor of English who races sports cars on weekends, or the executive who plays jazz piano, it becomes an avocation that brings new depth and excitement to their lives.

Retirement from the service may give you the chance to make that other role come alive. People with determination and willingness to make sacrifices for their dream have had some remarkable achievements. Albert Schweitzer, whose clinic in Africa became world famous, was an established theologian and educator when at age thirty-five he enrolled in medical school and began the career that made his name synonymous with humanitarianism. After a long career as a teacher, Helen Santmeyer became a best-selling author at the tender age of eighty-seven. And a semiretired actor named Ronald Reagan . . . well, you get the idea.

There are some practical limits to changing careers. The master armorer who can calibrate an M-1 tank gunsight with flawless precision is not necessarily ready to hire out as a brain surgeon, manual dexterity notwithstanding, and none of us on the far side of thirty-five are likely to pose a major threat to the Russian Olympic team. But opportunities do exist, and for someone finishing out twenty years or more of military service, the range of possible careers is much wider than it is for most civilians of the same age.

WORKING ON THE REST OF YOUR LIFE

Think back for a moment to when you first decided to choose a military career. Most of us made that decision after a few years on active duty when our initial obligation was coming to an end and we had to choose between signing up for another few years or making a start in the civilian world. We decided to stay on and at some point began to see ourselves as military professionals, committed by choice to a long-term career goal.

What prompted that decision? Individual motives may have varied, but in most cases two factors were important. First, you enjoyed your work. The hours were long, and sometimes the work was tough and dangerous, but you loved it. We all did. Second, you saw that there were rewards to be gained and the promise of a good future. There was potential for promotion, assignments were interesting and challenging, and after a time, you had a certain status and position. Fringe benefits and retirement were attractive, too, but at the time you decided on a military career, retirement was a fuzzy idea in a future that seemed a long way off.

Your situation now is not much different from what it was then, except that now you have accumulated more living experience and solid professional knowledge. You have already had a career that was more rewarding and interesting than most people's, and, most important, you have a clearer and more realistic idea of what you want from life. A vocational counselor would consider you a dream client. It may not seem that way while you are making difficult decisions about the future, but it's true.

The best way to start planning for a new career is to think of the reasons why you chose this one. Except for being older and wiser, you are the same person you were twenty or so years ago. Your goals and aspirations have stood the test of time, so begin with them.

It is a good idea to have some framework to guide your thinking and to help keep the balance between practical considerations and the never-never land of fantasy. This chapter will help define the framework of your planning. Even if you are one of the lucky ones who has known for a long time exactly what you are going to do after retirement and have a program under way, it is still a good idea to go through the process of planning for the future. No one thinks of everything, and most us tend to put aside those issues we don't want to grapple with. But now's the time to do your grappling.

Sources of Assistance

A remarkable amount of help is available for a person choosing a new career, and much of it is either free or inexpensive. Begin with the free part. Your transition-assistance office is the best starting point, followed by the educational-services office.*

---

*The names of various service-transition and educational-assistance offices vary, so generic terms will be used throughout this book.

Assuming you've done your homework, the DORS system will already have your mini-résumé on file and with your approval will send it out on the referral system's electronic bulletin board. In a way, you'll already be in the job market simply by filling out a few forms. Don't let it go to your head though. There's still a lot of work to be done.

A visit to the educational-services office is the next stop. In addition to helping you with the Education Evaluation form (DD-295) mentioned in the last chapter, this office will also have additional information on matters like local college programs and aptitude testing and will be knowledgeable about your eligibility under the Montgomery GI bill. And you'll get to fill out more forms.

While you're doing this, ask the people at the transition- and education-assistance offices for information on other VA, state, and local assistance programs. Get a copy of the VA's *Federal Benefits for Veterans and Dependents* and any other informational pamphlets or booklets that are offered. It's a lot easier than requesting information by mail, and reading the stuff will give you something to do in the evenings.

Individual research can take many forms. If you are not familiar with the reference section of the base or local library, take the time to go through it, and don't hesitate to ask the librarian questions. Most people who work in libraries love their work and enjoy the chance to help someone, especially on a slow, rainy day.

The firsthand experience of others is another valuable source of information. If you are considering going into a particular field or business and don't know much about it, ask someone. If the response is a roll of the eyes and a bitter little laugh, you might want to consider your choice. People who enjoy their work are usually glad to talk about it and can provide a perspective that you can't get from books. The civilian work environment is different in many ways from the military, and some jobs have hidden facets that can make them either unexpectedly attractive or completely unacceptable.

Career and vocational counseling is an expanding field. Changes in the nature of jobs and increases in state and federal programs have made such counseling a big business and attracted some very shady people. The yellow pages in the phone book and the classified section of the newspaper list dozens of counselors, employment specialists, and career managers, who will promise to give you everything but a key to Lee Iacocca's private washroom. Some of the classiest sounding operations, which advertise jobs "from $25,000 to $400,000," are not allowed to do business in half the states in the Union. Others are reputable services run by trained psychologists and counselors. The problem is that it can be difficult to distinguish the legitimate career specialists from the fast-buck experts until it is too late. For this reason, it is almost always a better idea for you to use the services offered by the military or the VA. And the price is right.

VOCATION, CAREER, OR JOB?

The French author André Malraux once wrote that the only true vocations were teaching, the military, and the clergy. He singled out those areas because they all require dedication far beyond any expected reward or recognition. A vocation is, by definition, a calling to some higher duty. The payoff, as career military people know, is a feeling inside that is hard to convey and can't be measured.

A career is a little different. In general, we use the term to describe work that has a progression over time, some system of expected advancement and reward, and a set of steps to complete. The old Romans had something called the *cursus honorum,* under which aspiring leaders had to get their papyrus punched by fulfilling a series of civic obligations before they could be considered for high office. The idea, as you may have noticed, is still around.

A job* is a job. It can be an important job, a dull job, or one that pays so well that no one cares if it is dull or important. It's something that we do to make money and if possible enjoy ourselves a little at the same time. It may or may not have a future, and unlike a vocation or a career, it is usually not part of a long-term plan or commitment.

The difference between vocations, careers, and jobs has a great deal to do with the role of work in your life, and at a time when you are making a major change in what you do for a living, it is worth considering. Each of the three categories carries its own set of rewards, problems, and limitations, and each requires a particular attitude if you want to avoid disappointment and unhappiness.

Vocations

True vocations are not limited to the three areas that André Malraux mentioned. Our society has a continuing need for dedicated people. In the social services, counseling, and helping professions former military people can offer a quality of experience that is unmatched. Even though we sometimes tend to raise an eyebrow at the civilian "touchy-feely" approach to human relations, most of us have learned more about counseling and dealing with human nature than we realize. There are few people, officer or enlisted, who have not been required at various times in a military career to help others solve personal problems or face life crises. We have been teachers, voca-

---

*Throughout this book the word *job* will be used for convenience to describe work that may be in the category of career, job, or vocation, but for the present discussion *job* refers to a specific category of work.

tional counselors, and substitute parents throughout our time in the service, and that has given us a background you can't get from a textbook. The civilian community has recently begun to recognize the value of this experience and now actively recruits retired military people for careers in teaching, counseling, and the social services. In some states, special programs have been set up at both the graduate and undergraduate levels to encourage military retirees to enter these professions.

Another area that offers a great opportunity for personal satisfaction is organizations such as the Peace Corps. The pay is terrible and the working conditions are often about the same as a Special Forces "A" Camp, but if you want to contribute to humanity, the rewards are magnificent. Here again, a military background is valuable. The Peace Corps and its private counterparts get more than enough applications from history majors and recent college graduates looking for something to do, but they are desperately short of people who can teach food service or arc welding.

The major disadvantage of most vocations is, of course, the financial compensation. You will not get rich teaching high school or helping dig wells in Africa. If money, "perks," and economic status are high on your list of priorities, you had best not get involved with a vocation. Following a vocation can also be tough on your family and, unless they share your dedication, can cause serious resentment.

Careers

A career involves a long-term investment of your time. The idea of a second career is relatively new to most of the civilian world, but it is gaining some popularity, especially with people who have had great early success and are looking for new worlds to conquer or those who have discovered in midlife that their careers are not living up to expectations. You have an edge on civilian career changers because prospective employers are not likely to wonder why you suddenly gave up your last job.

An interesting variation on career changing is the *ronin* approach suggested by Beverly Potter in her book *Maverick Career Strategies*. Using the example of the *ronin* (who were a sort of medieval Japanese gunslinger), she proposes a career strategy of moving among various jobs and job categories, seeking the best arena for each individual's talents, often without regard for normal career paths. This is a high-risk operation but not as farfetched as it might seem. The traditional idea that one should work for the same organization for an entire career is changing. The search for efficiency and increased competitiveness combined with constantly expanding technology are creating upheaval in the job market. Many traditional jobs and the security they provided are disappearing. New jobs requiring new skills take their place for a few years, only to be replaced in their turn a few years later. The *ronin,* alert and always on the edge of change, moves with new ideas and needs, capitalizing on opportunities and remaining flexible. This novel approach is definitely not for everyone, but for those excited by the challenge of new frontiers (and fast on their feet), it offers interesting possibilities.

Embarking on a new career is a major commitment to the future and has important advantages and disadvantages. Like your military career, it requires that you accept a set of assumptions that go with the job. In the service, you knew that at times you might have to live in dreadful places or that you could be on the way to a shooting war on very short notice. We all hoped to avoid those annoyances if we could, but we knew they were a distinct possibility. Civilian careers require acceptance of similar assumptions. You may start working for a company in a place and a position that are exactly what you want, only to find in a few years that company policy requires you to move or to take a different position from what you had in mind when you started working. This situation occurs when businesses merge, reorganize, or slim down. The standard practice is to offer employees who are high up the corporate ladder the choice of a new position or a severance package (if they are lucky), often on very short notice. If you are unwilling to accept their offer, you are out and often without much in vested retirement or medical benefits.

A second-career retiree is not in a good position when one of these corporate purges occurs. You will have less seniority with the company than most other people, making you subject to the last-hired-first-fired rule. Being a little different from other employees because of a military background may also mark you as a candidate for a cutback. You arc also less likcly to havc a good basis for a tcrmination lawsuit, and no matter what the company may tell you, your military retirement benefits will be a factor in the decision to let you go.

Job security can also be affected by the amount of time you have been out of uniform. Some defense-related organizations make a practice of hiring newly retired people to take advantage of their contacts and current knowledge. After a few years as civilians, when the retirees' knowledge is no longer fresh and the contacts have moved on, their value has decreased and they are let go. This is by no means a universal policy, but it does happen and is another reason why it is a good idea to check out a potential employer thoroughly before making a commitment.

Starting a new career usually requires committing more than time, and it is easy to get in trouble if you don't have your eyes open. Challenging jobs, the ones that bring the greatest rewards, demand long hours, time away from home, and sacrifice of your personal life. It's no different than it was in the service. For many people who are used to a fast-paced, high-pressure military career, it's easy to fall into the habit of fourteen-hour days and continual stress in the new civilian job. Chances are your new boss will love your dedication. Before long you may lose sight of the promises you made to yourself and your family. So before making a major commitment to a demanding new career, be sure that you have a realistic view of how much of yourself you are prepared to put into it. And get the family's opinion. They don't like long hours and separations any more than you do.

One serious point should be stressed. If you were proud to be called a workaholic while you were on active duty and then behave the same way in a new civilian job, maybe you should try to learn why. An obsession with work can be very unhealthy. In fact, it can kill you.

Jobs

For purposes of this discussion, a job can be defined as work that requires a clearly defined and limited amount of personal commitment. You do a job for a certain number of hours per day and receive a fixed amount of compensation, and that's it. You may or may not love the work, the pay may not be as high as you would like, but you do it because you have to earn money. Basically, it's what most of the people in the world do for most of their lives.

Plain old jobs have some obvious disadvantages and some not so obvious advantages. For someone accustomed to a military setting (which is both a vocation and a career), an ordinary job will probably seem bland and unchallenging. Coming as we do from an organization in which there is a constant effort to do things better and a permanent spirit of competition, it can be difficult to adjust to the idea that the boss expects you to do only certain specific tasks for a certain amount of time each day. The armed services recruit people by offering the opportunity to "be all that you can be" and promising that "it's not just a job, it's an adventure," but the plain old job calls for much less. An employer wants someone who is neither overqualified nor underqualified, not too young or too old, and, above all, who will show up on time every day. Such an employee makes the boss's life easier and allows for concentration on what is most important: making money.

Those are the disadvantages of a job, and to some people coming from a dynamic military career it may sound depressing. But there is another side to it, best expressed by a recently retired navy petty officer I know. As both a technician and a leader, he was accustomed to working as long and as hard as necessary to get the job done, taking care of his people, getting ready for inspections, preparing for the next overseas deployment, and handling the duties so familiar to us all. He retired and began work at a pleasant, well-paying job that required only his technical skills, and in the first week he almost went crazy. No employees worked late unless they were asked by the boss to accept overtime, and although the shop produced good-quality work, innovation and competition were not important to anyone, including the boss.

After a few weeks, though, my friend made a discovery. He found to his surprise that he liked the situation as it was. For the first time in years he could leave work at five o'clock on the dot and not feel guilty. He did not have to take the job home with him or worry about next month's inspection and the personal problems of his troops. His free time was his own, his boss was happy, and the paycheck was sufficient reward.

My friend is a wise and happy man because he realized that that job was exactly what he needed. He was not ready to choose a new career that would require a long-term commitment, he did not want to go back to school, and he welcomed the opportunity to take a break from twenty years of a difficult career.

WHEN MUST YOU DECIDE?

Choosing the direction of your future work life is too important a step to be taken in haste. Ideally, everyone should begin making job plans years in advance of retirement, but in the real world, many of us don't. There is too much going on in the here and now to worry about the uncertainties of the future, and we often don't know enough about what's available in the job world to make an intelligent choice. If you are in that situation it may be better to get a little experience at being a civilian before you make a move you might regret later. It is sometimes best to take a job, any job, for a while after you retire. This alternative will give you the time to do long-range planning and the perspective you will need to make a sound decision. That perspective is very important; one of the first things you will learn after you take off the uniform is that the military and the civilian approaches to the world of work are very different.

TWO DIFFERENT WORLDS: OR ARE THEY?

A famous story about humorist Robert Benchley gives an interesting insight into the difference between the military and the civilian points of view. Leaving his favorite hotel bar one night, after a few too many, Benchley turned to the elegantly uniformed gentleman at the hotel entrance and, assuming he was the doorman, asked him to call a taxi. The man glared at Benchley and icily informed him that he was not a doorman but a vice admiral. "OK," Benchley shrugged, "then call me a battleship."

The two men obviously had different perceptions of each other. The civilian view of the military is considerably different from your view of yourself, and civilian values can be very far from the ones you have lived with for most of your adult life. They are not necessarily better or worse, just different. This gulf between the two ways of life is more pronounced than it was a few years ago because fewer people have personal experience with military life. Since the draft ended and the all-volunteer armed forces was created, the number of people with even a few years' exposure to life in uniform has declined and will continue to do so. The aging of the World War II and Korean War veterans and the effect of the Vietnam experience have tended to isolate us from the civilian world. It is not realistic to expect that "they" will feel obliged to make an effort to understand us; after all, when we retire we are playing on their home field. It's our job to find out where the slippery patches are.

This is not to say that standards in the civilian world are completely different from those you are used to. A 1993 survey of fifty-six businesses ranked the top five qualities valued by employers as follows:

1. *Integrity*: Chooses ethical courses of action.
2. *Listening Ability*: Receives, interprets, and responds to verbal messages.
3. *Serves Clients/Customers*: Works to satisfy customers' expectations.
4. *Responsibility*: Exerts a high level of effort and perseveres toward goal attainment.
5. *Works with Diversity*: Can work with men and women with diverse backgrounds.

Not so different from what you learned in leadership training, is it?

Priorities

As you become familiar with civilian attitudes about work, the apparent importance of money will be obvious. Even if military people have worked in finance or have been involved in the budget process, they usually see money only as the means to perform the mission. Military pay is controlled by Congress and is based on fixed criteria such as rank and longevity. We do not negotiate our own salaries, we can't shop around for better compensation packages, and we can't go on strike or ask the boss for a raise. Thus we tend to take a matter-of-fact attitude about pay. We would always like to earn more, but the only way to do that is to get promoted and earn longevity.

In most civilian fields, money is at the top of the priority list. It is the lifeblood of the business world and the single most important measure of success or failure. Regardless of how pleasant a company's working conditions are or how much the company contributes to humanity, nothing counts unless it makes money. This is also true in fields in which the profit motive is not so obvious. Academic status, scientific research, social work, and success in many areas depend on the ability to secure grants and contracts. Even the clergy (although they don't like to admit it) use a reward system based on a minister's ability to generate healthy contributions.

Compensation for work also has a different meaning in the civilian vocabulary. In some fields, particularly in those that approach our definition of a vocation, pay is secondary to intangible rewards, but in others it may be the *only* good thing about the job. Automobile workers are paid well, not because the work requires great skill or dedication but because it is so deadly dull and repetitious. On another level, investment bankers who make spectacular salaries spend a great deal of time poring over stacks of incredibly dull financial data. And even though the image of the successful, hard-charging businessman has a certain glamour, his status may ultimately be based on selling lots of Hostess Twinkies. Money is the real glitter of most civilian achievement.

Imagine how you might have felt if the CO called you in one day and told you that the demand for C-130 flight hours was way down and the squadron would be laying off half the pilots and crew chiefs starting tomorrow. This happens all the time to civilians, so it should not be surprising that they keep a close eye on their benefit packages and frequently check their golden parachutes to make sure they open when someone pulls the string. There are very few guarantees in the private sector, and the tendency over the last decade has been toward reduced pay and benefit packages. Financial insecurity at all levels is common today, and no one will fight for your paycheck if you don't. So if it seems to you that people out there in the other world are preoccupied with money, you're right. They have to be.

Values

Philosophers and psychologists can argue about it for centuries, but generally speaking, our values come from two sources, the home and family and the external world. For career military people, the most influential part of that external world has been our service experience. Not everyone in uniform has the same set of values—we are still individuals. But we do share a common set of attitudes that over the years have become a basic part of our personality.

Patriotism. The armed forces are such an inseparable part of our country that patriotism is a natural condition of service. Military people are not necessarily flag wavers—our feelings tend to be more low key but closer to our everyday lives. There is little dissent over matters of ideology and government policy because very often we have been the instruments of policy. We carry out the decisions; we don't make them. We are very cautious about exercising strong opposition to government policy. The United States has a stronger tradition of an apolitical military establishment than any nation in the West, and for the most part it is a heritage to be proud of.

But you don't have to wear a uniform to be patriotic, and you don't have to support the government. After retirement, when your daily contact is mostly with people not in the service, you will quickly realize that there are a lot of folks out there who view the government, the flag, and many of the traditions sacred to you with suspicion, distrust, and open hostility. They are not bad people. They just see things differently than you do. Unless you decide to surround yourself with other military and former military people and spend the remainder of your life living in the past, you can expect to be exposed to a much broader definition of patriotism and loyalty to country than you ever dreamed of. This will be true on the job as well as socially, and if you let it upset you it can cause problems. In fields such as the arts and the social services, the protest mystique of the 1960s is still alive and well. Your coworkers and even your boss may be veterans, not of the Vietnam War but of the antiwar movement. You will have to learn how to get along.

This does not mean that you should abandon your basic beliefs and values to accommodate a new situation. On the contrary, you may use the situation as an opportunity to present the military's side of the story to someone who has never heard it on a personal level and in the process promote a little human understanding and mutual respect.

Commitment. No one takes an oath of loyalty to General Motors. That company undoubtedly has thousands of loyal employees, but few of them see their commitment to the company as a transcendent obligation. Nor does the company expect such loyalty. The difference between a civilian's responsibility to his employer and the military sense of duty is subtle but profound and too often misinterpreted by those of us who must make the transition from service to civilian life. As a result, we sometimes tend to apply our familiar standards of duty to the totally different requirements of the civilian work world. This tendency is one of the reasons why some employers are reluctant to hire retired military people for supervisory or management positions. Many of them feel that we are unable to get anything done without resorting to authoritarian behavior, which would bring instant resistance from their employees, not to mention strikes and lawsuits. Regardless of how inaccurate this belief may be, you can expect that you will encounter it in some form, and if you don't understand and accept the differences between the military and the civilian attitudes toward work, you might be one of those who perpetuate the misunderstanding.

It is equally unfair of people with a military background to sneer at the values of our civilian counterparts. As supervisor of a civilian shop or factory, you might be inclined to look down your nose at the employee who takes great pride in his or her work record simply because of always clocking in and out on time. In your military career, you think, you stayed around until the work was done and never went by the clock.

You might not realize that being on time every day for ten or fifteen years, never missing a day's work, and putting in a full eight hours is a source of pride to those employees, and rightly so. Incentives to do the job are much less compelling than they are in the armed forces. There is no reveille to start the day briskly, no sergeant or master at arms to urge one to awaken, and above all, no UCMJ hanging overhead. There is also less positive incentive. Going to work in the morning, a civilian employee is part of an undistinguished herd in coveralls or three-piece suits. There are no badges of rank, no decorations to wear, and no flag to salute. It's worse than the Pentagon. Going to work every day requires more internal motivation than most of us realize, and after you have done it for a while you will gain admiration for the secretary who for years has arrived at the same desk in the same office promptly at the stroke of nine because now you have to do it, too.

Professional Ethics

The era of corporate takeovers, dishonest bankers, and environmental and social activism has made ethics a subject of considerable attention. Professions such as law and medicine, which have built-in codes of ethics, have come under fire, and congressional representatives have found themselves under increasing pressure to establish ethical standards for themselves. We appear to be in an "ethics gap" like the missile gap of the 1960s.

Except for the issues raised by the Vietnam War, the military establishment has been immune to controversy in this area. Public opinion polls continue to show a high level of confidence in the armed forces, though trust in other institutions declines. People in uniform can be justifiably proud of this. As part of a military generation that endured some very rough public criticism in the Vietnam years, it is a pride you earned the hard way.

The problem you face now is to take that combat-tested ethic into a different world without either abandoning it or becoming a misanthrope. To do so, you will need wisdom and judgment. You may discover that there are some jobs and situations that you had best avoid because they will require compromising much of the pride in what you are and have been in the past. Yet you must be careful to avoid setting yourself up as a judge of other people's behavior or, even worse, developing a self-righteous, superior attitude toward ethical standards different from your own. The military ethic can teach the civilian world a few things if it is applied with tolerance. If it is not, you may find yourself being cast as the familiar stereotype of the "military mind," that is, as a rigid, inflexible dinosaur.

It's a tough world out there. Competition, whether for business or for a new federal research grant, can get rough sometimes, and the rules are often not as clearly defined as they are in the military world. In many fields the rules allow whatever the law does not prohibit. If that sounds shocking, consider why people hire experts to do their taxes. It's not to make sure that the Internal Revenue Service (IRS) gets every nickel it deserves. People want to pay as little tax as possible without breaking the law. Is it immoral? Not unless we lie or cheat. No one, not even the IRS, expects taxpayers to be dedicated to the spirit of the tax law. That's why taxes are not voluntary. The vague ethical code that covers much of everyday work activity is based on a similar assumption. If you want to believe that a bright red new car will do wonders for your sex life, don't expect the auto salesman to take you aside for personal counseling; his goal is to sell the car, not to straighten out your psyche.

These examples are simplistic, but they illustrate some basic principles of practical ethics. The first principle is that moral and ethical judgments should not be applied to situations that do not involve moral issues. The caveat "let the buyer beware" is not a cynical statement of the unethical salesman but a definition of the implied understanding between buyer and seller. The second principle is that in many civilian jobs, professional ethics have a more limited application than they do in the service. If everyone who sold women's fashions was completely honest with all customers, the miniskirt would never have become popular.

The Social Side. Television and the movies show the social side of military life as a combination of endless cocktail parties, tea with the colonel's lady, and interludes in an exotic port. It is a very unrealistic picture, and the TV version of corporate socializing is just as bad. Most people who work don't take two-hour lunches, are not required to join the country club, and usually behave themselves at office parties. Mandatory social activity, like the infamous "command performance" of the armed forces, is much less common than popular folklore indicates. Two-career families and changing social values have reduced the emphasis on social requirements in the civilian sector just as they have in the military, and only rarely or at the higher echelons of the corporate hierarchy are social obligations very important.

When there is social activity connected with the job, you will find to your surprise that everything you learned during your military career about etiquette and protocol will fit in perfectly. In fact, you will probably be more at ease than most of your civilian contemporaries, who can get unbelievably uptight about social nuances that are second nature to you. This is true whether you retired as a navy captain or a command master sergeant.

Social life in a work setting is common. You may have to learn to live with the "working lunch" or that more barbaric custom, the "working breakfast." In both instances avoid eating and drinking too much of the wrong things. The Italians and the French have won countless battles at the conference table by stupefying the opposition with a magnificent lunch and marvelous wine. In the same way, a 7:00 A.M. power breakfast when you are horribly hungover from the night before can be the most exquisite of tortures, as well as losing you all the marbles before the scheduled game even starts. The traditional three-martini lunch is passé these days, but some wily competitors will cheerfully urge lunchtime booze on you (while they drink Perrier) to make you more agreeable. For former military people, who are accustomed to the more austere boxed flight lunches and the Pentagon snack bars, the business lunch can be a pleasant change. But as the old Roman philosopher said, we should seek moderation in all things.

SELF-ASSESSMENT

You may be able to decide on the right job after retirement without any research or outside help. But if you feel no strong pull toward any particular line of work, it is very easy to drift through the classified ads almost at random in the hope that you will see something, *anything* that looks interesting. This is not a good way to plan your future.

People who have spent their active-duty careers in strongly military-oriented jobs usually have the most difficult time deciding on a civilian path. A quick glance through the paper will not reveal many openings for destroyer captains or artillerymen, and for someone who has spent years immersed in his own area of military expertise, the description of many civilian positions can seem foreign and downright incomprehensible. Faced with a discouraging prospect, we begin to doubt our employment value and can be easily tempted into jobs well below our abilities. Some people, believing that their military background is not marketable on its own merits, become convinced that they must disguise it as comparable civilian experience. By the time they have finished the cosmetic work, even *they* don't know who they are.

Neither of these drastic alternatives is necessary. A man or woman who has successfully completed twenty or more years on active military service brings skills and qualities to the job market that are much in demand in virtually every civilian field. What we have to do is to identify our special characteristics and learn how to use them to our best advantage.

Military transition programs now offer considerable assistance in skills assessment. Transition counselors can guide you through a skills inventory and, if you feel you need additional help, recommend more focused testing and counseling. The Transition Assistance Program (TAP) workbook also offers a step-by-step personal appraisal that will give you a good start. The TAP appraisal should be thought of as a foundation. For retirees, a more exhaustive exploration is a better idea.

Self-assessment is an important job even if you think you know what you want to do. It will help you put together a better résumé, assist you in presenting your skills at an interview, and, at the minimum, point you in the right direction. Be thorough. Whether you do a self-administered skills assessment or use someone else's system, the result will depend on how conscientiously (and honestly) you do the job.

Self-Discipline

Getting up in the morning, arriving on time every day, and setting and keeping to a schedule are second nature to someone with a military background. We take this high degree of self-discipline for granted. But in the civilian world punctuality is a prized commodity, valuable enough to be a significant job qualification in itself. Everyone has heard the warning about buying cars built on a Monday. Absentee rates in organizations from General Motors down to your local pizzeria are a major problem for employers, and the lack of personal self-discipline permeates all levels of society. There are executives at the highest levels of corporate management who have never learned to operate in a systematic, consistent way and cannot function without a phalanx of assistants and secretaries. In an era when most of the private sector is under pressure to become leaner and meaner (a slogan borrowed from the military), such a bureaucratic management style is becoming unacceptable. A job candidate who can present a track record that shows personal and professional self-discipline will have a significant advantage over the competition.

Leadership

Judging from the perennial controversy surrounding this subject in the armed forces, one might think that, like the American novel and the snail darter, it is on the verge of extinction. The civilian community pays much less attention to leadership as a requirement for success on the job. Library shelves offer hundreds of books on management but very few on how to lead, and despite all the self-improvement courses, seminars, and workshops available today, leadership is an almost nonexistent topic.

Why is this so? Outside the military establishment there is little appreciation of leadership as a useful attribute in daily life. Unless the subject is presidential candidates or pro quarterbacks, we don't discuss it much. The words we use to describe leadership, like "elusive qualities" and "indefinable something," suggest that it is so nebulous as to be impossible to learn or to measure. But we in the armed forces were never told this. Leadership was something you had to learn and practice. It was necessary for promotion and advancement. Unlike our civilian counterparts, we simply went out and did it, and after a while it became a habit.

That "habit of leadership" may be one of the most valuable assets you can take into your postretirement life. Success at practicing the art and science of leadership helped get you where you are. Learning how to lead and, equally important, how to follow has given you some distinctive abilities to bring into the job market. When you read chapter 5 and begin specific job search planning and cataloging your experience, you will see that leadership will be one of your big selling points, regardless of what your chosen field may be.

Dealing with People

All career people in all services are proven experts at working with people. Early in training we learn that people are one of the most important parts of the job. Leadership does not operate in a vacuum, and one of the earliest lessons of an apprentice leader is that skill in human relations is a *sine qua non* of success. Our competence in what the civilian world calls human resources was refined and tested through a range of situations much wider than is encountered in most areas of endeavor. The legal requirement of equal opportunity for women and minorities, the social upheaval of the Vietnam era, and current issues involving single parents and child care have all been confronted by the armed forces. We worked with those problems daily and in the process gained considerable insight into human relations. The training in human resources you received is recognized as the best of its kind. Combined with your practical experience, it should be part of the credentials you take into a new career.

Loyalty

Despite the dubious glamour associated with the barracudas of the business world and the popularity of the "me first" attitude, loyalty carries a lot of weight with employers. They don't expect the degree of commitment that is normal to military service, but they appreciate loyalty to the institution and, in good organizations, will reward it. Unless you have dreams of slugging it out at the very top levels of the corporate world, a reputation for loyalty will benefit you in most environments. It will help you sleep better, too.

Initiative

If newspaper job ads are a true reflection of employers' needs, initiative is in high demand. Pleas for "self-starters" abound. The columns almost seem to beg for people who can work without close supervision. In the actual work environment, the need is even more apparent. We have, unfortunately, become a nation of legalists, addicted to reading job descriptions in painstaking detail, more concerned with not doing too much than with not doing enough. Without an internal ethic to set a standard for themselves, people tend to do the minimum and to define their responsibilities solely in terms of what will satisfy the boss or fulfill their contract. Using initiative requires self-reliance and a willingness to take risks. It is part of an attitude that leads us to seek ways to do the job better and improve the quality of our work simply because we take pride in accomplishment.

Military people are expected to demonstrate initiative in every assignment of their active-duty career. The sense of pride in our command came from the knowledge that we had personally done something to make it better. It was nice to be rewarded, but even without the promise of a tangible payoff we gave that extra effort. Every student of military history can reel off the names of battles won because someone used an extra measure of initiative or lost because a leader did no more than he was told. The habit of using initiative stays with us even after we take off the uniform. It's no coincidence that retired military people fill many key positions in community and volunteer organizations. When you start making an inventory of what you can offer a prospective employer, don't overlook initiative.

Integrity

Your résumé probably won't reflect your integrity. You will not be asked to show integrity credentials, and the subject may never be mentioned in connection with a possible job. Nevertheless, it will be expected and its absence will usually ensure a quick ticket to the unemployment office. A reputation for integrity is as important to the smallest everyday dealings with people as it is to major decision making. We choose a particular lawyer, car mechanic, or real estate broker because we trust him or her, and though we are usually willing to overlook some shortcomings, even a hint of questionable integrity will end the relationship. Good organizations insist on integrity. Businesses and professions that make a practice of skirting the bounds of ethical behavior, on the other hand, are nothing but trouble for the people they deal with and will be for you if you are foolish enough to work for them.

Choosing a new career is not only a matter of discovering what you can offer the world; it also requires thought about what terms of employment you are willing to accept. A tradition of integrity, one of the cornerstones of the military ethic, is an attribute you will bring to any job you undertake. You have a right to expect that an employer will value this quality as much as you do. If you have any reason to believe he doesn't, it's time to do some serious soul searching. Integrity is too valuable to sell to the highest bidder.

ATTRIBUTES AND ABILITIES: FILLING IN THE PICTURE

The list of qualities common to most career military people discussed above is by no means complete. Other attributes, including reliability, flexibility, and the ability to accept change, will occur to you as you reflect on your service experience. Together they sketch out a unique profile of the characteristics you can bring to your next job. Don't be shy about bringing them to a prospective employer's attention. If modesty stands in your way, remember that you earned the right to be proud by paying your dues for a long time in a very tough, demanding, and exclusive club.

In addition to the special qualities your time in the service has given you, it has also made you highly skilled in one or more specialized fields. Exposure to experiences outside your own discipline has given you a richer and more diverse background than you realize. At one time or another all of us have found ourselves doing jobs that had little to do with what we were trained for. It's the nature of the service that, when a task comes up, we pitch in and do it. In Vietnam, military people built schools, raised chickens, and taught language classes. Some of us discovered that these "nontraditional" duties brought out aptitudes and interests we never dreamed we had.

Your skills and talents are a combination of those you have been using and developing for all these years and others that were discovered only because you happened to get involved in something outside your normal experience. There is still another category of aptitudes: those you don't know you have because you have never been in a position to explore them.

Proven Abilities

You have been paid for doing certain jobs and you have a record of accomplishments, promotions, and rewards to verify your competence. If you are lucky enough to be in a field that can be translated directly into a civilian job, and you want to remain in that field, your self-assessment will be easy. The main task facing you will be to identify the level of civilian responsibility that best corresponds to your credentials, then begin the job search outlined in the next few chapters. Count your blessings. You have the easiest assignment in the class.

People who have developed expertise in areas not so easily adapted to the nonmilitary world have a slightly harder job. Fortunately, many service career areas have applications universal enough to be useful after retirement. As a rule of thumb, the more technical a specialty is, the easier it is to find a similar civilian job. Electronics, aviation, logistics support, and engineering all have counterparts that often differ from the military arena only in terminology. But be careful. Job titles can have meanings entirely different from how they look. The best way to determine the civilian word for your job is to go to a reference such as the *Dictionary of Occupational Titles* or the *Encyclopedia of Second Careers*. Articles and advertisements in trade and technical journals will also provide an idea of what a job specialty entails and the qualifications and background normally expected of candidates. Don't confine your research to one job category, no matter how attractive it looks. List all possible applications of your career skills, including those you haven't used recently. When you begin identifying specific job openings (chapter 5), you may discover unexpected opportunities in areas you would never have thought of.

Review all the jobs you have held during your career, with emphasis on the most recent. Rereading your old performance evaluations, qualification records, letters of commendation, and award citations can help jog your memory. If this work is done thoroughly, you will develop a list of skills and qualifications that will become the basis of your proven skills inventory. The list will also be useful to match your skills to specific jobs and provide material for your résumé.

Generalists: A Special Case

Those of us still left standing in the back of the room after all the specialists and technical experts have gone are known as generalists. We are the "big-picture" people who always prided ourselves on being able to learn how to do any job that came our way. Generalists are much admired but seldom hired by civilian employers. Although top-echelon managers usually see themselves as generalists, on the way to the top they had to spend time in positions that most military officers would consider narrow and specialized. That was the way they paid their dues to get to the top, so it should not be surprising that they don't welcome with open arms someone who has not punched the same tickets. Except for very senior flag and general officers, the title of generalist will not cut much ice in the civilian world.

If you insist on portraying yourself as a true generalist and are determined to stay that way, be prepared for an uphill fight. The '90s is an era of the expert, and in some fields, calling yourself a "broad generalist" is a sure path to job rejection. Your competition will be selling themselves as experts in most situations, and many other career areas, like those related to defense, where employers didn't really care if you called yourself a generalist as long as you had a solid military background, are drying up.

People who still want to go into a new career as a generalist have three alternatives. First, you can review your background experience and divide it into areas that have some commonality. For example, an air force fighter pilot who served three or four staff tours in operations and readiness would probably discover that those jobs all had certain common tasks such as scheduling and coordinating operations. These tasks could be the basis for developing a profile that fits civilian positions requiring the same skills and experience. If this results in a match that offers realistic and acceptable opportunities, it may be worthwhile to continue more specific exploration.

The second alternative is to look at your experience from the perspective of which assignments and tours of duty you enjoyed the most. Write down the reasons why those jobs were attractive to you. Was it the location? The people you worked with? The day-to-day problems you handled? You may be surprised to find interests emerging that you have never consciously admitted were important to you.

The third approach is to ask yourself what it was about your interests, abilities, and professional development that led you to be a generalist. Your first reaction to that question may be a mental shrug and the conclusion that it just happened that way. Nothing "just happens" in an important part of life like your career. You ended up where you did for a reason far from accidental. The job now is to discover what that reason was and determine how it fits into planning for the future.

Collateral Skills

Collateral skills are those that are outside your specialty. The list can be long when you include hobbies, outside activities, and special assignments. Any area in which you have gained significant knowledge or skill should be included, even if it seems to be an unlikely foundation for a career. Many civilian jobs call for unusual combinations of background and qualifications. If your combination is what is wanted, you will be a standout candidate.

Go through the following list of collateral skills and write down everything you can think of, no matter how minor it may seem. Ask your family and friends to help, too. They may remember things that would not occur to you.

Additional Duties. Jobs you were assigned outside your regular duties might include membership on boards or committees, command representative for career or other counseling, exchange duties with other services or agencies, inspection teams, ad hoc working groups, and study groups.

Hobbies. This area can be a significant source of future achievement. Tom Clancy, author of *The Hunt for Red October,* used his knowledge as a war game enthusiast to produce a successful literary career. Hobbies and outside interests can sometimes be converted into a small business or job skill or they can back up your proven skills.

Part-Time Jobs. An advantage of part-time work is that it gives you experience in a civilian environment. No job is too insignificant. A few hours a day as a salesperson in an electronics store counts as retail experience. It also says good things about your ambition and energy.

Community Service. Volunteer counseling and other social service will add to your credentials for job opportunities in those areas and can be a help in other fields as well. Holding office in a civic organization demonstrates management ability and a talent for getting things done.

Organizations. Membership in special interest or fraternal organizations such as Toastmasters teaches you public speaking, computer clubs add to your technical knowledge, and other groups develop skills in sales and human relations. But be careful. A background in controversial or offbeat organizations can give you a label you might not want. "Survivalists," "New Age" enthusiasts, and other fringe groups give negative signals to prospective employers. Unless you are going to hire out as a mercenary, keep this information off your list of collateral skills.

Off-Duty Education. A course in tax preparation or creative writing or training in any technical area can give you the extra qualification that will someday get you a job. Review all of your past training and education for possible useful skills.

Hidden Talents

Everyone has untapped abilities that have never been developed into job skills. A flair for writing or the intuitive understanding of how machinery fits together are examples. Unexpected ability may have surfaced accidentally through your job, in recreational activity, or at home. Now can be the time to find out if any of these talents can be converted into a job. Some will be easy. If you love working on exotic cars as a pastime, or if others have often complimented you on your skill at interior decoration, you may need only a little push and some training to begin a career. Other talents will require definition and interpretation, perhaps by experts. Don't sell your innate talents short. Not many people are so fortunate as to be paid to do something they are naturally good at.

TESTING AND COUNSELING

Self-assessment is not easy for everyone. It can be difficult to evaluate all the experience of a twenty- or thirty-year military career objectively, and we are not always the best judge of our own abilities. There are some things we enjoy immensely but are not especially good at. There is also a little of the romanticist in us all, and the temptation to idealize some activity that gave us pleasure in the past can lead to very unrealistic expectations. If you don't believe that, think back to the time you met your high school heart throb twenty years later. It was not quite what you had expected, was it?

Your perception of the ideal job may be equally inaccurate. While you were on active duty you never needed to know anything about jobs outside the military establishment. When observing civilian counterparts at tasks you knew you could do easily, your exposure was limited to areas that were familiar to you. You didn't see that civilian's job as a whole, which may have included some requirements outside your expertise or ability.

We are also at a disadvantage because we often don't know any more about what civilians actually do in their jobs than they know about the service. Seagoing naval officers are amused when someone unfamiliar with hectic fleet operations asks how they pass all their spare time at sea, but they are likely to be equally uninformed about how a civilian manager runs his operation.

The realization that we may know very little about what we are capable of doing for a living and just as little about what most jobs require suggests the next step in self-assessment.

Testing

Aptitude testing, psychological testing, and skills inventory are parts of the process of identifying an individual's assets and matching them to possible jobs. At some point in your early service career you were tested and classified either through formal classification methods or by the selection process, and in all probability, the direction of your professional career was determined by the results. But that was a long time ago. Time and circumstances change our perspective on the world, and the experience of living alters our priorities. At this point in life, we possess more and different skills than we did twenty years ago, but exactly how different may not be easy to define without assistance. This is where testing and counseling come into the picture.

You will want to look into vocational or aptitude testing and psychological testing. In their broadest application, aptitude tests measure what you can do best and match those skills with job categories. The best aptitude tests are brutally honest; they tell you what you *can* do, not necessarily what you would like to do. For someone making a major career change this is an important distinction. The chance to strike out in an entirely new direction doesn't come along every day. In our enthusiasm to try something new, we sometimes let wishful thinking take the place of realistic self-appraisal.

Testing can assist in your career decision in several ways. First, it can suggest job possibilities you may not have considered. For someone contemplating a return to school, testing can point the way to the most rewarding area of study and give the extra measure of confidence needed to plunge into something new. The results of aptitude testing can also serve as a warning signal if they show a significant weakness in your abilities. Discovery of weak areas does not mean that you must give up a specific career possibility. It merely indicates that you will have to work harder at overcoming the lack of aptitude. If you are willing to do this, you can probably compensate for all but the most serious problems.

The most important benefit of testing is to outline a range of realistic possibilities. Career choice and a job search based on this foundation will be easier than if you are guided by guesswork or a "gut feeling" and more likely to produce a job that will suit you over the long haul. It's like a pilot's cockpit checklist. You can get off the ground without it, but it gives you a nice warm feeling when things get sticky.

Psychological testing can also assist in deciding on a career or a job. Such an evaluation will not offer any direct suggestions as to a career field, but it can tell you some useful things about yourself, particularly in areas you might not be willing to probe without assistance. An increasing number of employers require psychological testing for all prospective employees. They use the results not to test competence but to identify significant personality problems. Career counselors and placement specialists often use a standard psychological test to complete the initial workup of a client's profile. If the initial set of tests uncovers any problem areas, counselors will usually suggest a more detailed evaluation and professional help, if necessary.

If all this conjures up a picture of your mind being probed by somebody with a beard and a funny accent, relax. It's not like that at all. You have made it through a military career that tests you and imposes more psychological pressure than most other jobs, and if you had any seriously debilitating problems, someone would have found out by now. Psychological testing will fill out one more part of the picture of what the next career may be. Think of it as another look, from a different perspective, at the complex of skills, personality traits, and experience you will be taking into the market.

Counseling

Psychological and aptitude testing does not have to be accompanied by counseling, but you may want the help of a trained specialist to interpret the test findings and guide your career and job search. Free counseling can be obtained through your base transition office or the VA or may be offered by a state or local agency. Just because it's free does not mean it won't be of high quality, and even if the available support is limited, it is still better than going it alone. At the very least, VA and other public counseling services will stimulate your thinking and sharpen the focus of your career planning.

Private counseling is another possibility. It can range from basic testing and aptitude analysis to a full-service operation that takes you all the way through the job search. But the more you get the more you pay, and no one (at least no one reputable) will guarantee you a job. Should you decide that it is worth the extra cost to pay a professional counselor, be sure you know in advance, and in writing, what you will get for your money and how much it will cost. Avoid those who say job placement is the main part of their service; they are usually thinly disguised employment agencies or questionable pseudo-outplacement services. Remember, at this point in your journey to a new career, you are less interested in specific jobs than in deciding on a job field. Stick to first things first.

If you are thinking of going back to school, both the VA and most schools will offer guidance to help you get moving in the right direction. Schools also offer, and in some cases require, that you take tests to verify the suitability of your educational choice.

People pick up habits over twenty or more years. Some of the personality traits you have acquired during your career may have developed so gradually that you don't notice them yourself. If you have been in a leadership position, your idiosyncrasies may have been overlooked by seniors because you always got the job done and tolerated by subordinates because they had no choice. Now, though, some of those personality traits may jump up and bite you if you aren't prepared to recognize and do something about them. Testing and counseling may be the only way to solve these problems. We accept more graciously the criticism and advice of detached professionals than we do comments by concerned friends and family, and that is one of the great advantages of counseling. As uncomfortable as it may be to admit that after a long and successful career we are less than perfect, it is easier to make this discovery now than it will be after you have had a succession of failed interviews or, even worse, a string of unsatisfactory job experiences.

THE DECISION

The process just described should provide you with all the information needed to make a decision about the direction of your future work life. If you have done the suggested thinking, research, testing, and counseling, you have probably done more real career planning than most people ever do, and the basis for your decision will be as sound as the vagaries of human nature will permit.

Other methods of self-assessment and skills inventory are available. Books such as Richard Bolle's *The Three Boxes of Life* provide a step-by-step method of analyzing both life and work interests. Other systems, some in workbook format, can also be helpful. Adult education and minicourses on the subject are becoming increasingly popular. Don't overlook the seminars and workshops offered at military installations. They are designed to meet the needs of military people, and they are free.

But suppose you're still not sure? And what if you don't want to make a decision right now? Don't worry about it. For the first year or so after retirement you will be exposed to different ways of earning a living. There is no rule graven in stone that requires a firm career decision before or immediately after you leave the service. The thinking and self-assessment that you have begun and the tests and counseling you may have scheduled will get you started in the right direction but not necessarily right away. Some of us need time to allow the experience to soak in or to ruminate on the possibilities. An unexpected job opportunity may suddenly appear in a field you had not considered. If that happens, take the job even if you have no intention of making it your life's work. The experience gained from working at a civilian job is valuable in itself and will give you more information to help in the final decision, as well as a paycheck. There is no stigma attached to changing jobs one or two years after retirement, and job experience in the nonmilitary environment will only add to your qualifications for the right job when you are ready to make your move.

4

ALTERNATIVES

♦

Most of us define a job as working for someone else in a conventional business or professional setting. And in fact, that's what most jobs are. For that reason, books on job search strategy, management techniques, and other subjects associated with career planning tend to focus on positions in business organizations. Other fields are given only a light once-over or relegated to the odds-and-ends category, often with the implication that if you can't get a *real* job, here are some other possibilities.

In those dear, dead days when the steel mills still belched smoke and Charles Wilson reigned supreme at General Motors, that emphasis on the world of commerce was justified. In the last few decades, however, the American job landscape has changed drastically. Today only 20 percent of the U.S. workforce is employed in the manufacturing sector; 57 percent work in service or retail jobs and 17 percent are government employees. There are fast-growing career fields today that didn't exist twenty years ago, and new ones are popping up every day. As our society continues to change, the things we do to keep it running change too. Old jobs disappear and new ones take their place; areas where opportunity used to be limited, such as education and child care, suddenly blossom. According to a recent *Best Jobs Almanac,* the very best job in the country is an actuary's,* one of the least likely choices most of us could imagine.

For someone who has invested many years in a traditional business or commercial career, these great changes can be upsetting, even threatening. But for one who is moving into the job market after military retirement the possibilities are exciting. Retiring military people have an advantage over their civilian counterparts who are moving out of "soft" career fields; we are not under the same financial and psychological pressure, and we are making a planned and orderly transition from one completed career to the promise of another one. The specter of an uncertain future is not as scary as it is to someone being forced by circumstances to make a radical course change in the middle of a working life.

For this reason, a future in a less explored job area is an option worth considering. Whether your goal is a career, a vocation, or a job, the opportunity is there if you are willing to learn the requirements, take the risks, and accept the challenge.

This chapter will discuss the alternatives available to people who do not want a job in the business world. Some of these, government service or teaching, for example, are similar to jobs in the private sector but different enough to

---

*Actuaries figure out the odds on things (usually bad) happening to us, like being struck by lightning at your rich aunt's funeral. They work for insurance companies and are similar to respectable bookies except that they wear more subdued ties.

deserve special thought. Others, such as consulting or running your own business, demand an approach different from the normal career preparation and job search campaign. Going back to school is in a special category. It offers some of the greatest rewards but also demands some of the most difficult sacrifices and adjustments.

The alternatives discussed in the following pages are not exhaustive. Other fields such as the clergy, politics, arts and craft work, and, for the truly masochistic, writing for a living have their attractions. All of these career choices and the ones to be discussed differ from more conventional jobs in that they require some unique quality or talent. If your self-assessment suggests the presence of such an aptitude, you owe it to yourself to consider ways to put it to use. Your retirement has created a momentum for change and prospects for a new direction that do not come along often in life. If there was ever a perfect time to scratch that career itch, it is now.

BACK TO SCHOOL: THE FIRST ALTERNATIVE

Education has always been a ticket to a better future, but today it is almost a necessity. The job marketplace is changing so quickly that even people already well established in a career are going back to school to keep from falling behind. More and more, employers are looking for people with specific and current educational qualifications in their résumé; with the decline of the generalist has come the rise of the certified specialist. Other factors like the communications revolution and the growth of technology in general have pushed employers toward expecting skills that are more specialized and can be documented by some educational credentials. Colleges and universities now offer degrees and graduate education in specialized disciplines that didn't even have a name twenty years ago.

For many retiring military people there is a second reason for going back to school. It may be the only way some of us can get a decent job. As has already been mentioned, the decline of job opportunities in defense-related industries has thinned out the possibilities for jobs in that field. At the same time, the Baby Boomer generation (of which you may be a part) has glutted the market with qualified and experienced people. Boomers have also learned how to hang tenaciously onto their jobs. They've lived through almost a decade of corporate downsizing, takeovers, and reorganizations that has taught them how to survive in a tough, sometimes brutal, job market. The competition of the '90s will be just as stiff, and you will need every tool you can get your hands on to compete with the corporate veterans of the '80s.

Recent education gives military retirees another plus. It tells an employer that you are someone who is ready and willing to adapt and change, qualities that are highly prized in both the public and private sector. A fresh civilian diploma also helps leaven your military experience with a civilian flavor and can go a long way toward reducing the age disadvantage that often comes with being forty or older.

People in midlife are often reluctant to go back to school. We remember school as an experience of our youth, and as time goes by, students seem younger and younger, speaking a language of their own and living in a world very different from ours. The thought of becoming one of them is amusing but a bit threatening. It's much more comfortable to remain in our own familiar orbit and leave school to the kids, so we forget any ideas about becoming a student again, thereby depriving ourselves of one of the most rewarding experiences of adult life.

Talk to someone your own age who is back in school and you will be surprised. The intellectual stimulation of a modest educational effort is like a tonic to people. Whether they are studying landscaping or working on a Ph.D., the experience of learning gives people a new attitude toward life. It makes us think in ways we thought we had forgotten years ago, and association with students younger than ourselves helps to freshen up our own outlook. Returning to school can bring to blossom talents and skills we never thought we had. School will broaden your social and intellectual horizons at a time in life when a wider perspective is especially useful. It can be a buffer between your military career and a new role that might not be completely defined and a catalyst for a change in direction.

Financial hardship is another reason why we are reluctant to go back to school. This is not an imaginary problem. Training schools and colleges are expensive, and even with the best possible combination of scholarships and financial aid you will be on a tight budget if you are a full-time student unless you have substantial savings. But there are some ways to make the going a little easier, and with a retirement check coming in every month you will probably be better off than most of your fellow students.

If finances are a major factor in your decision about going back to school, sit down with your family and figure out how much it will cost and how expenses will be met. Here are some facts to consider.

Taxes

Going to school can give you a significant tax benefit. Money obtained through scholarships and service-related benefits is not considered as income if it is applied to tuition and fees. If it goes to cover food and lodging, it is taxable. Legitimate expenses for equipment and supplies required for education and training are deductible, too, so be sure to keep good records. Although the amount you will

save in taxes will not give you a free education, it will help
and should be added to the positive side of your balance
sheet.

Children's Education

If one parent is a full-time student, children are automatically eligible for more financial assistance under the federal government's financial aid formula used as a basis for
granting aid at most educational institutions. This can
make a significant difference in aid for both you and your
children.

Part-Time Work

There is no reason why you can't hold a part-time job
while you are in school. Most young students work, and you
are certainly better at organizing your time than they are.
You also have more skills to offer and may be able to find
an employer who will contribute to your education expenses if you agree to work for him later. Many schools
have work-study arrangements with companies and agencies, including the government and the public school system. Some schools operate co-op system that incorporates
one academic quarter of work in your field every year. The
co-op jobs offered under such a program provide valuable
experience and a break from the classroom, and they often
pay well enough to make a sizable dent in your expenses.
Remember, too, that unless you are attending school year-
round, you will be able to earn something during the summer break.

Veterans Benefits

The old GI Bill died quietly a few years ago and was replaced by the Veterans Educational Assistance Act of 1984,
better known as the Montgomery GI Bill. To be covered by

this law you must have been on active duty on 19 October 1984, and have served three years of continuous active duty after 30 June 1985. Almost all '90s retirees will fall into this category *except* for those who were commissioned from service academies or through ROTC scholarship programs *after 31 December 1976.*

Benefits can be applied to colleges and universities, apprenticeship training, and non–college-degree training such as flight training and cooperative courses. You may also receive benefits for correspondence courses and remedial or work-study programs. If you aren't sure if a program qualifies for GI benefits, be sure to contact the VA before you put any money down.

Eligibility under the Montgomery GI bill lasts for ten years after you leave the service. The program offers thirty-six months of education assistance at a current (1994) rate of $588 per month for single veterans and $624 for married people.

The positive aspects of going back to school can make the burden easier to bear, but you should be prepared to sacrifice time, leisure, and economic comfort. The rewards, however, are great. In addition to earning a freshly minted career qualification, you will come away from an educational experience with a new outlook on the world, more confidence in your abilities, and the foundation for an entirely different direction in life. It might be worth a try.

TEACHING

One of the most rewarding of professions, teaching has suffered for years under a bum rap. Bad pay, a perception of low prestige, and perennial horror stories about terrible teaching conditions have combined to create a negative image that is hard to overcome. Yet teaching has some advantages that make it an attractive choice for military retirees.

A few years ago it began to dawn on Washington and some state governments that retired military people might make good teachers. In 1988 the secretary of defense and the secretary of education formally recognized this potential and issued this statement:

> We are pleased to announce a new effort to encourage retired and retiring military personnel to consider second careers as teachers and administrators in the Nation's schools. . . . In second careers as teachers or administrators, many former military personnel can make outstanding contributions. . . . Their background, experience and character suit them to the challenge of teaching and administering. They have had years of experience; organizing, leading, instructing and inspiring—what good teaching is all about.

Since 1988 the states have also jumped on the bandwagon. Many places now offer teaching-certification programs designed specifically for former military people. In some states you can begin doing the required course work well before retirement, move into the classroom as a teaching intern or student teacher after you leave the service, and be fully qualified in a fairly short time. Your transition-assistance office or educational-service office should be able to help you learn about what programs are available for your area.

Even if you were never assigned to a training command or worked as a full-time instructor, you have at some time in your military career done everything a teacher is expected to do. Teaching, counseling, and evaluating people are duties that accompany every leadership position in the service. The ability to train people, to test their proficiency, and to set up plans to accomplish training objectives is a criterion for promotion that you have satisfied more than once. In short, you are already about 80 percent qualified for the job if you want it. Professional educators may disagree (they have unions too), but an examination of a teacher's job description will reveal several qualities that are, under slightly different names, very familiar. According to most authorities, the qualities of a good teacher are maturity and self-confidence, tolerance of others and a thick skin, good personal appearance and health, a sense of humor, love of learning, interest in working with and helping others, and awareness and interest in the community, the nation, and the world.

If you can't remember needing most of those qualities during your career, you have either a very bad memory or an odd background. For most military people these attributes were the meat and potatoes of career progression (and sometimes survival). We just called them by different names.

If you are interested in a career in teaching, one of your first tasks will be to translate the official description of a teacher's duties from "educatorese" into terms that describe your own experience. You will also be required to have your qualifications validated and perhaps certified by the educational establishment. This may seem simple, but as good old Clausewitz said about war, it isn't easy. It will require classroom time and training. A former infantry colonel or a submarine captain may find it less than thrilling to sit through a course on how to make puppets out of papier maché, but it goes with the territory. Courses in teaching methodology and educational theory are notoriously dull, but they are required. If you are seriously committed to teaching as a profession, you must accept their necessity and make it your goal cheerfully to punch all the tickets that must be punched. As a consolation, remember that in most cases, teachers' pay and promotion are directly related to the professional degrees they accumulate.

Military experience can often be validated using the DD-295 form (see chapter 2) to gain academic credit for required education courses. If you have been an instructor, attended an instructor school, or worked in any training assignment, you will probably be eligible for more credit than you think.

Education Administration

Not everyone in education is a classroom teacher. School systems are run by people who are more administrators, planners, and managers than they are teachers. The Education Establishment, like a lot of other things in the country, has become steadily larger, more technology oriented, and generally more "corporate." It hires facilities engineers, computer specialists, and systems analysts. And unfairly or not, the administrative and management side of education pays a lot better than classroom teaching.

Education administration usually requires an advanced degree in a specialty like education management or some other related field. State certification and a classroom teaching background may also be a requirement. In some cases, experience as a military instructor, especially in technical or vocational fields, may count as teaching credit.

Vocational and Technical Teaching

One advantage of this field is that vocational and technical instructors often do not have to go through the normal education and certification process and may be hired with only a high school education if they are knowledgeable in a high-demand specialty. Jobs are also available at independent vocational and technical schools outside the public school system. Because demand is high, pay is often better than it is for teachers of purely academic subjects.

Community Colleges and Junior Colleges

These two-year colleges have become a popular way to bridge the gap between high school and college. They provide teaching opportunities in both the academic and the vocational-technical area. Jobs in this sector of education often call for part-time or evening work under a contract arrangement. This can be an advantage if you are not ready to make a full-time commitment to teaching or if you want to test the water before taking up a career. The pay is usually a little better than it is for elementary and high school teachers, and there will be a bit more independence in choosing the curriculum material. Qualifications for teaching academic subjects are not as stringent as they are at the college level.

One way to find out if you like being a teacher is to work as a substitute. In most states a college degree is required to qualify as a substitute. After you have completed an application and been accepted, you will probably be asked to attend a short orientation course before you are placed on the substitute list. Daily assignments may come on very short notice so be prepared for calls at 7:00 A.M. Substitutes do not get to do the most rewarding work; their duties sometimes seem closer to baby-sitting than to professional teaching. But it is one way to get a feel for the environment and, by talking to other teachers, an idea of what the job demands.

Teaching at the College Level

College teaching has its own set of rules and requirements. Unless you have some special skill that is in demand, the competition will be very tough. Every year, hundreds of universities award thousands of advanced degrees. In disciplines like English, philosophy, and history, most of the freshly hatched graduates will be looking for academic positions. They will also have mentors and academic associates to help them along, which means that unless you are an exceptionally attractive candidate (or are willing to work for less money) your chances will be slim. Although no one in the groves of academe will admit it, you may also be subject to some antimilitary bias. A sizable proportion of today's faculty members were protesting the Vietnam War in the 1960s and 1970s, while you were you-know-where.

But there is a positive side to aiming for a college teaching job. A college campus is one of the most exciting and stimulating places imaginable. If you thrive on an atmosphere of intellectual ferment and enjoy the company of people whose primary currency is ideas, a career in college teaching can be ideal, regardless of the difficulty in gaining entrance.

Before committing yourself to any final decision on this career path, get some firsthand information on your prospects for employment, preferably from someone you know who is already established in the field. The next best thing is to arrange an appointment with the chairman or a senior professor at a college you might like to work at. Explain your situation candidly and ask for an opinion of your chances for academic employment in a similar department. Don't expect to be welcomed with open arms. Unless you have a doctorate, and a good one, you will probably be advised to go back to school or to reconsider your career plans. Reconsider. Then, if your mind is still made up, go for it. You only live once.

Teaching Overseas

For some people, finding a job overseas is a high priority and the choice of career is secondary. In cases like this, teaching can make available some options that might otherwise be closed to you because of a weak job market in your chosen area. There are pitfalls here too. You should not undertake a teaching career merely because you want to live in a certain place. If you have no enthusiasm for the vocation, you will soon discover that you can be unhappy even in your own personal paradise.

Teaching overseas is a special case. Our old employer, the Department of Defense, runs the DOD Dependent Schools. DODDS is one of the largest school systems in the world, and is always looking for new teachers. As in the armed forces, though, you won't always be sent where you want to go, at least not on the first assignment. Career teachers who have some seniority get first shot at duty in all the really neat places, so unless you get lucky or are in love with a country no one else can stand, you might not end up where you want to go. DODDS recruiters will not accept an application for a specific area, but after they accept you as a possible employee, you can turn down an assignment. Doing so will move you to the bottom of the list, however, and it could be a long time before you are called again. The DODDS booklet *Employment Opportunities for Education Overseas* explains how the system works and can be obtained from its recruiting office in Alexandria, Virginia, or through your service.

The overseas base reductions of the '90s have cut deeply into the DODDS requirement for new teachers, and it can be expected that for the next few years there will not be a lot of opportunities in this area. Remember, too, that future military force reductions could reduce job opportunities even further, leaving you with the task of starting all over again in the job market.

Overseas teaching opportunities are also available in the private sector and through other agencies. The International Schools Service (ISS) places teachers in

American schools overseas, and the Register for International Services in Education (RISE) maintains a computer data base to track teaching and other education positions overseas. Both of these organizations require an enrollment or registration fee. To round out our list of education acronyms, TESOL (Teachers of English to Speakers of Other Languages) operates a clearinghouse and provides certification in teaching the English language. This field, by the way, is growing quickly, especially in places like Japan, where there is a big demand for instructors. TESOL certification will improve your chances for an overseas teaching job and can also be an excellent source of part-time income for retirees already living overseas.

WORKING FOR THE FEDERAL GOVERNMENT

In some ways government employment is the least disturbing form of career transition you can find. A familiar looking treasury check arrives every payday, the working environment is reassuringly familiar, and except for the quirks of the civil service system and the change in uniform it's almost as though you never retired. Work for the government can enable you to live in an area you favor and may offer the only opportunity to remain active in a field you enjoy. There is a lot to be said for such a seamless changeover in work life, but there also are some disadvantages, most of them related to pay and to public law.

Almost all positions with the federal government are covered by multiple-compensation laws to prevent what is cynically known as "double dipping" by retired officers and warrant officers. As a general rule of thumb, half of your retirement pay over a certain amount is taken based on changes in the Consumer Price Index. The amount will vary* with the individual situation. A second reduction relates to the pay cap on federal executive compensation that prohibits you from earning combined retirement and government pay in excess of a given amount.

Because of variations, exceptions, and pending changes in the rules, it is a good idea to check out your individual situation before making any decision, but in essence, multiple compensation means that former officers will be working for less money than their nonmilitary colleagues. This is not always a major problem. The chance to work in a job you like at a respectable salary may be worth a loss in pay, and your time in service will count toward government retirement. The apparent pay cut is more of an emotional than a financial issue in many instances and should not be the sole basis for rejecting government service as a career option.

Legal restrictions also affect federal employment. This is something to take very seriously—a mistake can get you in a lot of trouble and maybe even jail. DOD Directive 5500.7, Standards of Conduct, supplemented by individual military service directives, outlines postretirement restrictions relating to employment with the government. For the most part, these restrictions deal with prohibitions on "civilianizing" one's last job before retirement, but they should be read carefully to be sure you are on the right side of the law.

To be considered for most federal jobs you will have to submit an SF-171 application for employment. People not familiar with government bureaucracy view these forms with an almost primal fear, but for someone who has spent a career battling military paperwork they are a piece of

*By using various simple computations based on your salary, retirement pay, the phase of the moon, and whether the groundhog sees its shadow, the government figures out how much of your money it will take. When you figure out the system, they change the law.

cake. If you have kept copies of all your important service records, filling out the SF-171 should require no more than an evening's work. Just get yourself some privacy, put soothing music on the stereo, and before you know it, it will be over. If you are applying for more than one federal position, be sure to make copies of a master form so you can simply fill in the blanks for each job and contribute to the paperwork reduction program.

Many people think that former military personnel get preference for civil service jobs. This is not always true. If you retired in a rank above O-4, you do not get veterans' points (although you don't have to return your combat decorations), and unless you are disabled, you will be considered along with everyone else.

The point system used for evaluating SF-171s is worth some research for anyone who plans to compete for a federal job. Most local libraries have books on the subject, and bookstores usually carry a selection of "how-to" books and pamphlets. Places that advertise themselves as experts at filling out SF-171s and locating job openings are not worth the money they charge. They can't do anything for you that you can't do better yourself with a little study and some legwork.

Job openings are most commonly advertised through vacancy announcements circulated to various federal agencies and state and local employment offices. The government sometimes places ads in newspapers and specialized trade and professional journals. Federal Job Information Centers (FJICs) are located in most major cities. The centers function as job clearinghouses and can assist you in application procedures.

Another good way to get a current listing of job openings is to go to the civilian personnel office on the military base closest to you. If you are seriously considering government employment, this is a good place to become acquainted with. It won't hurt to introduce yourself to the people who work there and to let them know that you are looking for an opening. You should also get an SF-171 on file with civilian personnel. Occasionally they are asked to screen their files for candidates to fill a specific job.

Agencies can sometimes fill jobs under something called "hiring under delegated authority," a legal way of getting around some of the paperwork of federal hiring. Technically, people employed under this authority are only temporary, but your foot is in the door, and after a year's experience you will be in a better position to compete for the job.

STATE AND LOCAL GOVERNMENT

Job opportunities also exist at the state and local levels, though they are harder to break into than the federal government. Depending on the state and the location, politics will play a bigger part in most jobs than it does in the federal government, and some openings are advertised publicly only to satisfy a legal requirement; the job has already been spoken for by someone who is only waiting for the required advertising and screening processes to be completed. Nevertheless, you should apply for every opening that looks promising. As government becomes bigger and our society more complex, state and local jobs are becoming more professional. For many positions traditionally filled by political cronies or "good old boys," qualification rather than influence is now more important.

The national trend toward decentralization of government has given state and local governing bodies an increasing share of responsibility for planning, managing, and executing programs. It has also made more money available to states and localities. No matter what local politicians say, in the '90s, government in general has been the fastest growing sector in the economy, and nonfederal bureaucracies have led that growth. The number of middle- and upper-level management positions has risen steadily in most areas, and so have salaries. The "pay caps" that Congress imposes on federal workers have kept the brakes on federal pay, while in many states the need for top-notch people has driven salaries to levels where some employees are paid more than the president of the United States.

Nonfederal government jobs also have the advantage of being unaffected by multiple-compensation laws. The pay scale may be lower than Uncle Sam's, but at least you get to keep it all. You will also be eligible to participate in a pension plan that in many states is exempt from state income tax, which your military retirement pay may not be. Veterans' preference is also more beneficial than it is under the federal system. As a general rule, the prospects for your obtaining employment in this sector will be highest in an area where military facilities are scarce. It's a simple numbers game. In an area with many military retirees, there will be more qualified people than the system needs. In other areas, especially in rural communities, your skills and experience may be distinctive enough to give you an edge.

The first thing to learn about local government is who does what and where. For a long time explosive growth and population shifts outpaced the ability of state and local authorities to adapt to changing conditions. Organizations set up for nineteenth-century rural communities were faced with problems beyond their capability, and the result was chaos. These problems are only now being sorted out, so you may find that your town (if it *is* a town and not a county, village, parish, or district) is run by a bewildering array of agencies, each with its own hiring system. So it will be back to the library again, this time to the reference section for information on how your local government is organized and run. This will be easier than you think because libraries are always funded by the local government and are obligated to keep more information than you can imagine on such subjects as mosquito control districts and watershed management.

Once you understand the organization, the next step is to locate its headquarters and apply for a job. It also helps to check on who works there. It might be someone you know, which could improve your chances considerably. Put in an application every place there could be a job, and don't hesitate to make the rounds now and then to say hello.

YOUR OWN BUSINESS

Mighty oaks from little acorns grow, and many financial empires began as successful small businesses. Americans like to see themselves as independent entrepreneurs, and the urge to strike out on one's own has been felt by almost everyone at one time or another. In recent years the majority of new jobs created have been a result of small business development. In an era of rapid social and technological change, new business possibilities arise continually for people who have the right skills and are in the right place at the right time. Running your own business is a way to get out of the familiar rut of working for someone else and replace it with the challenge of being responsible to the toughest employer in the world—you.

This choice is not for everyone. Starting a business demands a total commitment of your (and maybe your family's) time and a financial risk you never experienced in the service. No one will bail you out if you get in trouble, and even if you are successful, uncertainty will become a permanent part of your working life. The business can engulf you, taking away family life, leisure time, and peace of mind with no reward but more of the same.

If you can face these possibilities without flinching, maybe you should think of starting your own business. But first, take a look at some other factors, beginning with yourself.

Are You a Business Person?

Just as an aptitude test can highlight skills and identify potential abilities, other simple tests can indicate whether you are likely to be a success in business. The short self-test given in the Small Business Administration's (SBA) pamphlet *Starting and Managing a Small Business of Your Own* or those in the many books on the subject will give you some clues to your suitability. These little tests vary, but they all stress the same general characteristics:

• *Strong self-motivation and self-confidence.* You must trust in your own judgment and have the courage to act on it without outside support.
• *Leadership.* This quality was expected of you in the service. In business, though, you will have fewer established guidelines to follow. You must be able to make some of the rules as well as enforce them.
• *Organizational ability.* This includes the skills required to set up a new organization from scratch, not just the ability to run an established system.
• *Determination.* You must have the toughness and endurance to hang on for as long as it takes to succeed. This is the active side of patience.
• *Attention to detail.* You need to be willing to do the dull tasks like record keeping with the same thoroughness as you do the more interesting things.
• *Outgoing personality.* To be successful in business a person

must enjoy contact with other people and have the ability to impress, persuade, and convince them.

If you can answer with a ringing "yes" to all of the attributes just listed, you at least have the raw material to go into business for yourself. Any doubts about your strength in these areas should be cause for putting on the brakes now *before* you go broke.

The next factor to consider is the enterprise you will undertake. This is determined not only by what you would like to do but also by the skills you have to offer, the potential for success in a particular business specialty, and, equally important, the amount of money available. These factors must be assessed with hard, cold realism. A staggering number of people have gone belly-up trying to make money from quaint restaurants, cute gift shops, and scotch tape stores. Don't be one of them. Remember that business consists of supplying goods and services demanded by people other than your family and friends. If customers won't buy your hand-carved lawn ornaments, the business will fail, no matter how clever you are with tools.

According to the SBA, there are three broad categories of small business.

A New Business. These are most likely to succeed when you have found a niche in the market and a demand and you have the skills to meet the demand. It is the riskiest type of enterprise, but for the true entrepreneur it is the most exciting. You are on your own with no outside support and no existing customers. There will be a long list of decisions to make in the start-up period, and a talent for planning must be one of your strong suits. The need to choose an accountant, hire employees, select a location, and handle a dozen other tasks will come at you all at once. Most experts on small business recommend that you not make a move until you have worked out a detailed master plan to cover the start-up phase and at least the first year to eighteen months of operation. Developing the nitty-gritty details of the plan is also a good way to find out if the business venture is what you want.

For someone who genuinely relishes the chance finally to do it your way, the task will be an exciting challenge. But if the prospect of facing multiple unknowns begins to unnerve you, think twice about starting up your own business.

An Existing Business. First, the good news. For someone who is smart or lucky enough to find a healthy business with no hidden problems, this can be the most painless way to become a small business owner. The agonies and uncertainties of start-up are avoided, the business has an established reputation (a good one, you hope), and all you have to do is continue whatever the last owner did to succeed. Naturally, the healthier the business, the higher the price you will have to pay for it.

The bad news is that things don't always work out as hoped. The business may be failing. This can be an advantage for you if you know how to cure its problems and may enable you to buy it at a bargain price. It can also be disastrous. Such handicaps as a dying location, your predecessor's bad reputation, and a weak market may be insurmountable. Your motto should be "look before you leap." Be sure you know how to read a balance sheet or can get help from someone who does.

Franchises. Being a fried chicken king may not be as glamorous as owning your own aerospace company, but the chances of survival are a lot better. Investing in a franchise is like buying a frozen pizza instead of making one from scratch—it will not have exactly the ingredients you may have wanted, but when it comes out of the oven it will probably be edible.

A franchise contract gets you some support that other small business people do not have. There is a corporate structure behind you, complete with marketing experts, advertising agencies, lawyers, good accountants, and an array of high-priced help that you would never be able to afford by yourself. The product or service is already established in the market, and there are enough check-off lists to gladden the heart of a Rickover-trained engineer. A good company will exercise enough control to make it almost impossible for you to get into real financial trouble even if it turns out that you are not a very good manager.

That's the problem. Running a franchise is not like running your own business because it isn't your own business. When you sign a franchise agreement you are buying the right to sell someone else's product or service. Under almost all agreements the parent company retains the right to determine overall marketing strategy, to sell you inventory at a predetermined price, and to exercise some control over the way you run the store. Depending on company policy, that control can range from a simple adherence to quality and procedural standards to a requirement for reports, surprise inspections, and other wonderful things you used to do when you were in uniform. A national franchiser will have national policies that may or may not fit your situation. The company's objective is the greatest benefit for the greatest number. The profit of an individual outlet is not the first priority.

A franchise is the most foolproof way of jumping into the world of small business. The Federal Trade Commission requires the parent company to provide full disclosure of information to each franchisee, and many states have additional laws to prevent fraud. Someone who doesn't mind rudder orders from higher headquarters and who likes having a wise uncle hovering in the background will be happier as a franchisee.

The SBA, in cooperation with the International Franchise Association, now offers special services to veterans who are interested in franchising. The Veteran Transition Franchise Initiative, or VETFRAN, offers management and financial counseling as well as some breaks in financing. In some cases, franchisors will waive up to half the initial franchise fee or will finance up to half the fee at a rate comparable to the SBA's guaranteed loan rate.

MONEY MATTERS

Money is what goes on the bottom line. A plus or a minus sign next to the number tells whether you are a successful business or a sad statistic. No matter how much you may love your little enterprise, if the minus signs don't go away after a while, you will.

Money problems pose the biggest threat to a military retiree who starts a small business. We are not in the habit of weighing results in terms of dollars. Our measures of success are rooted in the basic military goal of winning, no matter what the effort, risk, and expenditure of resources it takes. Ulysses S. Grant would not have won a resources-management award, but he won the Civil War, and that was what he was hired for. In business there is no praise for being the last man left standing on the battlefield. The bottom line is the bottom line, and you must be prepared to direct your goals toward that end. Authorities such as the SBA can cite endless examples of small businesses that seemed to be vigorous and healthy, buying and selling at a gratifying rate, but failed because the owner lost track of overhead, cash flow, or other basic indicators.

Although the details of financing a small business are beyond the scope of this book, there are a few basics that are useful to know before you charge headlong into the world of capitalism. No one should even think about a future in business who is not prepared to learn about finances, beginning with the material recommended in the bibliography and including everything you can get from the SBA. Here are a few basics that can help get you started.

Shop for financing. Asking a bank or financial institution for business financing is not like applying for a car loan or a home mortgage. Be prepared to do an unabashed selling job. Call on all your talent and experience at briefing and persuading people. You are selling an idea, just as you did at times on active duty.

Know what you are risking. A borrower with a valuable high-equity home who is willing to pledge it can sometimes get money frighteningly easily. With such attractive collateral a lender who is not completely ethical will tell you your idea is wonderful even if he doesn't think so—as long as he's first in line to collect when you go bust.

Don't be afraid to ask for advice. The SBA and other agencies are chartered to help people like you. Reputable bankers have a wealth of knowledge and experience at their disposal and can be a great asset. But not all of them will be helpful; you may have to shop around to find an institution interested in working with a small operator like you. But when you find one, it's worth the trouble.

Exhaust every possibility. Banks, even the nice ones, may not listen to your argument. Pick the brains of every expert you can find to discover alternative sources of financing.

Consider partnerships, private investors, anything that will work. Remember, no one wanted to back Columbus either.

Do your homework. Take advantage of all the expert advice available but don't make any decisions unless your own independent research supports what others tell you. Shop around for accountants and tax lawyers. Check out every location, and even if you strike paydirt at the first lending institution you try, do more shopping for a better deal. In military survival training you learned that decisions made early in a survival situation can make the difference between life and death. In a small business it's much the same.

Once you have made up your mind to take the plunge, pause and think. When you work for someone else you always have the option to quit if you are unhappy, underpaid, or treated unfairly. Going out of business is completely different. Unless the business is attractive to a potential buyer (and if it were, you probably wouldn't be going out of business), you will be forced to sell it for whatever you can get or, even worse, go into bankruptcy. And unless you and your accountant have done a good job of separating personal from business assets, your creditors can snap up everything you own, including your firstborn child.

OPTIONS FOR INDEPENDENCE: SELLING YOUR SERVICES, CONSULTING, FREELANCING, AND OTHERS

Going into business does not appeal to everyone. The heavy financial and personal commitment needed to succeed in a small business definitely limits one's freedom. It requires accepting a long-term obligation that may not seem appealing in the first few years after retirement. Nevertheless, after working for someone else all our lives, many of us feel the urge to go it alone. The idea of swapping one uniform for another doesn't appeal to us, and at least for a while the absence of schedules and bosses would be a welcome change.

Selling your personal services is similar to going into business for yourself with a few important differences. It does not usually require the financial risk involved in a business. You can write poetry, for example, with little more than a pencil, paper, and a dreamy expression. The bad news, however, is that security and financial rewards can be very elusive. True, some independent consultants have incomes in the six-figure bracket, but they didn't get there overnight. Working independently takes a special mix of personal attributes and talents that not everyone has, and if these are not your strong points, you will fail.

Self-Confidence

This is a *sine qua non*. You must be convinced that the service you are offering is worthwhile. This is true for any endeavor, but when you are offering yourself as an individual package it is vital. When you are hired as an employee, it is assumed that you will undergo training for familiarization even if you are qualified for the job. In a business you have some latitude to make mistakes while you are learning. But when selling your personal abilities, you will be expected to perform on your own with a minimum of help and no excuses. Independent technical advisers are supposed to fix the problem without trial and error; consultants must know more than the people they are advising; writers must produce clean copy the first time around.

Insight

People are hired as outside experts because they can uncover problems and find solutions not apparent to those already working for the organization. As a consultant or an independent contractor, you must have the ability to analyze a situation quickly, reduce it to its key components, and figure out how it works. Someone whose strongest skills are in making a good organization better or managing a system already in place is not always comfortable with the critical approach required of an independent operator. If you are not sure which type you are, go back to your skills assessment and check it out.

Ability to Live with Uncertainty

There are few guarantees in any area of self-employment. As an independent you will be very susceptible to hiccups in the economy, corporate belt-tightening, and employment downturns. Unless you are working under an exceptionally solid contract, it is easier to eliminate the services of a hired independent professional than it is to lay off regular employees. Your living is much more at the mercy of individual decision makers than if you were salaried. You will have to sell yourself as the ideal candidate to do a job, not just once but each time you compete for an assignment or contract. Past successes will help, but they will guarantee nothing.

Self-Discipline

Military people pride themselves on being more disciplined than the average civilian. We are experts at living by timetables and schedules. Morning colors go at exactly eight o'clock. The battalion moves out on time. Each unit performs its assigned role keenly aware that a failure of discipline will be observed and noted. A well-disciplined military machine in operation can be truly awesome to behold.

Working for yourself demands a different discipline. No one will be looking over your shoulder with a check-off list or a stopwatch. There will be no directives from higher authority to set priorities and no operational-readiness exercises to test performance. Every bit of discipline must be imposed and enforced from inside, and that isn't easy. It is not unusual for people to come unglued when they have no external structure to support them. When you begin working for yourself, one of the first things you will discover is the challenge of establishing your own goals, setting your own schedule, and, most difficult of all, forcing yourself to stick to it. You will have to reward and reprimand yourself with the same relentless impartiality that was the norm on active duty. The key to making self-discipline work is self-confidence and an ability to call on your inner resources to generate the motivation that used to come from outside.

Exceptional Expertise

Selling your ability to provide a service requires two basic prerequisites. You must have a demonstrated record of results, and you must have exceptional ability in the field. Past performance is important because it establishes your credentials as a professional. No matter how good *you* know you are, others will rarely risk their time or money on anything but evidence of past success. Whether you are bidding on a contract or selling an idea, you will be competing against others who have as much confidence in their ability as you have in yours. In most cases the deciding factor will be past performance. Whatever form your portfolio takes, it will have to be better than someone else's. This is especially true when you are a new kid on the block, as you will be.

Marketing Ability

"Build a better mousetrap and the world will beat a path to your door." That may be true, but if you are not in the mousetrap game you will have to go out and hustle for work. Marketing your services is more difficult than in a product-oriented business because you are selling something intangible. Credentials are always necessary, but they still must be sold to a potential buyer. When you have established a reputation and the world is competing for your services, marketing yourself will not be a problem. Until that time, the selling part of the job will take a significant chunk of time. It is very important to understand this. The necessity to sell, sell, sell often discourages and frustrates inexperienced independents; they expect the luxury of working full time at something they enjoy only to find themselves out hustling like a used car salesman. Marketing yourself as a product is an essential part of being on your own. Accepting that fact is the price of survival.

Patience

Success can come suddenly like a bolt from the blue, but it seldom does. It is much more likely that your reputation will be built slowly on a succession of modest achievements over a long period. In some areas it may take months; in others, it can be years. To be a winner, you have to be willing to hang in there for as long as it takes without becoming frustrated or discouraged. If quick results and short-term benefits are important to you, think twice before you strike out on your own.

Consulting

This profession is worth more than $30 billion a year in the United States and includes twenty to thirty thousand people working in almost every sector of the public and private economy. Consultants can be part-time workers or really big fish who bring in seven-figure fees annually. They may work for a consulting firm directly, as an on-call associate, or they can be completely independent and do all their own marketing, bookkeeping, and administration.

The first reaction that many people have to the idea of becoming a consultant is "Who, me?" Lack of self-confidence and a tendency to take our own talent for granted can distort our perspective. Yet at some time in your career you probably worked with consultants who seemed to have no more expertise and ability than you did. In many cases their work consisted mostly of picking your brain and putting together a product consisting of information that was well known and easily accessible to anyone with the time to look for it.

Although consultants are usually thought of as operating at the managerial or professional level, this is not always the case. Technical consultants are in increasing demand in the high-tech world as well as in non-high-tech fields such as home handymen and assembling children's Christmas toys. (Don't laugh. There's a lot of money in it.) As a rule, consultants work under contract to provide their services for a certain length of time. They may take a one-time assignment contingent on accomplishing a project, completing a study, or making a final report. Long-term and open-ended arrangements are also possible with a consultant providing a continuing service. The latter is especially desirable because it gives the consultant a certain source of income and reduces the amount of time he must devote to selling his services.

An independent consultant does not have to face the heavy financial commitment needed to start a small business. But there are start-up and continuing overhead costs that must be considered. You will have to invest in office supplies, business cards, advertising material, and other basic administrative support. An office may be a necessity, depending on your specialty. In some fields it is perfectly acceptable to work out of your own home; in others, you will not be taken seriously unless you have a receptionist and an office with the right address.

The more sophisticated a consulting operation is, the more need there will be for accountants and record keeping. A bookkeeping system is mandatory not only to keep you informed but to keep the IRS happy. The IRS will expect you to keep complete business records no matter how small the operation is, and no exceptions are made for inexperience. A receptionist is an employee, which will mean withholding tax, social security tax, and any other requirements your state has.

A consultant is a temporary expert in a specialty for a client who cannot justify the time and expense of learning. A small electronics company, for example, would call on an expert to install a new data-processing system. Even though the firm may have employees with the technical ability to understand and install the system, it makes more sense to use their engineers' and technicians' time on work that will make money for the company.

To succeed as a consultant, you must have a proven skill that someone needs and is willing to pay for. Specialized areas requiring detailed knowledge of a subject are the best bet. As our society becomes more technically oriented there are fewer and fewer people who understand the complicated machinery and systems that make it work. Not long ago the corner filling station could completely tune up your car. Today the operation usually involves sophisticated testing equipment available only at specialized service centers.

How do you find out which areas are promising for an aspiring consultant? In addition to the books listed in the bibliography, there are trade journals and newsletters on what's going on in consulting. *Consultant's News* and

Consulting Opportunities Journal are two of the better known, and industry, business, and trade journals can provide good indications of where the action is.

In the first few years after retirement you should consider independent consulting as a career only if your expertise is in a high-demand and fairly specialized area and your knowledge is current. You should have civilian contacts in the industry in which you intend to work, and that can be a problem. Department of Defense (DOD) standards of conduct regulate how and when you can use your military experience in a civilian job. If you are a retired regular officer, your will have to file a DD 1357 Statement of Employment and keep it up-to-date. A mistake can get you into a lot of trouble.

If what you have just read suggests that independent consulting is a difficult field to get into directly after retirement, you are correct. Success will require big helpings of determination, sacrifice, and patience. For many who feel the lure of the consulting career, the best course of action may be to start out with an established consulting firm and get real-world experience or perhaps spend a couple of years working in the industry you would service as a consultant. Whichever way you choose, you will find it a fascinating profession that gives you more control over your work load and your earnings than most others.

Freelancing

Freelancing is a word that suggests rugged individualism, a bit of daring, and a devil-may-care attitude toward the world. The consultant wears a three-piece suit and a look of wisdom; the freelancer is envisioned with a camera slung around his neck or a battered portable typewriter at her side.

Like most romantic images, this one contains a bit of truth and a lot of exaggeration. Actually, the work is very much like that of an independent consultant. The major difference is that a freelancer sells finished work on a one-time, one-of-a-kind basis. When a buyer accepts the work and pays for it, the freelancer moves on to another job. Unless he is lucky enough to benefit from reprints, reproductions, and the like, his output is always sold in pieces. This can make earning a living a precarious business. Payment arrives in chunks at no predictable rate, and usually the work must be done before a potential buyer will consider it. This is why freelancers tend to be nervous, insecure people who always seem to be only a step ahead of financial ruin.

The demand for freelancers is always less than the supply. The range of the market is narrower than it is for consultants. With rare exceptions, opportunities are confined to such areas as writing, photography, graphic arts, and the communications/public relations world. Since there is almost no requirement for formal qualifications, many people attempt freelancing because it seems so easy. Unlike consulting, where experience and expertise limit the number of practitioners, freelancing is open to anyone with a camera or a typewriter. This is both good and bad. It's good because it allows anyone with ability and perseverance to have a chance at success, but it's bad because it increases the quantity as well as the quality of competition for every available opportunity.

Financial rewards are more meager and uncertainty greater than in almost any other form of self-employment, which is why almost every self-help book on the subject recommends that a beginning freelancer have a second source of income. Once you become established in your field, it will become easier. Instant success is about as rare as winning the lottery, and it takes more work.

If none of these gloomy facts discourage you and you have some talent, freelancing might be worth a try. Retirement pay and the fringe benefits that go with it will give you some advantages over other neophytes. Your service experience can also be an asset. You have traveled a good deal, have developed fairly steady work habits, and may have some unique experience or knowledge that you can put to use.

Begin by researching exactly what the job entails. Libraries are full of books on how to be a freelance writer, photographer, and so on (mostly written by freelancers who knew the chance for a buck when they saw it), and source material such as the annual *Writer's Market* will tell you where you can sell your stuff. Periodicals such as *Writer* provide hints on markets and techniques, and workshops are advertised periodically in most big cities. If you have more enthusiasm than experience, some classroom work, even only a minicourse in night school, is essential. The money spent will be worthwhile if you decide to pursue a career in freelancing, and if you don't it will give you valuable new skills.

A serious career requires a serious dedication of time and resources. Prize-winning photographs have been taken with the family Instamatic and developed in the broom closet, but it doesn't happen very often. Publishers don't read handwritten manuscripts, and *no* potential buyer will waste time on an offering that is not completely professional. You will need work space, basic equipment, and the determination to put in as many hours per day as necessary. Good work is not produced by the people who sit around in coffee shops looking pensive. It is produced, as one famous writer put it, "by sitting down at the typewriter until the beads of blood form on your brow."

Don't go overboard on setting yourself up. Some would-be freelancers use their enthusiasm as an excuse to spend staggering amounts of money on equipment and supplies, then spend all day mixing paints or sharpening dozens of pencils. They would be happier in the office supply business. Equipment and supplies can be tax-deductible only if you keep very good records *and* sell your work during the tax year. Writing off a $2,000 word processor[*] in a year you earned $10 from writing may work for one year. After that the IRS will eat you alive.

Freelancers collect rejection letters the way wine connoisseurs collect labels. They are like old combat wounds except that they don't hurt when it rains. The best way to avoid this becoming a permanent condition is to start out small. Local newspapers and other publications such as area tourist information bulletins and "What's happening this week" newspapers will not pay very much, but they do use art, photos, and writing by local people. This can be a good way to get started.

Having your work appear locally will give your ego a boost and also provide clippings to send along with your submissions to the more heavyweight segment of the market. Being paid for your work, no matter how little, establishes you as a professional. Everyone has to start somewhere.

WORKING PART TIME

All of the jobs, careers, and vocations discussed so far share one common factor. They demand a significant commitment of time. Some will require much more than an eight-hour day and will call for a level of personal dedication equal to that asked by your service.

---

[*]The first edition of this book was written on a $400 Brand-X word processor, hooked up to a used electronic typewriter bought in a pawnshop for $130.

Not everyone wants or needs so demanding a job. Many of us leave the service exhausted and burned out from years of stress, long hours, and heavy responsibility. The last thing we need is to jump head first into another job as tough as the one we just left. A decompression period, a time to reflect on what we want for our future lives and for our family, is sometimes the best thing for us.

At the same time, not working at all is not financially possible or psychologically healthy. Going from flank speed to stop can cause as many problems as overwork does. The working part of our life comes to a halt but our instincts and habits are still moving at the old speed. The scenario at the end of chapter 2, played over day after day, stops being frustrating and becomes depressing, perhaps dangerously so.

Part-time work can prevent this problem. The most obvious advantage of this option is that it doesn't take up all your time but still generates some income. Equally important, even a half-day job puts you on a schedule that will help maintain a structured life. Part-time work seldom involves much pressure. Because you don't have a major career stake in the job, potential irritants like difficult working conditions, low status, and an unpleasant boss seldom reach critical levels. If they do, you can quit and find another job. Part-time employment can also be a good way to ease into the civilian work world and to get some idea of what you like and don't like doing for a living. That alone can be a valuable experience.

Classified newspaper ads are the best way to locate part-time work. The offerings range from baby-sitting to delivering newspapers and include some unusual and potentially interesting work. As a military retiree you will be considered a very desirable candidate for part-time jobs because you are a proven quantity and, oddly enough, because you are not unemployed. Occasionally there will be an opening for part-time or temporary management or consulting assignments, but don't count too heavily on this. As a rule, part-time jobs are at the skilled and unskilled hourly wage level.

The "Temp"

More and more employers are relying on temporary employees, or "temps" to fill out their rosters. This option offers them flexibility in dealing with work loads, reduces time and risk in hiring (and firing), and usually saves money in fringe benefits. Most temps are hired through an agency that supplies people to fill jobs. Unlike an employment agency, the temporary specialist does all the paperwork and most of the selecting and interviewing and usually charges the employer a fee.

Until about ten years ago, "temps" were mostly hired for routine clerical, administrative tasks and as unskilled labor. In the late '80s, though, as the economy went through the agonies of restructuring and downsizing, employers began to discover that there was also a large and attractive pool of executive talent out there, waiting to be hired. People who had been laid off or given early retirement were having trouble finding new jobs, and many of them had decided to opt out of the corporate career rat race altogether.

The idea of "executive temps" caught on, and at last count there were more than two-hundred thousand managerial temps working at positions all over the country. These people are usually placed in jobs by temporary executive-placement agencies or by established executive-placement firms that have branched out into the temp field.

It's not easy for a recent military retiree to get into the management-temp game. The top placement agencies expect their temps to have a significant amount of experience—up to ten years, in some cases. Nevertheless, this alternative is worth a try. If you have experience in a high-demand field like communications or health care and you can do a good job of selling your qualifications, the executive-temp route may be attractive.

Some executive and management temp positions are a cross between temporary work and consulting. Instead of hiring on as a temporary worker on a week-by-week basis, you sign a contract to do a job for an employer for a specified number of months or possibly even years. Fringe benefits will be limited or nonexistent, but you will have assured work for a predictable length of time.

Temporary work at the clerical and administrative levels also has some advantages. Seasonal and short-term work at lower-paying jobs like assisting in inventories is usually available, and for those who want fresh air and exercise (and some colorful co-workers), some agencies offer construction and straight unskilled-labor jobs.

Don't turn up your nose at work that seems to be less prestigious than what you are used to. Getting a paycheck is better than hanging around the house, and a temporary job can give you some valuable insights into how the civilian world works. And for people going back to school after retirement, "temping" may be one way to help pay the bills.

One possibility worth considering is to learn a new skill that is in short supply. Someone who can use various word processing systems, for example, can command an hourly wage of $15 or more as a temp in places like Washington and Boston. If you have the right skills, the agencies will be calling *you* with job offers.

Seasonal and Cyclical Jobs

Part-year jobs range from glamorous ones like ski instructing to prosaic ones like delivering telephone directories. In parts of the country where business is highly seasonal there are many possibilities. After all, *someone* has to be inside the Mickey Mouse outfit at Disney World.

"Nontraditional" Jobs

We are living in what Herman Kahn once called the "Mosaic Society." All over the country people are working on little islands of unconventional jobs. Some work at home, on data-processing assignments or telemarketing. Others share jobs or work flexible hours, and a surprising number of enterprising folks still do what used to be called "odd jobs." Except for economically depressed regions of the nation, there are almost always more opportunities to make money than there are people to fill the needs. Almost every economic forecast indicates that this situation will continue and that the demand for reliable, intelligent, and experienced employees will continue to increase.

The communications revolution has made it possible to do a variety of work from your own home. FAX, interactive computer technology, and all that goes with them have made it possible to earn a living without leaving the comfort of your own work center. If you have the right skills and the necessary equipment, it's possible to do quite well at this kind of work. The advantages are obvious. You won't have to fight rush-hour traffic, you can live in an area that might be impractical for a normal commuter job, and, of course, you have more independence.

But there are some disadvantages too. Unless you already own the necessary computer, communications, and other equipment, you will have to buy a couple of thousand dollars worth of stuff to get started. You may also have to go back to school to learn how to use what you've just bought.

Another problem with working at home is isolation. For someone who has worked in a headquarters beehive or who has learned to loathe the endless corridors of the

Pentagon, working alone at home probably seems like a dream come true. But like many other things in this world, it's not so much fun after you've done it for a while. People who work at home often admit to feeling isolated—cut off from the everyday life of the community and from association with others. And like freelancing, working at home requires a lot of self-discipline and the ability to organize your work without outside help. You will also have to set some rules for family and friends, or you'll find that they will make it hard for you to get your work done. Friends who wouldn't dream of stopping by a busy office during "working hours" may see nothing wrong with stopping over for a cup of coffee when you're working at home.

However, there are an amazing number of ways you can earn money from a home-based business. One book on the subject lists more than 250 different jobs or services, including such varied occupations as woodworking, editing, and beekeeping. Most of these enterprises are actually a form of small business, so remember that unless you want some unwelcome attention from the IRS, you will have to keep books, pay taxes, and do all the things other business people do. The advantage is that with few exceptions you will not have to make the level of financial commitment that a conventional business requires.

It's a good idea to do some basic market and cost research before you launch into a home business. Your friends may think that those little birdhouses you build are the cutest things in the world, but ask yourself, will anyone else? Be careful, too, about ads in magazines and newspapers that proclaim you can make money at home. A lot of these "opportunities" involve work like stuffing thousands of envelopes at ridiculously low piecework rates. Unless you're willing to enslave your entire family and start up a homegrown sweatshop, it's not worth the trouble.

IN SUMMARY

The universe of alternatives described in this chapter is not exhaustive. New job and career possibilities are born every day and are waiting to be discovered. One may be waiting out there for you. The advantages and disadvantages of various options, along with your personal inventory of skills, goals, and talents, should have pointed you in the right direction. And if that direction happens to include a job search in the traditional sense of the world, it's time to roll up your sleeves and get to work. The next two chapters will tell you how.

THE JOB

This chapter and the next are about moving from the ideal world to the real one. Assuming that all the decisions have been made at least tentatively and you are tending toward a specific field of work, it is now time to begin searching for the one job that best fills your needs.

The operation is best done in two phases. The first can be compared to the marketing function of a business. A new product, in this case you, needs a buyer. But between the time it goes on the market and the final closing of a sale some intermediate steps are required if the effort is to be a success. You, the product, must be defined as a total package, your best points and special qualities highlighted. The potential market must be identified and means of access targeted and exploited.

The second phase consists of finding a buyer for the package and convincing him that you are exactly what he is looking for, even if he doesn't know it yet. You must negotiate a price for yourself and maybe even the terms of the final agreement.

To some this may sound a bit crass. Senior military people are accustomed to knowing precisely who and where they are professionally. On active duty we learn to expect that we will automatically be treated a certain way because of our seniority and rank. It is only natural to bristle at the thought of having to "package" ourselves. *We* know who we are; why doesn't everyone else?

Throughout a military career, your identity was a matter of record. Somewhere in a bureau or personnel directorate was a file containing the sum of your experience and qualifications and a detailed account of your performance in every job you ever held. Each time you were considered for a promotion or a new assignment, that file was reviewed and analyzed. Except for a little persuasion and maybe some string-pulling once or twice, your role in deciding a new assignment was limited to making a request and hoping for luck. The variable part of your "package" may have been professional reputation, timing, or the influence of a friendly mentor, but those factors were usually secondary. Compared to the situation you are about to encounter, the system was amazingly fair and objective. If you don't believe that, wait.

Preparing for a job search begins with developing a realistic view of what you can reasonably expect. Having identified your skills and your actual and potential ability and perhaps gained some additional education, you have a pretty good basis for zeroing in on specific areas. This is where reality rears its ugly head and you come face-to-face with the major disadvantage of being a military retiree.

For most desirable jobs you are either overqualified or underexperienced. You are overqualified because you held far more responsibility in the military than you can expect to be given in a civilian job. And you are underexperienced because your twenty or more years of service do not count the same as a comparable amount of nonmilitary time. It comes down to that tiresome but unavoidable problem of paying your dues. Most civilian employers will feel that you don't have the experience to be hired at the level of responsibility your military background suggests. Yet if they hire you at a level they feel comfortable with, you will be overqualified. That's not good either because overqualified people are often mistrusted. Conventional wisdom says that either they will move on as soon as something better comes along or there is a problem in their background or personality. As silly as this may seem to you, it is taken very seriously. Employers routinely pass up "bargain" candidates because of the aura of suspicion that surrounds the overqualified. The more impressive your qualifications, the more serious this problem becomes.

Human nature also plays a part in the over/under problem. The person across the desk from you at a job interview may have struggled for years at jobs he hated under people he despised. He's put in his time in purgatory. Why should you get away without the same suffering?

Your qualifications and background may appear threatening to a superior's own future. Someone who is insecure in his position (as many people are) and is hanging on by his fingernails to the best job he will ever have can be terrified by the heavy credentials that many former military people produce. If that insecure person is to be your future boss, he will be even more nervous. The easiest way for him to remove the possible threat to his position is not to hire you. And there you are, mysteriously out of the running for yet another job that seemed perfect.

Coping with this frustrating reality will be a necessity in almost any field you try to enter after retirement. That's why it must be factored in early in the job-search process. There is no point wasting your time and energy chasing jobs you will never get.

How do you avoid getting caught in this bind? There are two approaches. The first is to concentrate on jobs that are slightly out of the organization's promotion mainstream. Like the uniformed services, civilian careers have ideal promotion paths and certain key assignments. If you come from outside and compete for one of those slots, you may be innocently putting your hand into a buzzsaw. But when your interest is in a specialty or a staff function that does not put you in line for promotion to chief executive officer (CEO), your skills and experience will be genuinely welcomed. You will be seen as an asset and not a threat.

This may seem like a copout to those who are accustomed to fighting for the best assignments, regardless of the odds. But remember, you are making a transition from a military career, where you knew all the tricks, to a different neighborhood—one where you will be a forty-five-year-old with training wheels. The first job search after retirement will be enough of a challenge as it is. Don't make it harder than necessary. Set the boundaries of your expectations at the achievable, not the ideal.

Another way to prevent the over/under dilemma from working against you is to weight your job search toward larger, more established organizations. Their perspective will be closer to what you are accustomed to than that of a small operator. A Fortune 500 company will be interested, perhaps even impressed by your experience at managing a $20 million project; a little guy with a $2 million annual turnover may be terrified that you will break him in the first year.

Large organizations will have more specialized niches to fill, and as long as your job is not one that is earmarked for the company's golden boys, they will be more willing to hire you even if your military background doesn't fit their template. A single hiring exception is not a great risk for them as it is for a smaller organization, where every employee is vital.

The idea of starting your first civilian job search by moderating your expectations can be disheartening in the beginning, but it is better than coming to the same conclusion after six months of discouraging legwork. And there is a bright side. You are not married to the job. Because you are making a major career change, a move to another position in a couple of years will be seen by your second prospective employer as a plus. Then, after some seasoning in what they laughingly call the "real world," you will be more of a known quantity. A résumé from someone who has been retired from the military for only a few months automatically makes many prospective employers uneasy; one that shows a couple of years in a postretirement job will get more serious attention.

The first job search after retirement will be the hardest. It is not an easy experience for anyone, and civilian job changers fear it as much as you do. They do not have that emergency chute called retirement pay to count on. Their psychological problems can be a greater obstacle than the shock of career transition because many of them have been laid off, fired, or left their last position because of dissatisfaction. Your lack of civilian experience will require extra effort, but at least no one will ask you that most dreaded of interview questions: "Why did you leave your last job?"

PLANNING THE CAMPAIGN

The great amphibious operations of World War II were some of the most complex and ambitious endeavors ever made in wartime. Tens of thousands of men were trained, mountains of equipment were moved thousands of miles, years of research were done in months, and at H-hour all this effort converged toward one simple purpose—to take the objective. The newsreels showed what happened after the first wave hit the beach, but only military historians (and generations of suffering war college students) have paid much attention to the monumental planning that made the operations possible.

Finding your first job after retirement is similar to planning and carrying out a military operation. Books, seminars, and job seekers tend to place most of their emphasis on what happens after you hit the beach. Résumé writing, interview techniques, and other tools used in the operational phase of the effort are discussed in dozens of books, but the need for careful planning as a foundation to success receives much less emphasis. It is not difficult to put together a good résumé; a winning interview technique can be learned fairly easily. Yet people with good résumés and impressive interviews still have trouble getting the jobs they want. To go back to the analogy of the amphibious operations, they bring the wrong map, land on the wrong beach, and secure a hill that someone else has already taken.

Why does this happen? Usually it's because the candidate went after the wrong job. That error is often caused by not reading yourself well enough to know exactly how you want to present yourself for a particular position. This is not the same as evaluating your skills and special talents, which are more general in nature. When you plan a job campaign those general characteristics must be converted into specific qualifications for the job you are seeking. Résumés often describe job qualifications in lofty terms such as "experienced in decision making" without attaching that experience to anything concrete. The statement hangs suspended in midair with nothing to link it to you as an individual. Without a flesh-and-blood context, your abilities and experience are meaningless to a prospective employer. As a package to be marketed you are nothing more than a generic product in a plain vanilla box with black lettering.

Describing Who You Are

The first person to convince of your qualifications is yourself. Now that you are ready to target a set of possible jobs, you must test your experience and qualifications against the requirements of the position. At this point it is not necessary to go through an elaborate routine for each specific job; that step will come when you evaluate job openings. What you want to do now is to identify a set of qualifications and compare it to what you have to offer. This is comparable to doing a market survey. You are not selling to a specific customer but are uncovering what a class of customers is looking for. Once you have done that, the actual selling has a much better chance of success.

You will make two lists. The first one should be compiled from sources such as the *Dictionary of Occupational Titles* or the *Encyclopedia of Second Careers,* both of which contain detailed job descriptions for thousands of jobs including sword swallowers and palm readers. Since the descriptions in these volumes tend to be rather pallid, it is a good idea to use classified ads from the newspaper to develop a list of real-world requirements. You can save time here by using the *National Ad Search.* This handy little tabloid, which is published weekly, is a compendium of job ads from seventy-two papers around the nation. To make it easier to use, the jobs are broken down by category, for example, general management, human resources, engineering. The *National Ad Search* and its slightly classier counterpart, the *National Business Employment Weekly,* produced by the *Wall Street Journal,* will be good sources later in the job hunt when you are looking (at last!) for a real job.

As you begin reading ads and job descriptions it will become apparent that job qualifications fall into three categories: skills, certification, and experience. An example of a skill qualification might be "knowledge of laser communications techniques." Certifications can be either educational or professional such as "current teaching certificate required" or "licensed electrician." Experience is the least specific of the three and, as we shall see, is open to more interpretation. At this point in your job campaign, however, the three classes of qualification are most useful as screening devices to test categories of jobs against what you can offer.

A thorough self-assessment should have produced a list of skills and qualifications from your service experience and other sources discussed in the last chapter. Go back to that list now and add any items you may have overlooked. Using the job requirements from the list you have just made, begin looking for matches in your own background. Be thorough. No school or training course, including correspondence courses, should be considered too unimportant as a possible civilian job qualification. Service schools are highly regarded by the civilian community. Completion of a skills course, even if it is only three weeks of instructors' training school, can carry a surprising amount of weight. Major education such as attendance at a staff college can prop up a weak background in management training. All the service colleges teach management under various names. Depending on which course you attended, you may be able to claim up to thirty semester hours of undergraduate and graduate credit in management courses.

Experience with systems and hardware is another facet of your background to include on the second list. The Retired Officer's Association uses an excellent format for this information in its TROA Officer Placement Service (TOPS) registration form. This form, by the way, is a good check-off list to use even if you are not a member of the organization.

Your list will undoubtedly include some experience and qualifications that you have no intention of using in a future job. Resist the temptation to ignore these items. They can be of value in supporting weak areas, and if your primary job goal begins to look unpromising, they could turn out to be a useful fallback. An unusual qualification or bit of experience could tip the scales in your favor at some future interview. When there is a close race for a job, little things can make a big difference.

Don't forget to include experience gained outside the service. Teaching in night school or serving as a key officer in a community association can do double duty as a nonmilitary credential. You want all of these you can get.

When you have completed this exercise, you will have two lists in front of you and will have completed another major task. The next step is to place the list side by side and play a matching game, which is something like ordering dinner in a Chinese restaurant. It might look something like this:

LIST A	*LIST B*
(Your inventory)	(Job qualifications from ads and reference books)
Project manager, helicopter modernization program (three years)	Knowledge of COBOL
Corrosion control management school (five weeks)	Must be able to coordinate work of volunteers and professionals
Chair, church building committee	Requires experience in personnel interview selection techniques

LIST A	*LIST B*
Head, systems integration branch	Human relations background with emphasis on EEOC programs
Member, state ROTC interview board (one year)	
Speed reading course board	State engineering license required
Human relations seminar (one week)	Project manager for new maintenance system integration

This short list illustrates some potential matchups as well as a few very specific go/no go requirements. List A contains at least three qualifications applicable to the project manager job: a background in systems integration, project management, and a five-week school in a maintenance management specialty, corrosion control. That category of job and those qualifications would indicate an opportunity worth pursuing. But if you don't have a state engineering license or knowledge of COBOL, you won't get the job.

As you compare your List A with job requirements, a pattern should begin to emerge. Some jobs will always call for certain experience or qualifications. Those jobs will be worth pursuing only if you can present evidence in the "must have" areas to support your candidacy. No matter how attractive the job may be, it will be a long shot unless you can provide some exceptional alternative selling points. Put more bluntly, going for the job will be a high-effort, low-probability undertaking.

In the process of working your way through the two lists it will gradually become apparent that some aspects of your background are more marketable than others. Unhappily, the assets you would like to sell will not always be the ones in demand, and the skills that make you an attractive civilian package are not the ones that make your pulse race. As much as you wish it were different, there might not be too much civilian career potential in precision bombing, but there might be a bright future in designing bombing ranges. That realization is exactly why you are making those lists. If the work is done thoroughly and objectively, the outcome will be a catalog of what you have to offer to a real set of potential buyers and a grouping of job categories, which by another name are your market.

For almost everyone this analysis will complete one important phase of the job campaign. It is possible, however, that once the dust has settled and you have filed away the final version of those lists, you won't like what you have found. The most likely jobs to try for may bore you to death, and the most useful parts of your experience could be the things you never want to do again. If this is the case, you need to rethink where you want to go. Beginning a job search with a negative outlook is a formula for disaster. Before that happens, consider exploring alternatives like going back to school, taking a temporary job, or the others already mentioned. Don't commit yourself to the effort of a job search unless you are ready to undertake a tough and sometimes frustrating task.

ESSENTIAL PARTS OF THE JOB SEARCH

The most important tools are perseverance and a positive attitude. Without those attributes you won't find the job you want unless you are very lucky. Attitude is important because it colors your behavior. It communicates itself to others in many subtle ways. An experienced interviewer can spot a negative outlook in the first five minutes. Recruiters, who sometimes screen job applicants on the phone, can detect it, too, and will cross you off their list in a minute if they don't like what they hear. Most important of all is how the problem can affect you and your family. Fear and anger, which are usually the roots of a bad attitude, feed on themselves and can have a powerful impact on those closest to you. At a time in life when mutual family support is critical, destructive emotions can cause a tremendous amount of damage. If you have an attitude problem, do something about it. It won't go away by itself.

Perseverance will also be necessary. In his book *What Color Is Your Parachute,* Richard Bolles graphically illustrates the job-search process by a full page of "no's" ended by a single tiny "yes." That pretty well covers it. You only have to get one job. When you do, all those "no's" are quickly forgotten. It is easy to forget that halfway through a job campaign. When you have just finished mailing your hundredth résumé—and have had only five replies—and the ads are all beginning to look the same, that's the time to remember that the one worthwhile job is still out there waiting for you if you only stick with it.

FINDING THE OPENING

People who market products for a living spend a good deal of time and effort reaching potential customers. Even the rare and lucky ones who have a package so good that it sells itself must work hard to find the right need in the right place at the right time. The best sales pitch in the world is useless in an indifferent market.

There are five principal ways to make contact with the people who might have an interest in your qualifications and experience. They are networking, professional associations, recruiters and employment agencies, classified ads, and self-marketing. The books, seminars, and workshops on job-search techniques use different names and variations to describe these methods, but they all come down to the same basic ways of getting in touch with a prospective employer.

WHICH TECHNIQUE IS BEST FOR YOU?

One of the major differences between the job campaign of a civilian and that of a military retiree is the relative importance of the various contact methods. Networking is by far the best method of finding a job for someone who has been working in a particular field for a while and has lived in the same part of the country for a few years. Depending on which book you read, from 50 to 70 percent of jobs are acquired through networking.

Retiring military people rarely have the advantage of extensive contacts in the professional area of their choosing. Even though we may have lived in a community for several years, we are usually more isolated from its business and professional life than are our civilian counterparts. Therefore, networking is not as rich a source of potential jobs as it might be. A few years after retirement this will change; but for that important first job search, too much emphasis on networking can lead to disappointment.

Professional associations are of more value to us than to other job seekers. Groups such as TROA or NCOA have job placement services, which include nationwide referral systems, counseling, and other forms of assistance. Membership in one of these organizations is a worthwhile investment for the job service alone, and it is tax deductible. Other armed forces or defense-related professional associations can also be valuable sources of assistance. The Armed Forces Communications Electronics Association (AFCEA) and other groups publish newsletters, hold conventions where military and civilian members can meet, and often act as clearinghouses for jobs in the specialty. Participation in this type of association looks good on your résumé and, of course, is another tax deduction.

Recruiters will probably not play a dominant part in your job search unless you have a specialty that is in high demand. In fact, some of them will not touch a job candidate who is retiring or newly retired from the military. They consider you too much of an unknown. They will have to spend too much time preparing and selling you to an employer, and unless their area of concentration is defense-related they may have difficulty evaluating your qualifications.

Virtually every authority on job-search techniques will tell you that classified ads are not the best source of jobs. Nevertheless, most people begin their job campaign by going directly to the "help wanted" section of the paper. Some never get any further than that but continue week after week, mailing résumés to anonymous post office boxes and waiting anxiously for replies that never come. It is a discouraging and frustrating experience, but because it is the least demanding approach to locating a job we often tend to place too much emphasis on answering ads, even when the results are meager. Classified ads have a place in your upcoming campaign but should never be the sole source of job leads.

Marketing yourself by writing to potential employers is another technique for locating a job. Marketing letters, sometimes known as broadcast letters, are a way of distributing an ad for your skills and qualifications. They are usually done in volume; a market letter to one hundred companies is not unusual, and some job seekers send up to a thousand letters. Success depends on the appeal of your letter, the accuracy of your market targeting, and, like any mass campaign, the number of people you reach.

For each individual the blend of techniques and the amount of effort devoted to each one will be different. The important thing is to use all of the paths to locating a job. Some will demand more effort than others and require you to learn new skills. But at the very least, everyone should try each of the methods once. If one proves to be unrewarding or incompatible with your personality, you can consider abandoning it. But give all the methods a chance first.

Networking

Simply defined, this is a way of telling a large number of people who you are and what kind of employment you are seeking. It will mean getting your message to neighbors, old friends, friends of friends, and other people you know, such as your insurance man or your children's swimming coach. Although not as powerful a tool for retirees as for civilians, it remains the basis for actively spreading the word about yourself to as many people as possible.

Everybody knows something about an available job. The service manager at your car dealership may not be ready to hire you to tune Porsches, but it is possible that one of his other customers (maybe even the guy who owns the Porsche) is looking for someone just like you. Folks who come into contact with a cross section of society get all sorts of information every day. That's why beauty salons and country barbershops are such great sources of gossip.

In building and expanding your network, no possible contact, however humble or unlikely it may seem, should be overlooked. Sit down for a few minutes and start making a list of all the people you meet who might know about a job. Unless you have been operating undercover for the last few years, that list will be longer than you had imagined, and as you work on it, it will grow almost geometrically. It is your network or, to be more accurate, the beginning of your network. If you have been thorough it will consist of anywhere from fifty to one hundred names at the start and will grow as large as you want it to be.

The hardest part about getting a useful network going will be overcoming the initial reluctance that most of us have at "asking for favors" or being "pushy." These are simply not attributes a military career fosters. To most civilians, though, working through others and cultivating contacts are accepted parts of the daily business of life, and you too must learn to use them.

The techniques are simple and, once you get over the initial feeling of awkwardness, will gradually seem more natural. The idea of using a network will also be made easier if you remember that you are not going to go out and ask everyone on your list to give you a job. Instead, you will be letting them know that you are doing an active job search and getting leads on people they might know of who are in your field. In outline form this first phase of the networking process looks something like this:

• Starting with your initial list of contacts, let them know that you are in the job market and what kind of position you are seeking.
• Ask your contacts for names of people in companies or fields that you have targeted.
• If possible, ask your initial contact to let those people know you will be calling.
• *Don't* give them a résumé at this point unless you are lucky enough to get a definite job lead *and* your contact asks for a résumé to pass on to a specific individual. You want to keep running down job leads under your own control. As well intentioned as friends or acquaintances may be, they have more on their minds than finding you a job. At this point, all you are looking for is names.

• Start keeping records. Before long you will find you have a list of people in your job area to call. You will now be one step closer to the job market and ready to move into the next phase.

With the list of contacts as a starting point, the immediate objectives will be to find out where jobs might be and more names of people who might know of jobs. There will be many names on your list so set up a priority system to help you decide who to call first. Some leads will look more promising than others or be more appealing, or perhaps timing will be critical. Concentrate on those first.

The hard part begins with the second phase: picking up the telephone and going to work. Many of the calls will be to strangers, so you will have to establish immediately who you are and how you got the person's name. *Then* comes the reason for the call. Here's an example of how a typical conversation might open:

> *You:* "Good morning, Mr. Smith. My name is Bill Jones. Sally Williams suggested I call you. I'm doing a job search and Sally gave me your name as someone who might know the names of some people or companies to contact."

Except for the introductory call from your initial contact, the person you are speaking to is a total stranger, but in less than a minute you have told him that you are not selling him anything, that you know someone he knows, and that you are making a straightforward and reasonable request. He may even be flattered to know that his name was suggested to you.

Once the contact has been established and initial chit-chat about good old Sally is out of the way, it's time to get specific about what you want and then get off the phone:

You: "I'm sure you are busy now, and I appreciate your time. If you don't mind, I'd like to send along a résumé and call you back in a week or so, whenever it's convenient for you. What would be the best time for me to call?"

By assuring him that you won't take any more of his time right now, you have earned a little gratitude at the same time that you have gained his agreement to talk to you again after he has had the chance to look at your résumé. Congratulations! You have now completed your first networking call. That's all there is to it. Well, not really. There are nuances. You will find, after you become more comfortable with the mechanics of the thing, that some of the people you call are clearly not interested in helping you or anyone else. Cross them off your list and note the source of the lead. It may turn out that many of the names from one person are bad, which means that he is a lousy source. Cross him off, too. As your networking effort expands, you will have more than enough names to keep you busy. There's no reason to waste your time on losers.

Within a day or so of your initial call, write thank you notes and mail your résumé to the people you have contacted. Make the note short and polite, being sure to mention again the time and date that you agreed to contact the person for a second call. It is also useful to include a list of the companies and possible jobs in your area of interest.

After about two weeks, make your follow-up call. This time the object will be to get names of people who might know of jobs or, even better, generate an actual job lead or two. Don't be discouraged if all you get is more names of possible contacts. Remember that it is a numbers game and you are only in the initial round of a repeating cycle. Like parachuting, the first time is the hardest.

As a retired military careerist, it will be harder for you to establish and increase a network than it is for civilians. This situation makes it especially important that you use the first round of contacts to establish a beachhead in the type of companies you can expect to find a job with. It also points up the value of joining civic or service organizations where you live. Aside from getting together and eating rubber chicken for lunch every couple of weeks, these people make useful contacts through association. Membership gives you a good chance to join the world of civilian networking.

One way to break into the networking game with a minimum of anguish is to begin your campaign by contacting old service friends who have been retired long enough to have become established in the civilian world. Don't try this with anyone who's been retired for less than a year. They're probably as lost as you are—but they've had more time to accumulate misinformation. Instead, pick some people whom you knew and trusted when they were in uniform, and who seem to have done well in the civilian world, preferably in a field close to what interests you.

Call the people you select, and tell them that you are beginning a job search and that, since they seem to have done well, you would like the benefit of their experience and advice. Be sure they understand that you are not hitting them up for a job. Assure them that you just want to ask questions and learn.

If you use this approach, you will find that most people will be glad to help you. They'll be flattered that you've asked for their advice and, unless they have very short memories, will remember how they felt in your position. Be prepared to do a lot of listening. Since almost everyone who's been retired from the service for a few years has a pet theory about the best way to get started in the civilian world (often learned through painful experience), you'll get some revealing perspectives. Equally important, you'll get some up-to-date information on the job market and, with luck, some good referrals to help expand your network. You may even get a job offer.

Networking is the most time-consuming of the various job location methods, and because it is a continuing process, it is the one most likely to become tiresome after the first month or so. But if you allow your carefully built network to wither too soon, all of your effort will be wasted. It is best to begin as soon as possible, preferably before you have started using the other contact methods.

Professional Associations

Civilian job-search experts usually include professional associations as one of many sources of networking contacts. For civilian job seekers this is correct, but retiring military people are in a slightly different situation than other people. Our entry into the job market is a predictable event. The challenges we face as we make the transition into a new job situation are common to us all, regardless of rank and service. Recognition of this shared experience led to the creation of organizations like TROA and the NCOA, dedicated to assisting and protecting the interests of retired military people. Today a significant part of their work is related to job placement and career transition. The modest dues you pay to belong to one of these organizations give you access to an efficient, professional placement service with national scope. For the money it is a very good buy.

Both organizations provide services, which include résumé critique, job counseling, job fairs, and access to a computer-based job referral system. The referral system has the added advantage of listing positions for which retired military people are preferred. Many of these jobs are never advertised anywhere else, which gives you an advantage over the civilian competition that you will not find in any other aspect of your job search.

Specialized professional associations are another potential source of job information. For people with a strong background in engineering, communications, electronics, and other fields, they provide a powerful networking and job directory resource. Professional associations have the unique advantage of being a meeting ground between military people and their counterpart civilian professionals. Through professional symposia, conventions, and social events, unadvertised job opportunities can be discovered and valuable contacts established.

Less specialized associations of people with mutual interests in areas such as foreign affairs are another possible avenue of approach to job openings. Participation in these groups' activities will widen the scope of your nonmilitary acquaintances and provide access to people across a broad sector of society. The same is true of participation in political and special-interest organizations, but be careful. Membership in some groups will establish you, correctly or not, in a certain category. If that is to your advantage in a job search, fine. But if it is not, keep your political and ideological activities separate from your career.

Recruiters and Employment Agencies

Professional recruiters are paid by a client to find the best candidates for a position. They offer a service that has advantages for an employer who does not want to devote valuable time and effort to advertising, screening, and interviewing. First, they offer an expertise that the employer may lack. Finding candidates, evaluating résumés, and conducting interviews require skills and insights not normally used in day-to-day work. Managers and professionals who are brilliant at doing their own jobs are often uncomfortable interviewing others. Assigning this task to a professional gives the assurance that the handful of final candidates have already survived close scrutiny and makes the final selection process much easier.

If a company does not want to attract too much attention to its search for job candidates, recruiters serve as middlemen who can find people to fill the position with a minimum of publicity. Most of the newspaper ads that do not name a company and give only a post office box number for job replies are placed by recruiters.

There are more than two thousand companies in the recruiting business, ranging from large international operations down to one-person shops, and they cover almost every professional and management area imaginable. The *Directory of Executive Recruiters,* which is updated annually, lists them by functional area, location, and type. There are two types listed: conventional and contingency. Conventional recruiters work on a retainer paid by their clients to locate people for specific positions. Depending on the terms of their contract, they might provide one, two, or a dozen candidates whom they consider acceptable. They usually have a close relationship with the client and are well informed about job requirements and the client's specific desires.

Contingency recruiters operate much like an employment agency. They are not retained under contract by a client company and are paid only if their candidate is hired. This does not detract from their professionalism, but it does mean that they may have less inside information about specific jobs. They also may be more tempted to persuade you to compete for a job that you might otherwise pass up and, because they are playing a numbers game, to promote as many candidates as possible for each position they are trying to fill. Since you will be contacting a number of contingency recruiters who may be competing to fill the same position, it is possible that you will be presented to an employer more than once. This is not good. It creates the impression that you are shotgunning your job search and that you do not have any special interest in any specific job, a sure way to be dropped from consideration very quickly.

The best way to contact recruiters is by a straightforward letter telling them you are in the job market. To save time and effort for both you and the recruiter, tell her in the letter what salary range you are thinking of and any preferences you may have for a geographic area or type of organization. If you have not yet retired when the letter goes out, include the date you will be leaving the service. (Don't use the word *retiring*. It can give a negative impression.) Attach a copy of your résumé to the letter (see the sample letter in appendix A). A reputable professional will not pass salary information to a prospective employer but will use it as a screen to decide what jobs you will be eligible for. He will also appreciate your being up front with him. Less than reputable recruiters will either ignore you or try to interest you in a job that is clearly unsuitable. These people are rare but easy to identify and should be crossed off your list immediately.

Contact as many recruiters as possible with emphasis on retainer people because they are one step closer to the job you want. Try to send at least ten or twenty letters per week until you have exhausted the list of recruiters who handle your field and preferred location. An average list will include four hundred to a thousand names, so it will keep you busy every week for a couple of months.

The numbers involved in this effort make individual hunt-and-peck letter writing impractical. A personal computer or word processor with a mail-merge capability can be a godsend, but if you are not ready to buy one, don't despair. Typing and mailing services are available almost everywhere at a reasonable (and tax-deductible) price. Check the yellow pages and the classified section of the paper for the best deals. Many people operate secretarial services out of their homes and can often provide first-class support at a surprisingly low cost.

Don't expect a reply to your letter. Executive recruiters receive thousands of letters and résumés, and unless you seem like a possible candidate for a position they have listed, they will either file the information on you or discard it. Follow-up to your letter is not necessary, and telephone calls to recruiters only waste everyone's time. A recruiter who is interested in what you have to offer will contact you, usually by phone, to obtain additional information. His call—which will probably be very informal—is the first step in the screening process and can be either the beginning or the end of a rewarding relationship.

To handle these calls without shooting yourself in the foot, think of them as mini-interviews and act accordingly. Tell your family that you will be expecting recruiters to call. Ask them to write down any messages the caller leaves and explain to them why first impressions are so important. When a recruiter calls, be crisp, professional, and prepared to discuss your résumé and job qualifications. Pretend that you are face-to-face with him in an interview. If selling yourself without advance preparation is not your best point, tell your family to ask recruiters to call back even if you are at home to give you time to get your act together. People who live alone should consider getting a telephone answering machine to screen incoming calls.

Employment agencies have a role in the job campaign that varies directly with the level of employment sought. At the middle-management echelon and above, their importance decreases steadily. Few positions paying above $30,000 will be found through agencies; except for technical specialties such as engineering and computers, employers prefer to use executive recruiters to fill jobs above that level. For everyone else, however, the agency is too useful a source to be ignored.

Like recruiters, most employment agencies earn their money through fees from employers with jobs to fill. But there are exceptions. In some cases an agency will charge the job applicant a fee, either up front or as a percentage of the first year's earnings. Some contracts with agencies also call for an individual who is placed to agree to pay a fee if he does not remain in a job for a certain length of time. The possibility of encountering one of these situations makes it very important to read any agreement you make with an agency carefully before signing it. Usually, the agreement will be the first thing you see when you apply at one of these establishments. You will be given an application to fill out, which includes the terms of your agreement, often in small print at the very end of the form. The smaller the print, the closer you should examine it. If you do not wish to pay a fee for a job, be sure to note on the application *before you sign it* that you will accept only "fee paid" positions. Reputable agencies will accept this limitation. If they don't, you have saved yourself time and money. Unless you are a real basket case, there is no reason why you ought ever to pay a fee.

Don't be cagey or reticent with an agency. Like recruiters, they need to know your salary requirements and any other special restrictions or desires. When you are working with more than one agency at a time, be sure they all know it. Employers find it very annoying to see a person presented twice for the same job. It increases their paperwork and does not endear you to them as a possible employee. For the same reason, an agency must be given the names of any prospective employers or companies you have contacted by other means.

Unfilled positions don't make money for the agency so it may exert pressure on you to take jobs that you are not interested in. Resist this pressure whenever it comes. The agent will get the message quickly and give you less of a runaround. The agency may lose interest in you for a while, but if the right job comes along it won't hesitate to call you.

Personal appearance and the overall impression you create are important to success with an agency. Recruiting is a very competitive business, and agents do not want to get a reputation for sending losers for job interviews. A candidate who has made a positive impression on the agency interviewer gets first shot at the best jobs and wastes less time on the nonstarters.

State and local employment offices are often underused by job seekers who think that only the most desperate and stingy employers use these services. Although there is some truth in that belief, it is by no means universal. Public employment agencies have more extensive files and better-trained professionals than all but the largest private operators, and they never charge a fee to you or to the employer. They also have the inside track on many state and local jobs and can offer job counseling at little or no cost. The waiting room will not be as fancy as that of a plush agency, and the environment will be a bit less elegant, but at least you know that you will not be charged for the overhead.

Job Advertisements

As we grow older, we learn that most things in this world are not what they seem to be. That's the way it is with ads. No one in his right mind would waste money advertising a low-paying, dead-end job requiring someone with minimum intelligence and ambition. Instead, the job is presented as an exciting opportunity for the right person, who just happens to fit a profile common to 90 percent of the working population. By contrast, many job descriptions contain enough specifics, details, and conditions to make a Joint Chiefs of Staff (JCS) action officer blush, for the sole purpose of excluding all but the most qualified candidates. Between these extremes lie the majority of advertisements you see in newspapers, magazines, and professional journals. Interpreting them requires careful reading and educated guessing to discern what the employer is really looking for.

Job ads seldom contain outright lies, but they have been known to massage the truth in some ingenious ways. A low level of responsibility may be hidden behind a screen of impressive titles, bad pay disguised as an opportunity for advancement, and an innocent looking list of qualifications can actually be a minefield, carefully sown with phrases designed to eliminate undesirable candidates. Laws prohibiting discrimination based on race, sex, or age can be circumvented by the clever ad writer, and for some jobs in the public sector, a job description can be developed to exclude everyone but a candidate who has already been quietly preselected. Some of the more common techniques follow.

The weighted description. Ads frequently try to attract desirable people to low-paying, uninteresting jobs by describing the working environment in more detail than the job itself. Newspapers list more jobs for administrative assistants than for typists and receptionists, describing jobs as providing exciting opportunities to meet people and work in a glamorous setting. The real work is hidden away in the gushy prose and mentioned offhandedly. Ads for administrative assistant and editorial assistant are notorious for this tactic.

At the end of the ad they usually mention the requirement of a typing speed of fifty-five words per minute and a familiarity with filing systems, and that's the tip-off.

Silk purses from sows' ears. The advertiser is seeking "commanders for a fleet of vessels operated by one of the largest companies in the country . . . applicants must be experienced, good at dealing with people, wear a uniform well, and have a good speaking voice."

Is he looking for captains for "Love Boat"? No. The company that placed this ad is hiring people to run make-believe launches through a jungle safari attraction in its theme parks. It sure sounded good, though. Almost any job can be made to sound good when it is dressed up in Madison Avenue language. Ads that promise everything should be viewed with suspicion. Compared with some of them, military recruiters are masters of understatement.

Hidden discrimination. This is the nasty one. Without openly violating the law, an employer can convey the message that certain people need not apply. Ads sprinkled with words like "high-energy environment" and "fast-paced operations" often really mean "young applicants only"; a "traditional, shirtsleeves atmosphere" can be code for "no women."

The buried eliminator. A job ad must be read from start to finish. A job may seem to fit you like a glove at first reading, but when you get down into the grass you discover a harmless little phrase like "must be fluent in Urdu and Hindi." That's a buried eliminator.

The majority of job advertisements, though not intentionally misleading, will require some interpretation. The first piece of information to look for is qualifications, which usually appear in two layers: the required and the nice to have. Second to these is experience, followed sometimes by credentials or certifications. Special requirements such as willingness to travel round out the picture.

Critical reading of an ad consists of digging out the required qualifications and comparing them with what you have to offer. No matter how good a job may look, it is seldom worth a response if you do not have 80 to 90 percent of the must-have qualifications. Statistics show that an average newspaper want ad receives somewhere between one hundred and one thousand responses. Over 25 percent of these will be from people who are fully qualified for the job, and not all of them will get to the interview stage.

Experience and nice-to-have qualifications are more flexible and open to interpretation. Once beyond the mandatory items, an ad usually describes an ideal candidate in terms of the best qualities the writer would like to see in the person who takes the job. Different but comparable experience and qualifications are worth mentioning, providing that you can tie them to the employer's needs.

Formal qualifications are either "must have" or desirable. In the latter category, employers will often ask for the optimum knowing they are unlikely to get it. It makes the job and their organization look better and also scares off the timid applicant. Ads that call for a certain credential or its equivalent can open up a little more maneuvering room if you don't stretch the equivalent too far.

Some ads ask for an applicant's salary history as well as the compensation expected for the job sought. They may even say that applications without this information will not be considered. Don't give them the information unless you already have a good idea what the job pays or really want the job regardless of compensation. By telling you that they won't look at your qualifications unless you fit their pay limitations, they have suggested that they are seeking the best-priced and not the best-qualified candidates.

From time to time you will see an ad for a job that is absolutely irresistible. It's the dream job, the one you thought existed only in your fevered imagination. Everything about it is perfect except that under the cold light of reason you don't have the required background. Apply anyway. Long shots sometimes come in, and if you can convey your enthusiasm to a prospective employer, you might possibly get an interview. If you never hear from him, it is still better than lying awake at night wondering about what might have been.

When you find an ad with possibilities, the next step is to write a response that will get attention. Every serious contender who answers the ad sends a résumé and a cover letter. Many of the letters are boilerplate, some will ooze phony enthusiasm, and a few will be unbearably cute. None of them will get very far. A person who is screening responses to ads will quickly winnow out the ones that do not answer the mail, often without reading the résumé. To survive this first cut, your letter must get down to business right away by establishing three points:

You know what the job requires. In as few words as possible, summarize the required or must-have qualifications.

You have the qualifications. Under each job qualification you have listed, briefly describe your experience and qualifications with the same concrete examples used in your résumé (see chapter 6).

You have something special to offer. After listing the job's requirements and describing your qualifications, briefly outline the special attributes that make you more qualified than the other applicants. Special training, education, or experience might be included here. Do not invite attention to qualifications or experience you lack. Your candor will be appreciated only because it makes your response easier to eliminate.

The sample letter (appendix B) illustrates the recommended format for letter responses to ads. The letter should always include in the first paragraph the name and date of the publication in which you read the ad. Large organizations as well as executive recruiters often advertise more than one position in the same edition of a paper, so be sure to refer to the job by its full title.

Broadcast Letters

A broadcast or market letter is a flyer advertising that you are out there and have something to offer. At its best, this technique can gain access to jobs that are not advertised, not open to recruiters, and sometimes didn't even exist until you came along. At its worst, it creates expensive junk mail.

To understand how a broadcast letter works, take a look at the marketing material you get in the mail. You will notice that some of it is obviously shotgunned to everyone on your delivery route and that other items have been targeted at you and people like you. The most precisely aimed items come in an envelope designed to give the impression that it has been individually addressed. This arouses your curiosity enough to open the envelope and read the first paragraph. If it is a well-prepared letter, it will say something with which you immediately identify or would like to identify. Here is an example:

"As a SCUBA enthusiast, you probably spent between $200 and $500 on equipment last year . . . and paid too much money for it." Damn right, you say, and read on. The next paragraph tells you how the Captain Nemo wholesale house has saved money for hundreds of people just like you and cites a few examples of the great deals offered. You priced scuba gear just the other day so your interest is aroused and you continue on to the sales pitch in the closing paragraphs of the letter. You will not necessarily respond to the offer. Money might be a little tight or you may have decided to give up scuba diving. But if the letter happens to arrive at a time when you are considering upgrading your equipment and the deal sounds good enough, you may want to find out more about the sender.

Job seekers' broadcast letters work exactly the same way. They define a market of potential employers, discover what that market needs, and show by examples how they can fill that need. Since there is no way of knowing if each individual "buyer" is in the market at the moment he receives the letter, a broadcast mailing is done in volume. The normal goal is a reply rate of 3 to 5 percent. That may seem low at first glance, but a 3 percent response in your job campaign means three interviews per hundred letters mailed. That's not too shabby, especially when you only need one job.

Developing a broadcast letter begins with researching market needs. You should already have decided what category of organizations you want to work for so that part of the job is already done. Now you need to discover what problems your targeted market would like solved and what skills are in short supply. As one job-search expert puts it, you must "find out what keeps the boss awake at night."

That's not as difficult as it may seem. Trade journals and professional publications are constantly examining problem areas. Business and professional leaders make speeches on "challenges," and the mass media produce a surprising amount of material on issues in a variety of fields. Your own experience at handling difficult tasks is probably the best source of ideas. Firsthand experience is always a credible qualification and can also provide evidence of your past success. The opening paragraph of a broadcast letter might look something like this:

> Dear _____:
>
> Insurance costs out of control?
>
> If your company's liability insurance skyrocketed last year, you are not alone. A recent industry survey showed an average premium increase of 200% last year for firms of your size and no relief in sight.

Having gained the reader's attention, you can show how you can help get him do something about the problem. The next paragraphs do that:

> I can help get your problem under control. As a government-certified safety engineer and hazardous workplace consultant for Odoriferous Chemicals, Inc., I
> —Set up and administered a hazardous materials handling program that eliminated the requirement for special materials insurance coverage. Annual premiums saved: $6,000.
> —Established a safety awareness program that reduced the work accident rate by 35% in the first year. The insurance company awarded me the Safety Manager of the Year award and reduced the company's premium by 12% for 2 consecutive years.

And so forth. The letter has interest to an employer because it identifies a problem familiar to him and holds out the promise of a solution backed up by hard facts and figures. Its credibility is enhanced by the naming of a similar organization that benefited from your solution.

The final paragraph need only be a short invitation to contact you for more information. You should *not* mention that you are looking for a job. That can mean a short route to the circular file for your letter. The goal is to arouse enough interest to generate a letter or phone call to you and eventually the chance for an interview.

Broadcast letters should always be personally addressed to individuals in the organizations you have targeted. The names you need can be found with the help of your friendly reference librarian in directories such as *Standard and Poor's*. It will require some work to develop a mailing list this way but it is necessary. Unless a broadcast letter is addressed to a decision maker, it will end up in the hands of some giggling mail clerk who hasn't the faintest idea of what you are writing about.

You should send no fewer than one hundred broadcast letters, and the more the better. Follow-up is impractical because of the numbers involved and doesn't serve much purpose anyway. You will either rouse some interest and a contact or the recipient will forget the letter the day after reading it.

Broadcast letters are most useful when they serve as one part of a diversified job campaign. By themselves they are too much of a long shot to rely on. When you develop your plan of attack (chapter 6), you can determine how much time and effort you want to devote to this technique. But do it right or don't do it at all. A good broadcast letter must be polished like a gem and mailed in volume to the right people. Unless it is done right, it is a waste of time.

Creating Your Own Job

People have become millionaires by discovering an unfulfilled need and satisfying it. Henry Ford realized that the automobile was destined to be more than a rich man's plaything and sold the American public on the idea that everyone could own a car. In our own time, thousands of people have started small businesses and created new jobs because they foresaw that some service or product would be in demand. In a society changing as rapidly as ours, new opportunities are constantly springing up for people whose timing is right. Cottage industries like child care have turned into big businesses overnight, and obscure services such as hazardous waste disposal have become booming, high-tech industries.

Creating a new job opportunity is a high-risk undertaking that requires considerable research and preparation. The job must capitalize on a set of skills that you have already demonstrated. Your level of competence in the area should be exceptionally high. Before you can convince someone of the need to create a position, you will have to establish yourself as an authority in your field. In a way, you will be offering your services as a full-time consultant; if you are hired, you will be expected to be highly qualified in an area in which your prospective employer and your coworkers have little knowledge.

Defining and establishing a new position is a major decision for any organization. There must be convincing proof that it will pay off, which means that you have to persuade an employer that your proposal will result in cost reduction, more profit, or improved quality of output. To do this you must have a good insight into the general objectives and problems of all organizations in your targeted field as well as a grasp of the special circumstances of each individual organization.

If you don't have one particular organization in mind, broadcast letters are the best way to create interest in what you are offering. A modified networking campaign can also provide some leads: instead of searching out the names of people who might know about jobs, use the network to locate organizations that might have the problem your proposed job can solve or the void that you can fill.

Obviously, such an undertaking does not call for a superficial approach. New jobs and services are successfully established only after extensive research, analysis, and hard selling. From start to finish the process can take a long time. It is definitely not something you dream up on Sunday night over a few drinks and put into action Monday morning.

LAYING THE FOUNDATION

Finding the right job and getting it is a building process, and people making the transition from a military career to a civilian one will find that they must start from the bottom. The rules of the game, the vocabulary, the techniques, and even the job will involve new and unknown terrain. For a civilian making a job or a career transition the foundation is already in place. For us it must be built, stone by stone. The success of your job search and the quality of your new career will be in direct proportion to the care with which you construct that foundation.

6

INTO THE ARENA

◆

All the work you have done so far is preparation for the heart of the matter: getting a job. Everything else is window dressing. If that statement sounds extreme, think of all the people you have run across in your career who became so preoccupied with procedures and doctrines that they forgot what the mission was supposed to be. And then think of the ones who got results. You will probably agree that the latter group was distinguished by concentrating on the end objective without getting bogged down getting there. This is important to remember as you move from the planning stage to the point where you are trying to get real people to hire you for a real job. A stack of flawless résumés on the most expensive paper money can buy will be useless if they don't reach the right people and present you in the most effective way. Your skills, however marketable they are, will go undiscovered unless they are brought to the attention of someone who needs them.

A job search should be a full-time operation, which means eight hours a day, five days a week, and no cheating. This isn't easy. The transition from working in a structured environment to setting your own schedule requires self-discipline. No one will assign work or set deadlines for you. No support staff will fill your "in" basket to keep you busy. The little things you never thought of that helped you shift gears from home to work will not be there any more. Commuting, the first cup of coffee in the office, contact with other people—all the habits and activities that condition us to think work—will be absent. It can become very easy to get up a little later, putter around the house for an hour or two, and generally waste time. It wasn't only eccentricity that led the British to dress for dinner and punctiliously observe teatime wherever they were in the world; it was the recognition that at heart we are all a little lazy, and without the gentle urging of routine it is very easy to go native.

It's not likely that you will be tempted to spend your days sitting on the veranda sipping pink gins, but unless you organize and stick to a work schedule right from the start, time wasting can become progressively more insidious and habitual.

One of the most demoralizing things about being unemployed is the sense of alienation from others that comes with not having a scheduled place to go each day. Evenings and weekends, which used to be legitimate personal time, can now be sources of guilt and resentment. To someone who lacks an internal regimen, the pleasant sensation of unwinding after a long day or a hard week becomes meaningless, and seeing the rest of the family enjoy their well-earned rest can be like an accusation. This is another reason why you need to make your job search a full-time effort. Equally important, you should stop work at quitting time and look forward to weekends as a time of escape from the job.

ORGANIZING FOR A JOB SEARCH

First, make a place to work. Trying to run a serious job search from the top of the dining room table just won't make it. There will be constant distractions, the dog will eat your homework, and you will end up with guacamole on your résumés. It is absolutely vital that you carve out some place to be yours and yours alone for eight hours a day. If you are lucky enough to have a den or a study already established as your territory, make it your new office. If you are not so fortunate, find someplace that provides the environment you need. The following elements are necessary:

Privacy

If you don't have a den or other office space, use a room with a door that will close it off from daytime traffic. A phone extension is nice to have too. Be sure your family understands that what you are doing in there is *working* and that you don't want to be disturbed. Get into the habit of mentally changing gears when you enter the work room. Take coffee and lunch breaks if you have to, but put in a full day and treat your work time as just that—a regular work day. You'll be surprised how much this helps your self-discipline and improves your at-home work habits.

Any room will do. A guest room or spare bedroom is fine as long as there are no house guests wandering in and out. Even an attic or basement will do if it can be made reasonably habitable without a major home-improvement project. If no other space is available, use your bedroom. This may require a change in your spouse's sleeping habits, but that is a small price to pay for the wonderful job you're going to get. And if that argument doesn't sell, a few weeks of brisk early morning activity such as typing and loud groaning as you read the want ads will probably do the trick.

Working Arrangements

You will need someplace to sit, a desk or table or sit at, and a typewriter. A phone extension is handy too. Like recruiters, some prospective employers use the telephone as a screening device. Carrying on a conversation while the Top Forty is blaring from your kid's stereo in the background is not the ideal way to make a good initial impression. An answering machine can also be useful. A good technique, even if you are at home, is to let the machine answer for you. This allows you time to take the message, do some homework on the caller, and then return the call later, when you are fully prepared. Above all, do not use novelty messages on the answering machine. Would *you* hire someone who lets Count Dracula or the Seven Dwarfs answer the phone?

A word processor or personal computer is invaluable for preparing résumés and market letters, but don't buy one just for your job search. It will not pay for itself, and the IRS probably won't let you write it off as a job-hunting expense.

Some people have a fetish about freshly sharpened pencils, neatly arranged scratch pads, paper clips, and the other impedimenta that go along with the world of paper. If stocking up on office supplies makes you feel more businesslike, go to it (and keep the receipts for tax time).

Job-search experts love to argue about whether letterhead stationery is necessary. One group insists that you have to have it to look professional and organized; the other side points out that if you have it printed with a home address and phone number, everyone will think you've been out of work for a long time. In general, though, having some stationery printed is a good idea. If nothing else, you can use it after you get a job to write nasty letters to the local utility company. Just make sure that you choose the best quality paper and pick a discreet, dignified typeface for the letterhead. Cute or trendy lettering will create the impression that you are a lightweight, and paper that is any color other than white, ivory, or maybe gray can send some signals that you don't even want to think about.

Record Keeping

If a job search is done right, there will be a surprising amount of paperwork to keep organized. Good records are especially vital if you are doing an aggressive networking campaign. As your network expands, you will be making contacts with people who are three and four times removed from your starting point. If you can't recall who referred you to whom it can be embarrassing and could lose you good leads.

There is no one formula for setting up a record-keeping system, but there are some minimums you should stick to to avoid losing track of things. Some suggested formats for job-search records are given in appendix C. Whether or not you use these, you should maintain at least the following;

—a telephone log of all job-related calls
—a list of people contacted
—a record of all recruiters and employment agencies contacted
—a record of résumés and letters sent and received
—a reminder file for thank you notes and phone calls
—sales slips, receipts, and anything else useful for tax purposes
—an evaluation system for comparing jobs

At first this may seem like a lot of paperwork for one job search, but remember, finding that perfect position is a numbers game. An active, aggressive campaign can generate hundreds of leads, any one of which could be the dream job waiting there just for you.

Family Cooperation

Unless you live alone, most of the preparations described in the preceding paragraphs will require cooperation and understanding from the other members of your family. If you have never before had a study or private area and you suddenly blossom out with a fully stocked home office, they may suspect that you have come down with a new strain of midlife crisis. So in the interest of domestic tranquillity, it is a good idea to discuss your arrangements with the rest of the family. They will be reassured by knowing that when you are off by yourself in the "office" you are really working. You can benefit from your family's positive cooperation. When a recruiter or a potential employer calls you and reaches a polite, intelligent sounding teenager, he gets a good first impression, but if a "yeah, wait a minute" is followed by five minutes of waiting, he may not be so pleased.

You know that the job campaign is a full-time effort, but your family has learned over the years to associate your work with your being away from home. Unless you convince them that you are not just fooling around to keep yourself busy, it may be difficult to get the privacy and freedom from interruption that you need. Their understanding will help reinforce the discipline that you must impose on yourself.

NEW SKILLS

One of the differences between the military and the civilian worlds is the basic attitude toward the job. In the military profession we are constantly reminded that family and personal rewards notwithstanding, duty always comes first. It's not the same in the civilian world.

With the exception of professions that are devoted to helping or enlightening others, the focus of most civilian occupations is, to put it bluntly, on taking care of yourself first. This doesn't mean that you have to become a soap opera barracuda to succeed, but you will have to learn some new ways of getting from A to B.

The first thing to understand is that one of your top priorities is marketing yourself. Chapter 5 explained the difference between marketing and selling and showed how to identify and organize the traits you have to offer. Now it is time to get your message out to the people who can hire you. This means telling them, in the most convincing way you can, who you are. In less polite terms, you will have to blow your own horn. Everyone does some of this in the course of a military career, but we do not openly acknowledge doing it. Most of us believe that the selection system will take care of us with only occasional prods and pokes and now and then some help from our friends. For the most part, success in a military career depends on demonstrating performance in the right jobs and hoping that your abilities are recognized by the promotion boards, and unless you are a shameless hustler, you have probably done little unabashed personal hornblowing. In the civilian job market you won't have that luxury. Personalities and honest self-promotion play a large part in guaranteeing success, and self-effacement is not considered a practical attitude.

RÉSUMÉS

The Joint Chiefs of Staff's organization is not famous for brilliant innovation, but their system requires that even the knottiest military problems be presented in the right way. On any given day in the Pentagon, scores of tortured action officers can be seen desperately groping for new ways to express complex issues within the format of an 8" × 14" sheet of paper. Initial and final versions of work are printed on different colored paper to prevent the service chiefs from accidentally signing off on something the lieutenant colonels haven't approved. Red stripes are put on completed work to avoid the embarrassment of approving the same thing twice.

Résumés are to the civilian world what the JCS format is to the Pentagon. No one loves them, but everyone agrees that they are necessary. And although there is no single stylebook to tell us exactly how a résumé should look, there are some ground rules that are violated only at your peril.

At the very top of the page goes your name, address, and telephone number. This information can be a printed letterhead if you wish. The same considerations apply as for stationery. Use your home phone number even if you are still on active duty or are working at a temporary job when the résumé goes out. The reason for this is to maintain control of your calls. More than one interview has been lost by someone answering the phone for a job candidate and creating a bad first impression.

The Objective

Following the name and address, some formats show a paragraph variously called "Career History" or "Summary." Others begin with "Objective," specifying the type of position or even the specific job you are applying for. The first approach allows for broad interpretation by the reader; if you are writing a résumé to send to everyone except the Vatican this may have an advantage, but it may also leave a reader in some doubt as to whether you want to be secretary general of the United Nations or a missionary.

Very specific job objectives have their pitfalls too. They drip with insincerity and false enthusiasm if they attempt to create the impression that you have wanted this job all your life. To say that your job objective is "to be water commissioner in a city of two to three hundred thousand population composed primarily of single-family and small business clients" strains the credulity of even the most innocent. Ask yourself, Is this *really* what you dreamed about in algebra class when you were thirteen years old?

Summarizing your experience is not a good idea either. Busy people love to read summaries because it saves them time. A lead paragraph titled "Career History" that encapsulates everything else in the résumé will save them the time and trouble of reading the whole thing. This is very convenient for them but not so good for you.

The best opening is a clear statement of the kind of position you want and the background you offer for that job. A descriptive title or level of responsibility is ideal. Assuming that you have worked through the process described in chapters 4 and 5, your objective should now be focused enough to be expressed in a few words. If there is any doubt about standard names for job titles in your field, use the employment section of the newspaper as a guide or go to the *Dictionary of Occupational Titles*.

If you are job hunting in several fields, you probably should have more than one résumé. As a rule of thumb, a different résumé will be required whenever the body of the résumé (outlining your experience and skills) cannot fully support the objective at the top. If you need to do a separate résumé for each job, you have not zeroed in on your objective or fully defined your skills.

Experience

Summarizing experience is different for former military people than for civilians. Except for career changers, people who have worked in a particular field for most of their careers will have experience and skills that are easily recognizable as supporting their job objectives. The company names and job titles they list will be familiar to a prospective employer and can help establish their credentials. You, however, will have to convert your military experience into vocabulary a civilian manager can understand.

Some of the books and seminars produced for military career transition suggest camouflaging a military background with "civilian" titles, vague descriptions, and other coy devices. This strategy is useless. It dilutes the strength of your experience and, even worse, suggests that you are being evasive and deceptive. A few years ago it was in vogue for civilians to do almost the same thing by not mentioning the names of companies they had worked for. Résumé writers used euphemisms like "accountant for a large automobile plant in Detroit" instead of "General Motors" until everybody got sick of playing guessing games and went back to being honest. It is true that some employers will not hire retired military people. Trying to hide your background will not change their minds and will only waste their time and yours. Almost everyone who reads a large number of résumés can spot one that is concealing something, and if they can't guess that you spent twenty or thirty years in the service, they will certainly think you have something to hide.

Communicating the value of your military experience to a civilian reader is not as difficult as it may seem. Everyone watches television, reads the paper, and knows the difference between a tank and an aircraft carrier. As long as you stay away from jargon, acronyms, and technical descriptions, the people who read your résumé will understand what you are talking about. In some cases it may be necessary to provide a brief description to highlight the setting of your job (for example, "commanded a 5,000-ton destroyer manned by 20 officers and 250 enlisted personnel"), but if you do this thoughtfully it will not cause any problems and may even increase the impact of your résumé.

The purpose of describing experience in a résumé is to communicate the value of what you have to offer, not disguise it. Your task is to convert the language of the service into words that will make an impression on a civilian who knows nothing about military organization charts or equipment terminology but is attuned to recognizing qualities that produce results. Employers want to see experience that relates to their needs and evidence of performance that relates to their organization's goals and problems. If your track records stands out as meeting those needs, there is a good chance that a reader will be interested enough to find out more about you through an interview. But you will never create interest if your résumé is too vague to pin down. For example, experience as commanding officer of a helicopter squadron can be described as

Line Manager: Managed a line organization with 200 employees. Responsible for day-to-day operations, training, maintenance, and personnel management. Directed planning for routine and contingency operations. Controlled an annual budget of $3,000,000.

This sounds like a responsible position calling for someone with excellent management and organizational skill, but it raises as many questions as it provides facts. Did the writer manage a manufacturing plant or a large Chinese laundry? What were the routine and contingency operations? Were they changes in the assembly line or one-day service on shirts? There is nothing concrete to relate this experience to anything that might strike a chord with a potential employer. It describes the duties of thousands of people, not of an individual. Its vagueness creates an aura of suspicion.

If this person really held such a significant position, why doesn't he explain what he actually *did*?

The same experience, honestly described, looks different:

> *Helicopter Squadron Commander:* Led a unit of 20 officers and 180 enlisted technicians. Planned and directed daily flight operations of 8 transport helicopters from home base and on extended short-notice deployments to Europe and South America. Responsible for scheduling simultaneous training and transport flights. Accountable for $3,000,000 operations and maintenance budget.

That tells a reader something about *you*. He may not be hiring helicopter squadron commanders, but he might be looking for someone who can work well in a rapidly changing environment and can train people without shutting down the production line. And chances are he knows exactly what accountability means in terms of the good old bottom line.

Presenting yourself honestly in a résumé will help you later in an interview. Rather than wasting your time and the interviewer's explaining what you meant by a line organization or a contingency operation, you can get directly to the heart of the matter, convincing him that your experience and qualities are just what he needs.

Experience alone does not tell your whole story. A résumé also has to paint a factual picture of what you did in the job you describe and the tangible results your talents produced. A clear exposition of the job, as in the second example, will make this much easier. When you hide behind a smoke screen of generalities it becomes very difficult to highlight the achievements that make you special, but when you can cite actual results your qualities will stand on their own merit.

The mysterious "line manager" will say something like

Successfully completed scheduled and nonscheduled operations within budget despite increase in annual requirements. Received award for this achievement.

This colorless account does not say anything that a prospective employer can relate to his needs. But if he reads that the helicopter squadron commander

Successfully completed 450 out of 500 assigned flight missions. Sixty of these were conducted in response to emergency or two-hour-notice conditions. Absorbed requirement for 20 percent increase in number of missions (an additional 100 missions) without additional funding. Personally decorated by commanding general.

He now has some facts to sink his teeth into.

List A in the personal inventory recommended in chapter 5 is a good foundation for describing your experience and communicating your qualities. In addition, books like Keith Nyman's *Reentry: Turning Military Experience into Civilian* (Bibliography, chapter 3) and others offer good information on how to present your abilities. The "Experience" section of your résumé is its most critical part, and you should spare no effort to make it the best possible.

As a rule of thumb, use only your assignments for the last ten years or so unless something further back is especially significant. Civilians in the job market generally summarize all their earlier positions in one paragraph to establish their background. This technique also leads the reader to concentrate on your most recent accomplishments, which are probably the most significant.

Experience and qualifications can be described in either of two formats. The straight chronological method begins with the most recent position and works back, giving the inclusive dates that you held the job. This system is usually best for civilian job seekers whose career progression is in the same field. A military retiree can seldom use this format because our assignments are generally divided among operational, staff, and schools, or in the case of the navy, sea and shore. A chronological résumé written for a nonmilitary position will either include some military experience not relevant to the job, thereby wasting space, or leave out some nonpertinent assignments, creating unwanted gaps in the chronology. This creates doubt in a reader's mind and starts your résumé on a one-way trip to the circular file. If you are among the minority who can benefit from a chronological résumé, by all means use it. Recruiters and employers are accustomed to seeing this format, and it will work to your advantage.

Most of us will have to use the so-called functional résumé, which groups our significant experience and achievements by function, such as personnel management or quality assurance. Functional areas *must* support the objective stated at the top of the page, and they should be as specific as possible without being restrictive. For example, "Planning" standing alone as a function is too broad; "Small Machine Shop Maintenance Planning" is too restrictive (and too wordy). "Maintenance Planning" would be just about right.

Resist the impulse to stick in a functional area that doesn't support the job objective, just because it is one of your strong points. When you are applying for a job as a systems analyst, no one will care how well you play the piano, even if you did win a prize.

Other Résumé Information

With the hardest part out of the way, all that remains is to list other vital information about yourself in a way that will support your qualifications for the job. You must avoid volunteering intentionally or unintentionally any data that might disqualify you. Here are some things to watch for:

Age. If they really want to, readers will be able to guess your approximate age from the dates given in the "Experience" paragraph. There is no reason to attract attention by including it in the "Personal" section.

Education. Don't indicate dates, although service schools, if they support your job objective and gave you a significant qualification, should be listed. Make sure that the title of the school is self-explanatory. A parenthetical statement of the civilian equivalency of education at service war colleges should also be included. This information can be found in the *Guide to Evaluation of Educational Experience in the Armed Forces.* A ten-month course in residence at the Naval War College, for example, is considered equivalent to twelve semester hours of management at the graduate level. If you have too much or the wrong kind of education in your background, leave it out.

Hobbies. These and community activities can be a trap for the unwary. Dangerous hobbies such as auto racing or sky diving will raise eyebrows in conservative organizations. Sedentary pursuits such as stamp collecting can create the impression of passivity. If you have any *really* weird hobbies, like collecting Elvis Presley commemorative whiskey decanters, don't mention them. In general, hobbies should reflect the person you want to market in the résumé or they should not be mentioned.

Participation in community activities, especially in leadership positions, is usually a plus, but here too you can get into trouble. Too much involvement with too many organizations will suggest that your attention will be somewhere other than the job. Membership in organizations that are controversial or offbeat can also kill a beautiful résumé, so if you are president of the local Star Trek fan club, keep it to yourself.

References. The statement that references are "available upon request" is another piece of useless information. If an employer wants them, you will have to come up with references whether you like it or not, and he knows it. Do not mention references in your résumé.

Personal. Information on family and marital status is useful only if you have been married for a long time and have a few children. Too many children or none at all can be a minus. Any other indication of marital status will be damaging. Single, divorced, separated, or, heaven help us, "undecided," are categories to avoid.

RÉSUMÉ FORMATS

The example in Appendix D and those given in the books recommended for this chapter show the most common résumé forms. You will have to decide between a chronological and a functional approach. Some job-search professionals recommend that retired military people always use the functional approach, but this is not always the best. If your background lends itself to a chronology stressing the last ten years or so, that is the way to go. No résumé, of whatever format, should be more than two pages long.

With the advent of computer word processing and high-quality printing, there is no reason why a résumé should not look neat and professional. The costs to get résumés made up and printed are modest and, of course, tax deductible. The paper should be good quality, twenty- to twenty-four-pound laid bond, in white, ivory, or gray. If possible, have your résumé put on a computer disk so it will be easy and inexpensive to make changes in the future.

Cute and novelty résumés are useless. They usually end up decorating the bulletin board in a company's personnel office before being recycled as waste paper. The best of them are passed around the office for a few laughs *and then* thrown away. Unless you are going into advertising or public relations, stick to the standard format.

THE INTERVIEW

My local library lists sixty-two titles under the heading "Interviews." That should give you some idea of how important they are. Between the covers of those sixty-two books you will find a whole universe of advice, some of it useful, some a bit strange, and some downright silly. Various authorities on the subject caution readers about the danger of using the wrong body language; the Freudians hint darkly at the significance of playing with your tie; and the assertiveness trainers seem to stop only at pistol whipping the interviewer. If a job candidate tried to follow all this advice at once he would probably end up in one of those places where you lie on the couch to do your talking.

Interviews are not really so terrifying. For you, as a retired military professional, they should not present an overwhelming problem as long as you understand what both you and the interviewer are trying to accomplish. This is where the people who concentrate on the psychological and social aspects of the event often lose the bubble. By paying too much attention to peripheral matters, they lose sight of the real objective, which is to convince the interviewer that you are the most qualified candidate for the job and that you can offer the organization exactly what it is looking for.

The Purpose of an Interview

By the time a candidate gets to an interview, he is already at the small end of a funnel that began with dozens, perhaps even hundreds, of people submitting résumés and has narrowed down to selection of a few finalists. People along the line have been impressed enough by your qualifications to include you in that small group, so they must think you have something to offer. In the interview they will try to discover which one of the finalists comes closest to the organization's ideal and at the same time uncover, if possible, any weaknesses in your qualifications or glaring flaws in your personality.

Your goal is to convince the interviewer that you fit the ideal closer than anyone else and that any deficiencies in your background either are minor or are balanced by more important strengths. You must also avoid ringing any alarm bells by the way you dress or behave, but you don't have to be perfect. In fact, if you are perfect you may be classified as overqualified and you will be out of the running.

Preparation

Interviews, like great battles, are often won or lost before the first shot is fired. Your work so far has accomplished its purpose, which is to get you an appointment for an interview. Now that you have come that far, it's time to go into high gear and make sure that you are completely ready.

Find out all you can about the company and the people who might hire or interview you. A few hours in the local library with the same references you used to identify companies will give you a good idea of what makes the organization tick, who the key people are, and what special needs they might have. Try to get a current annual report. If there is enough time, ask the company to send you one. If there is a business school in your community, it may be on file there. Newspaper files and trade magazines are good sources of information and can offer insights into special problems or plans the organization may have. Don't hesitate to do a little discreet checking with friends who may know something about the company or its management.

The thought of doing this much homework for each interview may seem overwhelming at first, but remember, it is not something you will be doing every day. Even the most energetic job search will generate only about a dozen interviews, and if you are one of those rare people who have recruiters beating on the door day and night, don't complain. No one will feel sorry for you.

On the day of the appointment, reread your résumé carefully. Be critical and try to put yourself in the place of an interviewer who will have nothing to base his judgment on but those few pieces of paper. Probe for weaknesses and soft areas. It may have been some time since you first drafted the résumé so make sure you are thoroughly familiar with its contents. As obvious as this may seem, job candidates sometimes get so preoccupied by the interview that they forget what they wrote about themselves three or six months ago. If you have been suckered into paying a "professional" to write the thing, shame on you. Read it extra carefully. You never know what you may find, and drawing a blank on questions about your own background is a sure killer for any job.

Plan on arriving at the interviewer's office about twenty minutes early. This will give you time to catch your breath and a final chance to go over your notes. It will also give you the opportunity to be polite to the receptionist or secretary, which can be very important. You already know that front office people on military staffs have influence with the boss; in civilian life it is no different.

Take the time to look around you. The office atmosphere can offer clues about the organization and the personality of the interviewer. Plaques and pictures on the wall reveal information about company priorities, history, and the interests of the person you will be meeting. Trade magazines and house publications may contain features about important events and people and might even have a profile of the interviewer or something he has written.

Offers of coffee or refreshments while you are waiting should be politely declined. If you are a smoker, be prepared to suffer until everything is over and you are out of the building. Smoking is a big issue in many places and can, by itself, cost you a job offer. A briefcase belongs on the floor, not on your lap, and for the actual interview, plan on carrying only a thin portfolio with your résumé and vital papers.

If these details seem excessive, try picturing what might happen if the interviewer were suddenly to pop out of his office with his hand extended to greet you. Then imagine yourself, open briefcase on your lap, prune danish in one hand and cup of coffee in the other, trying to figure out how to get on your feet and shake his hand. Well?

YOUR NEW UNIFORM

For the Men

If you are the kind of guy who has worn the same polyester blazer to every wardroom party in the last ten years, you probably have a lot to learn. Believe it or not, civilians take their clothes very seriously, and unless you are planning on a second career in poetry or construction, you will have to take the matter seriously, too, especially for an interview. After you get the job, maybe you can wear rumpled tweeds and play the lovable eccentric, but until then plan on following the rules.

Much folklore surrounds the subject of dress. John Molloy's *Dress for Success* has gone through several editions, and the title has achieved a niche in the language. It is still a good book to read because it is unselfconsciously pragmatic and has a clear message; if you want a certain job at a certain level there are some things to wear and others to avoid like an uncharted reef.

Because this area has been so thoroughly explored by Molloy, there is no reason to repeat here what has already been written. There are, however, a few special considerations for former military people and not so obvious pitfalls to avoid. Here they are.

Don't throw away your old wardrobe. Molloy's book is invaluable if your target is the corporate world, banking, or the law. But if you are a shirtsleeves engineer there is nothing wrong with looking like one (but not at an interview). If a job makes it reasonable to wear one of those plastic protectors over a pocketful of ballpoint pens, go ahead and do it *after you get the job.* Check on what is acceptable in your chosen field. You may find that every suit you own is fine.

Wear clothes that suit you. Some people should not wear some colors or styles. Your wife has been telling you this for years. I never wear dark blue suits because they make me look as though I'm on my way to arrest someone or do a surprise audit of the company's books. And think about the last time you saw one of those huge pro football players on

TV wearing an oh-so-conservative three-piece suit. They look as though they're one of Frank Sinatra's bodyguards.

Be careful about shirts. Permanent press shirts look OK without starch, but that's all they look—OK. Before an interview have your shirt done by a good professional laundry. Collars can look just right or really terrible. A tiny collar suggests that the shirt you are wearing is the only one you own, and excessively large collars are too "show-biz." Do not wear your white uniform shirts no matter how new they are because they will look like white uniform shirts. Don't wear a shirt that came in the same box as a tie unless you are selling aluminum siding door to door. Don't wear a short-sleeved dress shirt with a suit unless you use one of those plastic protectors for your pocket, carry a lot of ballpoint pens, and are a brilliant technical type. In that case the combination may be tacky, but at least it's consistent.

Never wear a brown suit to an interview. This is because in England before World War I, men wore brown suits only in the country and never in the city on business. That may not be a very good reason, but it's the best I've heard so far. Just don't wear a brown suit to an interview, regardless of what men's fashion writers or anyone else tells you.

Pay attention to your tie. For some of us, choosing a tie can cause incredible agony and soul-searching. The best way to avoid this is to go to the best man's store in town,* bringing your suit jacket with you if necessary, and have the best-

---

*Good men's stores have well-dressed salesmen and oak paneling on the walls and are expensive. If there is hard rock on the Muzak, strobe lighting, and the salespeople have names like Trish and Jeffrey, you are probably in the wrong place.

dressed and oldest looking salesman in the place pick out a few ties for you after you have explained the situation to him. Wear the ties he selects for you whether you like them or not. Be very, very careful about school or "regimental" ties. In England, wearing the wrong tie is almost as serious a social offense as putting ice in your drink. Graduates of Princeton and Harvard can get mileage out of the old school tie, but for the rest of us, forget it. Even though all of the uniformed services, as well as institutions such as the Naval War College, have distinctive ties, you should wear them only at reunions, the Army-Navy game, or a yacht club where nobody knows you. But never at an interview.

Jewelry. The miniature Legion of Merit or aviator's wings in your lapel is jewelry. So are service tie tacks and cuff links. The trouble with them is that they suggest to an interviewer that you are inextricably rooted in your military past, and this is not a good impression to create. Also, as unpleasant as it may be to contemplate, the person across the desk from you may turn out to be a veteran of the so-called movement of the 1960s and have strong feelings about the military. It's all right to make a statement of your allegiance as long as you understand the possible consequences. Sorry, but that's the way it is.

Trends. Ignore them. Red suspenders, power ties, and watches made from chunks of pure gold have their place, but it's not at your interview. Anything you wear that hints that you are not what you seem to be will work against you. The men's fashion gurus may dictate that everyone is wearing brown double-breasted suits with big shoulders this year, but they are talking about men who are under thirty or rich enough to wear what they damn please. That's not you.

For the Women

A couple of years ago the job-search experts made the amazing discovery that women were actually being interviewed for positions other than secretary and schoolteacher. This was no news to the women who were already embarked on successful business and professional careers. But there are always a few people who don't get the word. Today, woman's place as an equal in the workforce is being accepted, and although many equal rights issues remain unresolved, one area of agreement is that everyone, male and female, has to play the job-search game.

Robert Molloy, the *Dress for Success* guru, covered this part of the subject in *The Woman's Dress for Success Book*. This is an eminently sensible book and, like his other work, provides an almost bulletproof guide to dress in the workplace. It is "must" reading before an interview, even if you think you have the fashion sense of Coco Chanel. Other advice on the subject should be taken with a grain of salt. The articles in women's magazines are often misleading or are written for nineteen-year-old airheads who have to be reminded not to chew bubble gum during the interview. *Anything* written in a magazine sold at supermarket checkouts should be viewed with deep mistrust.

Women who are retiring from a military career have some advantages over their male counterparts and a significant edge over many of their civilian competitors in the area of interview preparation. As a professional military person, you have learned more about self-discipline and organization than most nonmilitary women. You have been exposed to a wider variety of social and professional settings than most of your contemporaries, and chances are you have more experience in high-pressure, performance-oriented jobs. The same unequal opportunity that slowed promotion for many years pushed women into many military career fields out of the mainstream and ignored by men. Areas such as computers, telecommunications, and public relations were scorned by the red-blooded males as not being sufficiently career enhancing.

After retirement, though, woman gets her revenge. The career specialties you entered in the military because they were accessible are, on the whole, a superior foundation for a civilian career. And your military background is an advantage in itself because it is one of the best proving grounds for the qualities most sought after in a job marketplace still dominated by male work values. But you probably already knew that.

Dressing for an interview is merely an extension of the qualities that made you a success in the military. The objective is to present yourself as exactly who you are: a woman who has completed one significant career and is ready to move into a new one. The advice in Molloy's book is sound and covers the ground thoroughly, but there are still a few things to be aware of.

Counter the stereotype. Interviewers of either sex will probably not have had any military experience. Older men who were in the armed forces before the 1970s often have weird attitudes toward women in uniform. The impression of professionalism created by your dress must work to overcome this misconception. If this requires you to move up a few levels in the investment you make in clothes, do it. Expensive, well-tailored clothes usually look the part and will contribute to the first impression you make.

Jewelry. What goes for the men goes double for women. Unless you are going into law enforcement, do not under any circumstances show up for an interview wearing lapel pins that are miniature ribbons or miniature insignia such as jump wings. An insecure male interviewer will dislike you immediately, and things will go downhill from there.

Sexual Messages. Don't send them, even accidentally. Molloy and other writers on dress cover this subject, but it is especially important for military retirees. To many interviewers, you are more of an unknown quantity than other women, and you must make an extra effort to avoid creating curiosity or questions in the mind of the person across the desk. You are neither Mary Poppins nor the Happy Hooker. Don't dress like either of them.

H-HOUR: THE INTERVIEW

The résumés have been written and read, the preparations completed, and you are sitting in the outer office wearing your interview uniform and reading, for the fifth time, an article about the company picnic. The door to the interviewer's office opens and you rise, sickly grin on your face, to meet the person who has suddenly become the arbiter of your future career. The hour has arrived.

It's really not that bad. Most of the sixty-two books in my local library on interviewing were written for people who have never done a serious interview or been placed in a position that required them to perform one-on-one in a high-pressure situation. But if you have retired from the armed forces after twenty or thirty years, you learned to handle such situations a long time ago. The dynamics of an interview are very much the same as those used in briefing a military senior; you do the convincing and he tries to find weak spots in your argument. There are only a few differences between the two situations, and once they are understood there is no reason why anyone who has survived a service "murder board" shouldn't be able to do a successful interview.

Who Are You Talking To?

In the service you always knew who belonged where in the organization. That information made it easier to tailor a briefing to the specific interests and needs of each listener. At an interview, you may find yourself talking to a personnel specialist, an executive who has been given charge of interviewing all candidates, your future boss, or a designated hitter. Each of these people may have a different set of priorities and objectives for the interview. It will be your job to discover, early in the process, what they are. A human resources specialist may have a graduate degree in psychology but not the foggiest notion of what your job will require, whereas a line manager may intuitively know exactly what he wants in a candidate but be incapable of stating his needs in an interview.

During the first few minutes of the encounter, try to discover the perspective of the interviewer. If he wants to ask questions about your interests and personal background, answer him but steer the subject back to the present by relating those responses to your qualifications for the job. In an interview with a line manager, particularly if he may be your future boss, help him define the person he wants in the position by asking questions about the scope and nature of the duties of the job. Try progressively to draw out a profile of his ideal candidate, then describe your experience in terms of those characteristics.

Avoid Digression

People are naturally inclined to place emphasis on the things they find most comfortable and familiar. When the person across the desk from you is not experienced at interviewing, it is likely that he will be looking for a subject area in which he feels at ease. If he discovers a topic of mutual interest, he may seize on it like a drowning man and be perfectly content to stay with it for the entire interview. Although it is helpful to find some common ground with an interviewer (mutual friends, personal interests, and the like) this can cause problems for you if you are not careful. A delightful discussion about the best places to fish can make the time pass pleasantly until you notice that the interview is almost over and the business at hand has not been discussed. The warm glow of comradeship fades quickly when you realize that you have found a kindred spirit but lost a job opportunity.

To avoid getting into this situation, answer background or personal questions briefly and, as you finish each answer, direct the conversation back to the job. You can do this either by relating your personal experience to your present qualifications or by ending your answer with a question to the interviewer to refocus his attention on his job needs. Let him know that as much as you would love to talk about fishing, what you are really interested in is finding out more about the job.

Problem Interviews

Most interviews will be fairly predictable. If you have done your homework and can get the interviewer interested in what you have to offer and at least partly convinced that you fit his need closer than any other candidate, you will be almost home. Occasionally, though, something may happen to derail the entire process. In those cases, you will have to decide whether to continue the interview or write it off as an educational experience. Examples of situations you might encounter follow.

The wrong person for the wrong job. Halfway through the discussion you both realize that either the employer didn't know what he wanted or someone misinterpreted your qualifications and you are not the one for this job. This is best handled by acknowledging the situation gracefully and ending the interview to avoid embarrassment and a further waste of time. It might even be possible to get a lead, since you are already there, on something more appropriate that might be available. Your candor and honesty might not be enough to get the job you expected, but it may impress the interviewer enough to help you somewhere else.

The hostile interview. This, thank goodness, is no longer a popular technique, but some people never change and others enjoy making people squirm. The military experience of being on the wrong end of a world-class chewing-out should get you through most hostile interview situations, but at some point you may realize that an interviewer is so unpleasant and obnoxious that you wonder if the whole thing is worth it. It's not. Unless you are being considered for a job as a CIA agent or a school bus driver, an excessively hostile interview should be considered a hint of the way the organization is normally run. You don't need that.

Bad chemistry. It happens. Sometimes the social chemistry between you and the interviewer is so poor that it overshadows everything else. One recent retiree I know (a former O-6) innocently walked into an interview conducted by a team of two women and one man, all young enough to be his children. Although they had copies of his résumé and knew his military background, they had been directed to work from a scripted interview that included a lot of generic questions like "Have you ever been in a stressful situation?" "Yes," he said, and described some of his combat experiences. The team looked annoyed.

"Have you ever been a supervisor?" they asked.

Now *he* became annoyed. "Yes," he answered. "In my last assignment I had command of about one thousand men and women."

The interview ground horribly on. They wanted to know if he had ever traveled outside the United States, if he had ever held a security clearance, and finally, when the script called for it, they blandly inquired whether he had ever served in the armed forces. His tongue-in-cheek reply guaranteed that he'd never get the job, but they wrote it down anyway. It was an unhappy experience for everyone concerned.

Bad chemistry in an interview is a rare experience for most people, and usually it's accidental. It just happens that the people involved rub one another the wrong way or are communicating on two completely different levels. If it happens to you more than once, though, it may indicate that you are the one with the problem.

Between you and me. . . . A strong sense of professional and personal ethics is so ingrained in most career military people that it is almost second nature. This is not always true in the civilian world, and it is possible that during the course of an interview you may be confronted with a situation that calls for an on-the-spot decision about an ethical or legal issue. This can arise when an interviewer says something like "We obey the law on equal opportunity, but between you and me, we only hire _____ to fill our quota and keep them off our back." How do you respond? Only you can decide, but before you do, think of the years that you wore the uniform and saluted the flag, when words like *honor* were part of your job. Then decide.

After you have (I hope) told the interviewer that you would find it impossible to work for an organization with such an outlook, you may find that his comment was bait, to test *your* ethics. If it was, you passed. If it was not, you should be on your feet. A parting handshake is optional.

The suggestion during an interview that the organization is willing to overlook or knows how to work around the legal restrictions on employing retired military people is another warning flag. Aside from the unpleasant possibility of being involved in something illegal, ask yourself, If a company is ready to deceive the government, how do you think it behaves toward its employees?

Closing the Interview

One of the most valuable qualities of a salesperson is the ability to "close." When the merits of the product have been sold and the buyer convinced that it fits his needs perfectly, the time comes for the salesperson to close the deal and get a commitment from the customer. Without that, his selling effort is wasted. Vague promises to "think it over" or call back are signs of failure. As time goes by, the immediacy of the sales presentation fades and the unique qualities of the product are forgotten. To return to the analogy of a military arena, this one is a "decision brief." You can probably remember more than once when you gently had to urge the boss toward making a decision, or at least promising one by a certain date.

Successfully closing the interview is vital to a job candidate. It is deceptively easy to be lulled into euphoria by a pleasant interview only to discover, after you have shaken hands and are on your way out, that you have no idea where you stand. If you have not gained a specific promise of a follow-on interview or set a time and date to call back about one, there is no reason to believe that you will ever hear from the employer again. In his mind the relationship between you and the job remains purely theoretical, and his need to begin the decision process has been postponed until some time in the future. If you have drawn a commitment from him, however, such as the name of the next interviewer you will be seeing or the time and date of a call, he will be nudged toward looking at you as a possibility for the position. If you don't have a chance of getting the job, nothing short of physical violence will help you, and an interviewer's refusal to make a commitment should tell you not to hope for much.

THE FOLLOW-UP

You have dodged all the minefields and defused all the booby traps that the interviewer has strewn in your path, and suddenly it is over and you are on your way out the door, satisfied that you have presented yourself in the best possible light and ready for the next step, or maybe even a job offer. The toughest part is over, but work on getting the job isn't.

As soon as possible, sit down and reconstruct the interview, making notes on areas in which you felt weak or unsure and writing down any points brought up by you or the interviewer that may come up again the next time you meet. If time did not allow you to bring out a significant skill or qualification, note it to be emphasized in a possible follow-on interview or negotiation. Try to think of ways to improve your interview technique. Even if you are sure you won't get the job, no interview opportunity should be wasted. We learn a little more with each experience.

Within a day or two, write a thank you note. It is surprising how many fairly civilized people forget to do this. It is a small gesture, but in a highly competitive job market it can be the deciding point between two equally qualified candidates. Thank you notes are also a good vehicle to confirm in writing the commitment for another interview or remind the interviewer of when you will be calling back. In addition, you might want to include in the note a short paragraph to cover, as an "oh, by the way," some additional information about your qualifications or experience that wasn't fully covered in the interview. Make this short and informal and don't try to resell areas already covered.

NEGOTIATIONS: THE HOMESTRETCH

The decision to accept a job is not as simple as it may seem. When you are on active duty, negotiation centers around the job itself and whether it is good for your career, interesting, or something you have always looked forward to doing. Location may enter into the discussion, or family plans may make the timing of an upcoming move a factor. But unless you have been in some very unusual situations, salary and benefits were a fixed point that neither you nor the service controlled.

In the civilian world things are almost the opposite. The job is the starting point, but everything else may be negotiable. Except for positions in government and other highly structured organizations, the salary and benefits package may be more uncertain than anything you have ever experienced. Salary may be traded for pension plans, medical coverage for insurance policies, and moving expenses for profit sharing. At the upper levels of the corporate world, negotiating an executive's compensation package can be a major undertaking, involving offers, counteroffers, lawyers, and everything we normally associate with such very important people as twenty-one-year-old basketball players and rock musicians.

For most of us, the negotiable items will fall somewhere between the rarefied atmosphere of the boardroom and the familiar black and white of a military earnings statement. Current trends in pay for most positions are toward cost-cutting and simple, closed-end packages; that is, the old salary plus stock options plus tax shelters is a thing of the past. People who don't already have a golden parachute are not likely to be issued one.

The "lean and mean" mind-set of the late '80s and the continued surplus of qualified job candidates has restricted the amount of maneuvering room available to you. Cost cutting has also put an end to many benefits that used to be standard. Relocation allowances, for example, are no longer offered by many employers.

The global marketplace has brought about some other changes in traditional benefit negotiations. Today it is quite possible that you may be offered a job in an organization owned or controlled by a multinational or foreign company. Be aware that the corporate culture and standards of compensation can vary a great deal in situations like this. Some foreign companies will be amenable to considerable individual negotiations; others (the French, for example) are very hard-nosed.

Despite this gloomy situation, retired military people have a few cards to play which are not available to their civilian colleagues. Your service retirement benefits are assured regardless of what plans an employer may offer you, and that may give you trade-off leverage. If, for example, you are facing high college expenses for your children in the near future, it might be worthwhile to load your compensation package so that it provides more cash now, when you need it, in place of future pension benefits. Or you may want to opt for a lower-coverage medical plan to supplement your CHAMPUS benefits, rather than duplicating coverage you are already assured as a military retirement benefit.

Individual needs vary greatly, and it is almost impossible to describe a single package that fits everyone's requirements. The 1986 tax law is changing the relative importance of traditional compensation options in ways still not fully understood. It is important to know which components of the package offered to you are negotiable and which are fixed. That will be your starting point. It is also a good idea to get the advice of a family lawyer or accountant on what benefits are most advantageous to you. Groups like TROA and NCOA can also provide useful advice.

The Military Trap

Your military retirement benefits can provide some negotiating opportunities, but they can work against you if you are not careful. Some employers, particularly those in defense-related businesses, will want to pay you less than someone else because of your benefits. No one ever admits doing this, but it is remarkable how often employers will offer a package that, when added to your retirement pay, comes suspiciously close to what you were earning on your last day of active duty.

There is no way to avoid this problem completely, but there are two things you can do to minimize it. First, you can stay away from defense-associated jobs. Once you move into the purely civilian-oriented economy, you will find that prospective employers know surprisingly little about your retirement benefits, and you are under no obligation to educate them. You can use your benefits to best effect in the negotiating process in this sector.

An alternative approach, if you really want a job in the defense industry, is to beat the employer to the punch. Be up front about the relationship between your military retirement benefits and his compensation package. This may enable you to work out a deal beneficial to both of you without wasting everyone's time pussyfooting around the issue.

Timing and Judgment

Unto everything there is a season, and salary negotiations are no exception. Between the time you have your first interview for a job and the day you are welcomed aboard, there are right and wrong times to talk money. If your timing is off, you may not only lose out on pay; you might talk yourself out of a job.

Before an interview, you should have some idea of how much the job pays, either from the advertising or from your own research in the field. Your own minimum figure (which will probably be too modest) should be within striking distance of what you think the company's figure will be or you will be wasting your time. It is unrealistic to expect a prospective employer to negotiate his offer beyond about 10 to 15 percent, so that should be your rule of thumb.

Don't ask about salary or benefits in the first interview even if you are burning with curiosity. If the interviewer raises the subject, tell him you would prefer to have a better understanding of the job before discussing pay, but if he persists, give him a figure, hedging it as much as you can. Suggest that your figure is, of course, flexible, subject to the nature of the rest of the compensation picture, and that in any case, you would rather discuss it later. Unless he is making a job offer on the spot, that answer should satisfy him.

It is rare for an employer to expect that an offer will be accepted without thought. Take as much time as you can to decide, no matter how much you want the job, and continue your job search while you are considering. Something else could come along tomorrow, and the good feeling that comes from having another offer in your pocket does wonders for your self-confidence when you interview with other companies. If you are considering more than one job, use the matrix suggested in appendix C to make a comparison.

Negotiating Points

Once you have decided that an offer is in the ballpark, the real negotiation will begin. By this time you should have established your own bargaining position and which areas of compensation you will stress. The next step is to find out, if you can, the other side's position on the same points. In some fields such as health care, company policy may be locked in and not a subject for discussion. If that turns out to be the case, there is no point asking for concessions. Shift your emphasis to another subject on which you will have some room to maneuver.

Find out how much latitude the negotiator has. The president or CEO of the company can make his own rules, but below that level a negotiator will be working from guidelines that may or may not be flexible. He might also be required to clear certain items with the people in charge before agreeing to them.

Get something on paper. Employment contracts are not popular these days, and you will probably not be offered one unless the job is at a fairly high level and includes an elaborate compensation package. Most organizations do, however, make an offer in letter form. This will become the basis for negotiations. Once a final package has been agreed upon, ask the company for a new letter to reflect the final figure that you have accepted. Although this will not have the force of a formal contract, it will at least be on letterhead paper and signed by someone in authority. Every little bit helps.

Don't count promises of raises or promotion as a benefit. A company may try to get you to agree on a lower starting salary with a promise of future increases but will almost never put this in writing because it's too risky. First, you are not a known quantity and there is no guarantee that you and the position will be a good fit, regardless of your abilities. Second, organizations can change very quickly these days, and written promises of advancement reduce the company's flexibility and increase the threat of that great modern curse, the employee lawsuit. Future benefits should be viewed as an incentive, not a guarantee.

"TAKE THAT JOB AND LOVE IT"

Money isn't everything. The job that really excites you may also be the one that offers a marginal salary, a mediocre benefits package, and not much chance for advancement. But sometimes the pleasure of doing what you enjoy can far outweigh the drawbacks. Moving from the military to the civilian world is a big transition under the best of circumstances. Accepting a job only because it pays well can put you in a situation in which you hate the work, loathe the environment, and can't stand the people around you. Within months you will be wishing you were back in the service. Your personal life (that new adventure you have been promising yourself and the family) will turn to ashes, and you will be thoroughly miserable.

Life is too short for that nonsense. Take the job that suits you best and enjoy it.

YOUR NEW LIFE

◆

It is easy to let concerns about a new job or career over-shadow other important changes that come with the journey from a military career to civilian life. The service has been close to the core of who you are. Its sudden loss creates a vacuum that demands filling, sometimes at the expense of other facets of your life. But at some point you will get a job, begin a new career, and start to settle into the work part of retirement. You may arrive at this point soon after you retire or it may take a year or more, but sooner or later you will get there. That's when it's time to think about the rest of your life.

First, a little philosophy. In the most general terms, after military retirement one set of fixed assumptions in your life is replaced with another. On active duty you expected change in your assignment, rank, and location at fairly predictable intervals. Most of this change was imposed from outside. Your service set the policy for promotion, tour length, and so on, so despite frequent change, there was little uncertainty.

In civilian life you will find that the system has been turned upside down. Once you are settled into a new job, there will be less change but more uncertainty. This can be disturbing at first. Driving to work in the morning, you look around at the traffic jam and are suddenly struck by the depressing realization that this will be your daily lot for an indefinite time into the future. The old consolation of knowing you didn't have to live forever with an assignment you disliked is gone. No hand will reach down from the assignment office to pluck you from Camp Swampy and deposit you, family, furniture, and all, at an exciting new duty station. The permanence longed for so many times over the years is now yours. The future has arrived, and you're not sure you like it.

At the same time, it may dawn on you that your life is much less certain than it used to be. News reports of layoffs, downtrends in the economy, and budget cuts affecting your job take on a new significance. You begin to understand why civilians always seemed to worry so much—they have plenty to worry about. And now you get to play too.

The first and most normal reaction to these gloomy insights is to wish you could go back to your old life. It's easy to forget the long family separations, the anxiety and fear in combat, and the misery of rain and mud and green water over the bow. At least you knew where you stood. The hardship and stress that gave you those gray hairs begin to take on the rosy glow of nostalgia, and the unknown, confusing civilian world assumes a bleakness you never before imagined. The dread that you will be working at the same address ten years from now is made worse by the fear that you could be fired tomorrow.

These are not unusual feelings. For most of our lives we look forward to the future, expecting it to be better in some undefined way, while remembering the past with a fondness it often doesn't deserve. The word *nostalgia* literally means a return home. It's the same feeling you had on the first day of summer camp. Then it was homesickness; now that you are grown up it's more a sense of sadness and loss, a small mourning for things gone.

These feelings can be powerful enough to affect your entire outlook on life or they can be a passing twinge, felt for only a short time. For most of us the experience will be somewhere between the two extremes. Make no mistake about it, though, the constellation of reactions and emotions that goes with a major change in life such as retirement from a long and proud career will leave some mark on everyone. The real question is, Will it be a help or a handicap?

So much for the philosophy. The meaning of change in life is not an abstract theory for learned debate. It's a real event that can be either a jumping-off point for new and exciting growth possibilities or a little worm that eats away at the future. Your ability to handle change, especially in midlife, will profoundly affect the quality of your years to come. Growing into the future is a process requiring both thought and action. Tomorrow will come no matter what you do. The question is, Whose hand is on the throttle? Will it be yours or the rest of the world's?

CONTROLLING CHANGE

Change is unsettling to everyone, but people retiring from the armed forces have some advantages. Areas of change that can be threatening to others are not even issues for us unless we create problems for ourselves. The task is to make sure that we don't create new headaches that are not necessary. In other words, take care of the easy stuff first.

Financial Changes

A list of the important life issues in this category has to begin with finances. A civilian making a major change in midlife is faced almost immediately with the challenge of economic survival. Except for the happy few who drift gently down under golden parachutes, most people who cut loose from a job are on their own. There is no safety net. That is why books on surviving change devote much of their attention to financial planning and coping strategies.

The safety net for military retirees may not be as springy as we would like, but at least we know it's there . . . unless we do something to screw it up. And that is easier than you might think. Every year tens of thousands of people go bankrupt. They are not all unemployed or stupid; many of them are successful and hold good jobs. In a large percentage of cases they got a little careless or after surviving on the edge of financial ruin for years were forced over the brink by an unexpected setback. The road to hell, they say, is paved with good intentions. In our society it has been resurfaced with shiny plastic credit cards.

Avoiding this trap is a matter of planning and self-discipline at the right time. The simple financial review discussed in chapter 2 ought to be high on the list of things to do before retirement. If you have completed this review with a reasonable amount of care, you will be aware of the fixed portions of your monthly expenses and have them under control. Nevertheless, expect to make some adjustments in the first six months or so after retirement. A job search will cost more than you expected. Lunches, even if you are a fast-food addict, can become a significant expense. There won't be any allowance for your new civilian uniform, and since you will probably be spending more time at home for a while, you will use more groceries.

People who always had a secret yen to shop may find that their new feeling of freedom brings with it an urge to hit the shopping malls.

But there is also good news on the financial front. In the period before you begin working full time at a new job, you will have time to do for yourself some things that you used to pay for. Most military installations have auto hobby shops that are seldom crowded during the working day. Doing simple tasks like changing your own oil or spark plugs will save money and will make a therapeutic break from the daily grind of a full-time job search. After a week of wearing your best smile for interviews, the chance to get your hands dirty and curse at the car can do wonders for your disposition. Household repairs, previously done by a succession of surly prima donna handymen at outrageous rates, can now be attempted. No one will call you in the middle of a rewiring job to go TDY for three months.

Individual situations can vary widely. Depending on the length of service and rank at retirement, you will know long before the day arrives whether you can survive on retirement pay alone. Even though you have every intention of finding a new job, it is a good idea to have a contingency plan in case you are unemployed longer than expected. The plan doesn't have to be detailed, but it should take into consideration the following points.

Required expenses. Mortgage or rent goes at the top of the list. It's hard to plan for the future when you are sleeping in a tent. Insurance is the next item. Sometimes when things start to go wrong they *really* go wrong. Don't let the insurance lapse the day before your car burns to the ground. Utilities must also be paid without fail. A prospective employer may wonder about you if he calls and finds out that your phone has been disconnected.

Budget cuts. Anyone who has worked with the DOD planning and budgeting process knows how budgets work. You spend the first part of this exercise listing all the things you absolutely, positively must have and the second part cutting half of them from the list and figuring out how to do without them. Somehow it always worked out and the job got done. It will now, too, but it should be a cooperative effort including all family members. Arbitrary belt tightening, scolding, and recriminations only cause resentment, as the average congressional budget hearing proves. A team effort can produce heartening results and will make everyone feel better.

Groceries are one area in which expenses can be cut, and you don't have to send the children out into the woods to forage for roots and berries to do it. Home economists say it is possible to reduce an average family's grocery bill by up to 20 percent by shopping carefully, using coupons, and buying in bulk.

Deferred items. If things are really tight, installment payments can be reduced without getting in trouble with creditors or hurting a good credit rating. If you followed the recommendations in chapter 2, your credit card payments should be small enough not to cause any major problems. But things don't always work out according to plan, and those little plastic devils may have you firmly in their grasp. Professional financial planners often suggest going to the creditor when a required payment can't be made and working out a schedule of mutually agreeable minimum payments. This is a good idea, but it must be done the right way. Major credit card companies are like any other large computerized organization. Below a certain level it is difficult to find anyone who is authorized to make a decision. Working out an arrangement to defer or reduce payments will require you to penetrate, with all the patience at your command, through successive layers of company bureaucracy until you find a decision maker. For some companies this will mean only one or two calls to the 800 numbers; for others it takes more perseverance. Most of the larger international credit card institutions have programs designed especially for people who inform them *before their account becomes delinquent* of problems with meeting payments. If you have a good credit record with no delinquent payments in the past year, the company will set up a special plan to reduce your payments for three or six months. But the time to take action is before you get in trouble. Once you become delinquent, you will receive less sympathy.

Emergency employment. In regions where the economy is healthy, it is easy to find a few days' work or a short-term job. Those who work in financially precarious professions like freelance writing are experts at this. Temporary employment agencies are always looking for people who have salable skills. For the rest of us, the temps can offer unskilled work of all kinds. Digging holes for a few days a week might not be great for your tender ego, but the pay can keep the wolf from the door. You may even get a nice suntan and meet some interesting people.

Help. All the uniformed services offer financial planning assistance. Don't hesitate to use it. An objective, trained professional can often suggest ways to improve your situation that never would have occurred to you. Military credit unions, which most of us belong to, will also assist you. For years you have kept a savings account, borrowed money to buy cars or put the kids through school—and paid a lot of money in interest. The credit union has a stake in your future and will probably be happy to provide counseling, advice, and even loans if necessary. Retiree organizations such as TROA and NCOA also offer help in financial planning.

To close this discussion of unpleasant contingencies on a bright note, remember that hard times can happen to anyone. As a military retiree you will be insulated from complete disaster even in the worst of times. Because the retirement retainer will always be there, creditors will often give you extra maneuvering room. A twenty-to-thirty-year career in the service is an unequaled character reference, and they know it. You are a solid citizen, and they want to have your goodwill in the future. Providing you are honest and don't wait until disaster is stalking your heels, most reputable businesses will work with you.

Excessive fear of financial uncertainty clouds judgment. Unchecked, it can spill over into other areas of living and create a mushrooming set of problems. It can affect your family life and stampede you into accepting a job that you really don't have to take. A simple contingency plan will prevent that from happening.

MEDICAL PROBLEMS: FACT AND FANTASY

There is a considerable body of folklore about all the terrible things that will happen to medical coverage after retirement. Some of the rumor is based on fact but a great deal of it is caused by misunderstanding and a lack of knowledge. This is not hard to understand. In the last two decades, government policy on medical benefits for retirees has been changing continually. Congress attempts to cope with rising military personnel costs by passing new legislation every year, and since most of these laws are written by staff specialists the result is often incomprehensible to anyone but another specialist. Were it not for retiree advocate groups like the NCOA and TROA, which monitor the status of legislation and attempt to explain it, the situation would be even more confusing than it is.

Another reason for misunderstanding is the perspective that comes with our new status as a retired military person. During our time on active duty, our role in the medical establishment was usually limited to showing up for shots when we were told to. When medical problems needed attention they were taken care of without too much trouble and little thought of the expense. It is not until after retirement that we begin to notice the signs at the clinic reading "Active duty and dependents will be treated first." Until now, CHAMPUS drifted in and out of the health-care picture, and the thought of getting medical attention at a VA hospital never entered our minds.

All at once those unknown entities have become the basis for almost all the medical care we receive. That realization alone is enough to disturb many people, creating an impression that somehow we have been cheated of what was promised us. The wait for a prescription to be filled seems endless. Waiting rooms appear to be filled with other retirees, just as grumpy as we are, but older. People in uniforms, many apparently still in their early teens, are taken care of while we cool our heels. No wonder everyone complains about vanishing benefits!

Viewed objectively, the medical benefits afforded military retirees are better than most civilian plans. It's true that many employers offer health plans that seem, at least from the outside, to be more comprehensive than the DOD's. But they pay for the coverage, and the charges go up every year. There are also millions of people who have no significant medical coverage and live in a constant state of fear that some medical emergency will overwhelm them, consuming everything they own.

The military health-care system for retirees is not perfect. In all probability you will be paying some bills you never had to worry about before, and as "reform" of the system progresses, health-care costs may go up even further. Fortunately, there are ways to adapt to the changes you will encounter and reduce their impact on your digestion and your bank account.

Foresight

The preretirement medical planning discussed in Chapter 2 is a starting point. This advance action should include verification of enrollment in DEERS, documentation of unusual or critical medical problems, ensuring that you have copies of every scrap of medical records you can get your hands on, and a current physical for you and every member of your family. With that out of the way you have a fighting chance.

Education

Much of the vague apprehension about postretirement medical benefits is caused by a lack of information. This not surprising. Reading the regulations concerning CHAMPUS and other forms of health care is not the most exciting pastime in the world. Understanding it requires effort, but the peace of mind to be gained is worth the work.

Priorities of treatment at military medical facilities are not established arbitrarily. Chapter 55 of Title 10 U.S. Code directs the armed forces to give priority to active-duty members. The medical facility has no choice in the matter. CHAMPUS benefits are also determined by law. Active-duty people pay 20 percent of hospital and outpatient costs over the deductible, and retired personnel pay 25 percent. So when the smoke clears, the "loss of benefits" really amounts to a loss of priority at military facilities and a 5 percent increase in CHAMPUS contributions. Dental benefits and some specific programs for the handicapped are also lost to retirees. But beyond that, the safety net is still firmly in place.

Read the CHAMPUS handbook again. Individual service bulletins for retirees also should be required reading, as well as the information put out by TROA, NCOA, and others. The weekly service newspapers such as *Army Times* cover changes in medical benefits as well as pending legislation. All that reading may seem like work, but remember, doctors spend a good deal of time keeping current on changes in their profession so they can figure out new ways to bill you; some homework on your part will help you stay even.

Activism

As a group, military people are politically submissive. Our tradition of staying out of politics helps justify old-fashioned laziness in the area of medical care, and we often don't get as involved as we should in issues affecting our welfare. Politicians often float the most outrageous proposals relating to military benefits by using a variation of the old smoke test. If the proposal doesn't raise any smoke and smell from the constituents most likely to be hurt, it can become law before anyone realizes what has happened. Political activism is a perfectly acceptable way to bring problems to the attention of the people in Washington, and sometimes it's the only way. Don't hesitate to make your feelings known on pending legislation affecting benefits. As of this writing, the number of military retirees is in excess of 1.6 million. That is a powerful voting bloc.

Insurance

When all else fails, pay. As a rough rule of thumb, it is wise to assume that all medical care given to retirees through sources other than military or VA facilities will cost something. Fees can range from small amounts (just enough to make you mad) to payments big enough to hurt. Future changes and new concepts in medical care (catastrophic medical coverage and contractor-supplied medical care, to name only a couple) can cost you more money out of pocket. Supplementary health insurance, once thought unnecessary for military people and retirees, is quickly becoming desirable. Many of the various retirees' associations sponsor CHAMPUS supplemental insurance. The premiums are a modest price to pay for peace of mind. The health plan offered by an employer may overlap or duplicate CHAMPUS and supplemental coverage. What is important is to know exactly what benefits you have from various sources and which ones give you the best deal at the least cost. Take the time to read and compare the details of all your policies. Insurance documents are intimidating at first, but consumer laws require the paperwork to include an explanation, in readable English, of what the policy does and does not do for you.

Support

After studying the labyrinthine provisions of CHAMPUS and dutifully examining your insurance policies, you may still be confused. Don't despair. Every military health facility has a resident expert on the subject who will be able to help you. These folks are trained and experienced at dealing with medical ignoramuses like you and me. They can untangle almost magically the most intricate problems and usually do it with a smile. Visit one of their offices sometime and you will see a waiting area filled with poor souls, clutching in their sweaty hands sheaves of indecipherable medical documents. They shuffle meekly in to see the CHAMPUS person and emerge a few minutes later wearing expressions of relief and joy. It's more fun than going to the dentist.

NEW RESPONSIBILITIES

One of the things that gives civilians the idea that military people are as free as wandering minstrels is our freedom from the little trials of everyday life. After retirement, when you have settled into a community, these little surprises will begin arriving as messengers of change in your life. Throughout your active-duty career, great changes have been going on in the states and communities where you have lived, but chances are you have taken little interest in them. The biological clock of most military people is set to go off every three years or so. It is not easy to become deeply interested in a ten-year road-building plan or a sewage treatment plant scheduled for construction next door five years from now. For those who have lived in military housing for a great part of their career or have spent long periods overseas, the disassociation from the civilian community will be even deeper and the shock of exposure to the new world greater. This aspect of change can be unnecessarily upsetting. Coupled with the other changes and new areas of uncertainty that descend on us, it can cause resentment and an unhealthy case of nostalgia for the days of "Who Cares? We're being transferred next year."

But that won't make it go away. There are new things to learn and some surprises, not all of them pleasant. If you did the advance planning recommended in chapter 2, you already know about state and local income taxes, property taxes, and similar goodies. But if you have not checked into these requirements or have moved to an unfamiliar area, there are some things you will have to find out. The best way to do this is to prepare yourself; the worst way is to get official-looking mail from people with titles like tax assessor and sheriff.

Taxes

State tax regulations vary and can be complicated. The best to be said about them is that they are usually simpler than the federal regulations. Some states tax military retirement as straight income, some don't, and a very few have no income tax. For the carefree and uninformed, state and local income tax can bring an unpleasant surprise at the end of the year and blow the best financial planning out of the water. The service finance office responsible for keeping retirement accounts will take care of federal deductions for you but will not deduct state income tax unless you request it. Thanks to the miracle of computers and information exchange, states and municipalities will discover your existence sometime during your first year of retirement and eventually present you with a tax bill. Unless prior arrangements for deductions have been made, the self-employed and those with no taxable income except retirement pay will be hit at once with a tax liability guaranteed to get attention. The solution is to make arrangements as soon as possible (preferably before retirement) to have these taxes deducted from your check. It will hurt less than that big bite at tax time.

A change in status from active duty to retired will also make you responsible for other taxes and fees. In many areas military people are exempted from personal property taxes, city automobile decals, and the like. These breaks end with retirement. No one will chase you down until an ominous looking bill comes in the mail or Officer Friendly writes you a ticket. Make a few phone calls to state and local offices to determine what new taxes and fees you will be expected to pay. They will be glad to tell you. In fact, some of them will be downright gleeful. Membership in one of the retiree organizations can be a big help, too. It will be able to give you an accurate rundown of what you have to pay and who you must pay it to. Pick the brains of other retirees who have been around for awhile, and the picture will be complete. Not cheery maybe, but complete.

Community Affairs

Bond issues, new water supplies, air pollution, and similar issues will take on new significance once you begin to realize that you will be part of the community for a long time. Inconveniences like traffic were endurable when that short-timer's chain was in the desk drawer. But now as you gaze out over a sea of automobiles and blue exhaust fumes and think about driving the same road for the next ten years, the problem comes closer to home.

Back in the days when we lived in caves we slowly learned that one of the best ways to keep saber-toothed tigers from eating our children was to band together and find a common solution to the problem. The challenges are different today, but the old approach still works. Community action can cut problems down to size and give us a feeling that we have some control over what is going on around us. It is also an excellent way to take charge of our changing circumstances. The slightly uncomfortable sense of newness that accompanies a move from military to civilian life seems less threatening when we become active members of the community instead of outsiders. Military people are welcomed in most places. We have a well-deserved reputation for being steady and responsible. We are also accustomed to taking charge, and here a word of caution is in order. Plunging enthusiastically into a community organization is fine, providing you don't forget that you are a beginner. Civilian organizations do things differently—not necessarily better or worse than the military, just different. Participation in a community or civic group is an excellent way to learn these differences but requires the ability to accept what may seem to be disorganization and a lack of discipline. You won't make friends by wading in with both feet, acting impatient, and behaving like the stereotype of a military bore. Learning to live with different ways of doing things is part of your postretirement education. Make the most of it.

Loss of Status

There is no way to avoid losing the status your military rank gave you. Ruthless honesty right from the start is the best way to cope with it. To many, especially more senior people, this can be the hardest change to accept, the one that causes the deepest discontent. We have all seen sad examples of those who could never get used to the idea that their position in the world has changed. That old nemesis denial gets so deeply rooted in them that they simply quit trying to adjust to the reality of their situation and shut themselves away in an imaginary world of how it used to be. That attitude does not bode well for the future.

In the last months before retirement we sometimes find ourselves paying surreptitious attention to the retired people we see at the commissary or the exchange. The slight irritation we used to feel standing in line behind one of "them" during a hurried day is replaced by the first stirrings of a new feeling. Soon, we ponder, that will be me. It is not always a good feeling. The stripes and decorations we wore when in uniform defined a big part of ourselves, not only because others had to salute but also because they represented our history. A navy officer lunching at an air force base cafeteria could instantly learn a great deal about a tablemate's life history from the pilot's wings and the air medals worn by his neighbor. In many ways it was a very comforting, orderly universe.

The rest of the world doesn't define itself so conveniently. Our egos, already tender from the many other changes brought by retirement, are not helped by the revelation that no one can tell who we are and that most don't care. We have lost one of the intangible benefits of life in uniform and have nothing to replace it.

Time and an acceptance of our new situation are the only cures to this problem of change and adjustment. As you adapt to civilian life, you will see that the rest of the world does indeed have its symbols for status and that many of them are too silly to worry about. In fact, you will be at an advantage. Having learned to accept yourself without the familiar uniform, you will probably have a much more realistic attitude toward status symbols than most of the people around you.

NEW RELATIONSHIPS WITH YOUR FAMILY

From the time you first decide to retire you may tend to become preoccupied with yourself and the changes happening to you. This is understandable. In the course of an active military career your attention has been directed outward to your duties, the people who look to you for leadership, and your family. Self-discipline and subordination of self-concern are fundamental to the professional ethic that gradually becomes part of your personality.

As the impact of retiring from the service makes itself felt, involvement with the job and with your people begins to decrease. Planning, thinking, and worrying are directed toward the future, *your* future. The service will go on without you. An hour after the retirement ceremony someone will be folding the chairs and stowing the podium. Business will continue as usual.

Preparing for and organizing a job search focus attention on self-examination, self-inventory, and self-marketing. As time goes on, the process of adjustment may seem like a problem that you alone must struggle with against an outside world in which most relationships have changed. In this period in your life, you are the number one priority.

Fortunately for everyone, that situation doesn't last forever. Except for people who have serious psychological or emotional problems, things eventually get sorted out and a more healthy, balanced outlook on the world returns. A new job replaces the old one, new challenges are met, and you begin to feel more comfortable with the different life you are now living.

But what about your family? On that day when the decision to retire was first announced, their lives changed too. While you have been rushing around doing the chores you have had to do, they have been faced with major change, new experiences, and the loss of a way of life as important to them as your career was to you. And they probably have had to do it with less help than you had. Even if you have been thoughtful enough to involve them in every step of decision making during the retirement process, it has nevertheless primarily centered around you. They have been the supporting actors while you held center stage.

They might be a little tired of that role. Considering the level of dedication normal for most career military people, it is likely that the family has taken a back seat to the service for some time, not because you were ruthless or unfeeling but because the demands of a military career absorbed so much of your time and energy. Civilians must walk the same tightrope we do in balancing domestic and job concerns; if the books and studies on family problems are any indicator, civilians don't do any better than we do. Long separations, frequent transfers, and classified duties that make it impossible to discuss your work raise additional barriers between you and your family. No matter how understanding and supportive they may be, they know inside that they have been excluded from parts of your life. They have come to accept it over the years, but they probably don't like it.

The situation just described is not intended to make you feel guilty. It has been well documented in studies of the military family as well as in numerous books on midlife changes in general. Issues arising from the adjustment to retirement must be faced even if they make you feel uncomfortable and perhaps a little guilty. The major change that retirement brings to your life did not happen in a vacuum. The environment, the rules, and the surroundings changed for your family, too.

One of the most exciting opportunities open to us after retirement from the service is the chance to deepen and enrich family life. The ability to retire at an early age with some measure of financial security is a reward given not only to you but to your entire family. Chapter 2 discussed the value of including family members as participants in the decisions made early in the retirement process. As time goes on, the importance of doing this will become more apparent. If everyone knows what is going on, there will be fewer surprises and less fear and apprehension as changes begin to take place. But when family members feel that they are being towed along in the wake of an experience that is exciting only to you, they will be resentful and angry. The changes in their lives, like the changes in yours, should be seen as positive. If they are not, something is wrong.

The average library contains dozens of books on every aspect of family life. Most of them discuss stresses in the family, and without exception they list a lack of participation in family decisions as one of the main causes of problems. Interestingly, the issues we might expect to be high on the stress list turn out to be not so critical. One typical survey, discussed in the book, *Stress and the Healthy Family*, discovered that retirement, change in work patterns, and even unemployment consistently failed to rate high on the list of stress-producing events. In commonsense terms, this evidence suggests that most people can accept hardship, inconvenience, and change as unpleasant but necessary parts of life, but they get very upset when they aren't told what is going on.

This does not mean that your retirement and all the change that goes with it will glide along without a murmur from any family member if you only keep them informed. That would be too much to expect from human nature. It does suggest, though, that there is no reason to believe that everyone in the family will have to sign up for counseling because of your retirement. If serious problems already exist, transition from military life to the civilian world can exacerbate them and professional help might be needed. For most of us, though, it is less a matter of coping with problems than it is of moving on to new horizons. But first, let's take a look at where the family is, now that a new way of life is an established fact.

Family Roles

Psychologists and sociologists are fond of drawing diagrams composed of circles and lines to express roles and relationships. They are fine for the professionals but too complicated for us simple folk to worry about. Changes in family roles caused by retirement are not usually earthshaking unless you drop out of life completely and do nothing but hang around. Minor changes and adjustments will take place, however, and you should know what to expect.

You will be at home more often. With the exception of those masochists who leap immediately from high pressure and long hours in uniform to the same rat race in the civilian arena, working hours will be shorter and your attention focused more on what is happening at home. This is good for everyone, providing that you don't suddenly decide to make up for all the time you missed being with your family and break out in a case of Superdad or Supermom. Get the feeling of the terrain first. The rest of the family might not *want* to rise at 4:00 A.M. to go fishing with you.

Some of the authority you had by virtue of your rank and position will no longer exist. This will be a welcome change for your family because it makes you more accessible. At the same time, they may hold a tiny bit of resentment at the loss of status now that you are a civilian like anyone else. Your attitude toward the change will affect how well everyone handles it. A sense of humor and the ability to take the situation in stride will ease the tension for everyone.

Finances are bound to be a more visible issue when the paycheck is reduced. Before, your role as breadwinner was so secure that no one gave it much thought. Now you will be paying more attention to the subject, and so will everyone else. Concern about finances, real or imagined, will become a topic of conversation. This can cause others to worry, especially if you react by becoming an instant Scrooge.

Of all the family members, your spouse will be the one most affected by changes in family roles. Overnight he or she may become the family breadwinner if you are in school or not working at a regular job. Starting a family business will place both of you in a new relationship that demands patience, honesty, and the ability to admit error. This is not always easy. Working together can provide an opportunity to deepen a good relationship, but it places additional strain on one already in trouble.

Change in family roles does not have to be a problem. Most healthy people will adapt to the new situation without thinking much about it. Military life has already given everyone in the family a remarkable ability to adapt to new external situations. Changes *within* the family resulting from your new role will be new to everyone, but even these can be handled without much trouble if you are prepared to make an effort.

Set an example. Time and mutual tolerance will do wonders in aiding everyone's adjustment to a new life, but it doesn't hurt to give them some help now and then. Taking the lead in adapting to change, and even initiating it, is a nice way of showing your family how important they are. A positive attitude and willingness to take the initiative will also encourage family skeptics to see the advantages of cooperating. All it takes is leadership from you.

Be willing to learn. Out of uniform for the first time in years you will be a little less intimidating to the kids, no matter how old they are. There might be some things they can tell you for a change. Knowing that you are willing to listen and learn will encourage them to share more, and everyone will be better for the experience.

Swallow a little pride. Loosen up and try your hand at a role no one expects of you. One retired woman officer I know of periodically takes a day off and heads for a local fishing pier. No one else in the family shares her enthusiasm, but they have discovered a new side to her personality and admire it.

Encourage others to grow. Permanence in the community can offer your spouse the chance to make a commitment to a career that has remained on the back burner during all your moves. Family members who were reluctant to get deeply involved in an activity because of frequent changes in duty stations can participate now without the fear of having to drop everything and leave on short notice.

Initiate change. The surest way to show that you are sincere in your intention is by action. Promises made but postponed can now be fulfilled. Something as simple as participation in the PTA after years of excuses and too many late nights on the job will demonstrate that you really do have a new set of priorities.

Have patience. Don't expect instant enthusiasm for changes. You may be fired up about a new challenge, but other family members might be less willing to change. Their priorities are not necessarily the same as yours.

Don't try too hard. Sometimes the best way to cope with a new situation is to do nothing. If it's not broken, don't try to fix it or you may have an experience like that of one new retiree who decided that he was going to start helping out around the house. With the best of intentions, he reorganized the pantry, the linen closets, and the cleaning supplies. No one could find anything for days.

UNFINISHED BUSINESS

The Latin motto *carpe diem* has nothing to do with fish. Translated literally, it means "seize the day," grab today by the throat and don't let it get away because it will not be back again. The first year after retirement from the service is a "day" that cries out for seizing. Some of the biggest, toughest decisions of your life are behind you. The family has weathered great changes, learning from the experience and in the process gaining confidence in their (and your) ability to cope with some of life's most difficult challenges. Like a combat unit that has just completed a tough training exercise, they are as ready for the future as they will ever be.

Now is a good time to do something that we seldom have the opportunity to do in our busy lives: sit down and plan for change. It is our natural inclination to solve urgent problems first and to ignore the others in the hope that they will go away. The same thing happens to many dreams and aspirations. There are always good reasons not to take an action involving risk and change, even if it is something we want to do. We make excuses like "when the kids get older," "next year when we have more money," or that ultimate copout "when things settle down." Years later, when it is too late, we look back and realize with the painful clarity of hindsight that if we had only just *done it* everything would have worked out. But then it's too late.

Captain Joshua Slocum dreamed of being the first man to sail around the world alone. But in the year 1894 it did not look as though he would ever see that dream come true. He was forty-nine years old, a sea captain who had just lost his ship. He was on the beach, dead broke, and because of advancing age his prospects for the future were dimming rapidly. It was time to put his dreams on the shelf for a while, maybe forever.

Three years later, he was halfway around the world, well on his way to becoming the first solo circumnavigator. Captain Slocum did not win the lottery or inherit a fortune. He just went out and did it. He found an old boat, bought it cheap, and repaired it. When he was satisfied that it was ready, he scraped up enough money for provisions and set sail. Just like that.

Not everyone has dreams as bold as Captain Slocum's and not all of our unfinished business has to do with dreams for the future. It can be old problems from the past, which have never become big enough to cross our discomfort threshold but nevertheless continue to hang around, inhibiting our ability to move forward and grow. They will probably never kill you or ruin your or your family's lives, but it would be nice if they could be resolved.

Unfulfilled dreams and unresolved problems are not always big ones. A minor but persistent weight problem may be preventing you from looking or feeling your best. Dreams of completing an education, writing a cookbook, or hiking the Appalachian Trail sit on the shelf for years, never disappearing but never getting any closer to fulfillment. On the more serious side, there may be old family conflicts, issues that have been too difficult to face but not serious enough to demand immediate attention.

Where to begin? Discussing change in her book *The Big Switch,* Rochelle Jones suggests, "Wherever you are right now is, in fact, the best place." The military retiree who is still in the early years of retirement has a "now" much more favorable than most other people can hope for. A plan for change may not bring about any profound changes in your life—and profound change might not be needed—but it will freshen up everyone's outlook and improve communications among family members. That alone is worth the effort.

To begin investigating some of the possible ways to deal with unfinished business, authorities on the subject recommend using some simple techniques.

Make a List

Since this is both a family activity and an individual one, get everyone to list things they would like to do or change, no matter how unrealistic or silly they may seem. At the same time, ask them to make lists of the things that bother them. Keep this one within limits. Issues that bother people deeply or would upset another member of the family should not be mentioned at this time. There are better ways to handle really serious problems.

Discuss the Lists

It can be more fun than a board game and everyone will learn something. Discussion will generate ideas. When enough ideas have been discussed, agree to arrive at conclusions and make decisions. Determine which items are easiest to accomplish and deal with them first.

Set Goals

Actions that will take considerable time, money, and preparation will need more thought by everyone, which will lead naturally to planning more discussions in the future. Set aside issues on which there is disagreement and let everyone think about them for a while. Ask for suggested solutions and compromises.

Agree to Have More Discussions

Once this process has been started, you will either have raised some expectations and be obligated to follow through, or you will have found out that everyone thinks it's a dumb idea and unnecessary. There's nothing wrong with the latter conclusion. People may be satisfied with their own lives and with the family. They may not be interested in any new plans. But at least they know you care.

If you decide to try this approach, keep it light. No one will enjoy it if you begin assigning homework or if the participants are unwilling. Discussions can occur casually at the dinner table or become subjects for conversation in the car. If it appears that sensitive issues are being raised, give them some thought and talk privately with your spouse.

IF YOU DON'T HAVE A FAMILY

Our society now has a higher percentage of single-person households than at any other time in the nation's history. Changes in Americans' perception of the family, a high divorce rate, and greater acceptance of living alone as a normal way of life have made this lifestyle common. Single people have distinct advantages as well as special problems, and retiring military people in this category will find that both the advantages and the problems become bigger issues when they leave the service.

It used to be that a fairly high number of career people never married. In those days clever phrases like "if the service wanted you to have a wife you would have been issued one" reflected a military subculture insulated from the rest of the world and in many ways downright misanthropic. But now that we have, thank goodness, moved into the mainstream of American society (whatever that is), retired single people are no longer misfits venturing fearfully into a hostile world. Nevertheless, singles making the transition from active duty to retirement can encounter problems that require thought and action.

Isolation

Those who live alone are used to a little loneliness. It is one of the prices of independence. As long as it does not become a burden, most of us can live with it. But retirement brings changes. On active duty, isolation and extended periods of loneliness were unlikely. There were usually other people around and plenty to keep us occupied. In retirement, more of our time will be spent without the company of others.

Until we learn to cope, this may be a depressing experience. Solitude as a permanent way of life can have psychologically and physically crippling effects. Unless a new center is established and new activities and interests found to replace the old ones, an isolated life will become first a habit, then a disease. Samuel Johnson recommended a long time ago, "In solitude avoid idleness, and in idleness avoid solitude." The transition from a life of activity, when you are surrounded by other people with whom you had close professional and social ties, to one in which everything is new and strange can intensify loneliness; it can be even more intense if you are not working.

The best antidote for isolation is activity. Work itself is a tonic. Getting a job keeps us in the mainstream of life, regardless of how good or bad the work itself may be. Those who do not plan on another career after retirement should seriously consider volunteer activity or self-improvement. Building new social ties should also be on the agenda. In the past, you may have been content with centering your whole social and leisure life around military-related activities. Now it will be more difficult to do that without becoming stuck in the trap of continually trying to relive old times.

You don't have to get a face-lift and haunt singles bars. Opportunities for new social contacts are everywhere, but you have to do your own footwork. Sports, hobbies, continuing education, and travel all provide fertile ground for meeting new people. Job seekers get an extra benefit from being socially active because it can dramatically increase the scope of their networking. Special events and cultural activities in the community are another way to get out and meet other people. Even former workaholics with no outside interests whatsoever can find something going on in the community. Almost anything is better than getting your social stimulation vicariously from the television set.

Support

Married people have an advantage in being able to encourage each other through life's difficulties. Single people do not have this benefit built into their lives, but they have as much need for a friendly ear or a gentle critic as their married counterparts. After a long day of filling out job applications and waiting to see interviewers, it's nice to have someone who will listen to your troubles. And the dog just won't do.

Fortunately, there are enough single men and women in today's society that it is not necessary to go it alone if you don't want to. Whatever your interest or problem, there is a support group out there somewhere made up of people in exactly the same situation. Forty Plus organizations were formed with the specific objective of helping in career transition and job search. At an informal level, you may find it helpful to get together occasionally with other retirees to compare notes or talk. Knowing that others are experiencing the same frustration and uncertainty you are seems to make things easier for all of us.

Self-Discipline

Although this subject has already been discussed, it is of special significance if you live alone. If you are surrounded by a family, you get caught up in their routine even if your own changes. Alone, you set the schedule. When the old structure provided by the service is gone, it will be up to you to construct a new one. Without such a framework, your everyday life may quietly begin to come unglued. Procrastination gets easier, little things start piling up, and before you know it your life is a disaster area with you in the middle of it.

A military career has given you training in self-discipline and organization, but after a few months of a less structured lifestyle the old discipline can begin to fade. With nothing to replace it, you risk an imperceptible slide into sloppiness, boredom, and, if the psychologists are correct, serious depression. Keep to a routine. You don't have to write a plan of the day for yourself, but it is important to stick to regular meal hours, a fairly steady schedule for sleeping, and, if possible, physical activity. Do these things even when you don't want to. Do them *especially* if you don't want to.

Relationships

This is not a book about how to meet wonderful people and have a fantastic love life. Single retired military people are a special category that can present certain hazards. The old-fashioned words were *gold diggers* and *fortune hunters,* and they referred to ladies and gentlemen who made a career of separating affluent and trusting souls from their cash. Such people are still around. A more sophisticated society has made their tactics more subtle, but the game is the same. Your retirement pay can be an overwhelming temptation for them, and laws that treat retirement benefits as property create the possibility that an opportunistic marriage followed by a cleverly orchestrated divorce can deprive you of some of that property and cost you alimony and other benefits. This can happen to anyone, male or female, and it will not be fun. It is a classic illustration of the old adage "Marry in haste and repent at leisure."

CHANGE ISN'T EVERYTHING

This chapter has examined change and uncertainty as natural products of the retirement process. Change is an inevitable reality that cannot be ignored. If we choose to grasp the opportunities presented by the transition from military to civilian life, we can steer change in the direction that is most beneficial to us and our families, while minimizing the disruptive effects that new experiences can bring.

But change for its own sake has no inherent value. An individual or family who can make the transition from contentment in a military environment to easy acceptance of the civilian world has achieved an important accomplishment, regardless of whether he or she has taken an active role in effecting the changes. Instead of choosing to confront change and play an aggressive role in managing it, it is sometimes wisest to absorb it, letting it grow slowly on you like ivy on a pleasant cottage. Some of the happiest people in the world are those who simply do their best, trust life to come out reasonably well, and go about the business of living day to day. Those who possess that ability need not feel obligated to rush into change. They can live and prosper calmly, like the quiet people in Gray's "Elegy in a Country Churchyard," who,

> Far from the madding crowd's ignoble strife,
>   Their sober wishes never learned to stray;
> Along the cool sequestered vale of life
>   They kept the noiseless tenor of their day.

8

PERSPECTIVES

◆

The first year of retirement will be a time of transition from a military perspective to one that reflects a new direction. The transformation takes place gradually, and we are not always aware that it's happening. It is not always a smooth process; all change is accompanied by varying degrees of discomfort. As we discover unexpected differences between our new environment and the way things used to be in the service, it may seem that we are being required to devote inordinate effort to learning the rules of the game.

Relations with our service are changing. Although we are no longer in uniform, our center of gravity does not shift suddenly on the day of retirement. Hardly anyone cuts the old ties completely. A twenty- or thirty-year military career represents a major investment in life, and separation from that familiar world does not automatically put it out of our lives. But as the months go by, we become accustomed to seeing our old home with more detachment, reluctantly accepting the fact that we are no longer an active part of it.

Change from outside comes upon us whether we like it or not, but we ourselves determine how rewarding or painful the experience will be. People can live for years in misery because they cannot understand change and are unable to accept it. Thoreau's famous comment "The mass of men live lives of quiet desperation" referred not to abstract, philosophical discontent but to the everyday malady caused by low-key unhappiness in our work. Although most of us are realistic enough to understand that no job is ideal and don't share the quiet desperation Thoreau talked about, we do sometimes allow ourselves to be bothered when it isn't necessary.

THE NEW JOB

Retirees new to the civilian world often feel this discontent more strongly than others, especially in the first months. Having survived the sometimes difficult experience of finding the right niche, we expect things to settle down into a more comfortable pattern. Instead, we find that much of our energy is devoted to figuring out how the game of work is played, what the new rules are, and where we fit into the picture.

Chapter 3 discussed the contrasts between military and civilian careers. Those differences apply in varying degrees to most jobs. Once you are aware of them, there shouldn't be many big surprises in store for you, but you may find that the difference between reality and expectations is greater than you had anticipated. The priorities of the workplace may have little to do with what you thought was important about the job. The work values of your colleagues may be alien to those you were accustomed to in the service, and the sense of mission, which made everything understandable to you in a military organization, might be difficult to discover.

Military retirees in a new job are in an unusual position. On one hand, we are mature and experienced with a track record of career success. On the other, we are as new to the environment as an entry-level employee. Unlike someone new to the workforce, however, allowance will not be made for our inexperience. Learning the ropes will be our responsibility, and unless we take the initiative, our best effort to adjust can become a frustrating uphill battle. Trial and error will eventually solve the problem, but there will be some bumps and bruises to the ego in the process. In the most extreme cases it can mean quitting in disgust or being fired. There are easier ways to learn.

In planning a military operation, commanders insist on the best possible intelligence on the enemy and the combat environment. No combat leader would suggest that intelligence wins battles by itself, but without it the risk of failure increases and the difficulty of reaching an objective becomes much greater. A good captain can bring his ship into any port in the world, but he insists on having updated charts, and when necessary he uses a pilot who knows local conditions.

The observations that follow can be looked at as a guide to the terrain of the civilian job world or, for the sailors, a set of pilot charts. Understanding them will not guarantee that you will be happy or well adjusted in your new job, but at least you will know what is going on around you.

Appearance and Reality

Things are not always what they seem to be. Mistaking the *appearance* of a work situation for the *reason* for it can put you out of step with everyone else. You *think* you know what is going on, but you really don't. For example, Ann is a newly retired electronics specialist working at a high-tech company. She is going crazy because her "real" work is interrupted constantly by the necessity to attend repetitious, time-wasting meetings and presentations. Her department head spends hours persuading the big boss that these meetings are vital, and the head man seems to agree. Ann's frustration is compounded by the inconvenient location of the meetings; her department is located in an old building remote from the executive offices, requiring a thirty-minute round-trip for each meeting. Co-workers don't seem to mind the trip or resent the time wasted, and Ann begins to feel like an outsider because she does. Finally, an old hand takes pity on her and explains what is going on.

The real purpose of the meetings, she is told, is to create visibility. Their department is important, but its location is remote and the building a standing joke in the company. Without the meetings, their visibility would be zero, the budget and staff cut, and the department possibly eliminated. The department head has to fight constantly for his position, and the big boss wants the board of directors to authorize a new building and takes every opportunity to highlight the need for it. Ann still thinks it's a little silly, but she remembers doing things in the service that were no different. And there is one less frustration in her work life.

Job Security

There are no layoffs in the uniformed services. If a command is reorganized or its functions eliminated, everyone is transferred somewhere else or retrained. Service members are even rewarded for devising ways to eliminate their own job or reduce the amount of work their unit has to do. Not so in the civilian world. When a company is reorganized or its functions are reduced, employees lose jobs. The lucky ones may be transferred or offered new jobs, and those who are released are sometimes given a severance and outplacement package, but in any case their careers and lives will be disrupted and their future in doubt. That's why job security is such as emotional issue. People will go a long way to keep their jobs and can get very upset with anyone who seems to pose a threat to them. Your reasons for recommending that the size of your branch be reduced by half may be altruistic, but don't be too surprised if someone slashes your tires in the parking lot.

Accept the importance of job security to others. If the means used by co-workers to keep their jobs bother you, try placing yourself in their position. You always have retirement benefits to fall back on. They may be only a few years from being vested in their retirement program. Job loss will cost them years of pension payments.

Illegal or morally dubious attempts to keep a job are another matter. Your response will have to be governed by what is ethically and professionally acceptable to you. Nothing says that you have to sell out. The ethical standards that were a source of pride during your military service are a valuable possession. Not many careers are important enough to justify sacrificing them.

Game Playing

Everybody plays games. The ancient Greeks were experts. When they got tired of trying to capture Troy by the book, they invented the Trojan horse, which brought results overnight. In fifteenth-century Florence, Niccolò Machiavelli wrote a tech manual on the subject, which is still used by politicians and real estate brokers. The military environment is not free from game playing either; we are just a little more hypocritical about its existence.

The civilian world is not so squeamish. Political maneuvering is considered acceptable in all areas of endeavor, including the church. Lofty academics can fight as dirty as anyone. The problem for second-career people is not that office politics exist but how to understand the rules and, having done that, deciding whether to play.

It is interesting that though there is not a single book or seminar on how to play the game in military organizations, there are dozens on the subject in the civilian sphere. In uniform we do many of the same things that everyone else does but are always defensive about it. Power and promotion games are a secret that we prefer not to discuss, although everyone who has spent time on active duty has seen them in operation. The senior who insists on excessive staffing of an action to cover his six o'clock and the top noncommissioned officer who is careful never to be around when risky decisions are made are part of a familiar landscape.

The difference between military and civilian game playing is its importance on the job. Despite its imperfections, the military promotion system comes very close to being genuinely objective. Seniority, formal examinations, and a rigid professional code guarantee that a person with ability will usually succeed. There are no such guarantees in civilian jobs, and to avoid frustration it is vital to understand and accept game playing as a part of the real world of work life.

Insight into office politics can be developed by a combination of observation, research, and a friend to explain the rules. The latter is the most useful and the hardest to come by but can teach you more about your organization than any book and keep you out of trouble at the same time. Books on the subject are very useful, though. Titles like *You Can Win at Office Politics* and *Having It Your Way* make it clear that these people aren't fooling around. Scan two or three of these books, and what you observe happening at work will begin to make more sense.

Deciding whether you want to jump into the pool and play with the others is an important step in the transition from a military to a civilian perspective. Experienced politicians in uniform will have no problem once they understand the new rules and nomenclature, but the majority who prefer to consider themselves above that sort of thing will have to draw some lines. Either do it or don't. Being drawn passively into a political power game is about the worst thing you can do—you draw the opprobrium of being a game player but have no control over the rewards.

Ultimately it will boil down to another ethical distinction. You will have to decide for yourself if you are willing to pay the price and if the compromise is worth the reward. But you can't pretend the issue doesn't exist and you had better not jump into the pool unless you know what you are doing. The sharks will eat you alive.

Ruthless People

The atmosphere of a work environment depends on how people choose to behave. The majority will find some comfortable middle ground on issues like job security and office politics, but there will always be some who are simply SOBs no matter where they work. Handling them can be a chore. On active duty the misery was bearable because one of you would eventually be transferred out of the situation. But if the SOB happens to own the company you work for, the prospects for relief are not good. How do you cope with a situation like that?

First, you must realize that nothing you can do will change the person. As one writer on the subject puts it, "The issue is irrelevant. The shark is permanently committed to being a shark, you are not." If the "shark" is a competitor or an equal in the hierarchy, all you can hope to do is avoid him, defeat him on a particular issue, or convince him that crossing swords with you is not worth the trouble.

A ruthless person who is your superior is a different challenge. You cannot wait for him to be transferred. Voodoo dolls and prayers for just a tiny coronary are generally considered to be a long shot, and most other ways of getting rid of him are against the law. What you *can* do is find out why he is ruthless and work around it or establish the limits of his ruthlessness and try to live with them. An executive with a reputation for firing people at the drop of a hat may actually do so only when a certain button in his personality is pushed. Pinpoint that button and you can keep out of his jaws.

Other superiors may feel that you are a threat to them. In the military it is almost unheard-of for a senior to be fired so a junior can take his place. In many civilian fields it is common. Your position as a retiree, especially if you are in a staff or specialist role, will not be as threatening to the ruthless person. Make sure that the boss knows that (unless, of course, you *do* want his job, in which case you're on your own). Finally, bosses sometimes have a good reason for being hard to live with. When the last two people to hold your job were fired for dipping into the till, it might not be surprising if he shows a galloping case of paranoia about your honesty.

Superiors, co-workers, and subordinates who are ruthless people can upset you only if you let them. You don't have to play their game. If the situation gets too bad you can always walk. They do not have the power to send you into combat and get you killed, and you don't have to become a mental case because of them. Life is too short for such nonsense.

Money

The Department of Defense has a terrible reputation for wasting money. Justified or not, the Congress, the public, and the news media assume as an article of faith that people associated with the military services look upon money as something to be spent by the fistful, preferably in multiples of a billion. Of course, we know better. Anyone who has endured a New England winter in a drafty World War II "temporary" building or tried to coax one more effort from an ancient generator realizes that the Defense Department is not always rolling in the green stuff.

Military professionals do, however, have a distinctly different attitude toward work and money than civilians do. There are several reasons for this. First, we are one of the few groups in the workforce with no power to negotiate our pay or to pressure our employer. Pay scales are set by law and, like it or not, we receive whatever the government decides on. We can't form unions or walk off the job. Our compensation is a matter of public record down to the penny. There are no Christmas bonuses, no salary discrimination, and no hidden goodies.

The role of money in achieving our institutional goals is that of an input and never an output. The armed forces need money to accomplish their missions, but with few exceptions we do not produce any goods or services used by the nation at large. Our product is national defense, and it is very expensive to produce, so we are accustomed to thinking in large amounts of money. There is often little direct relationship between the cost of defense items and their visibility. Nuclear weapons and ballistic submarines are big-ticket items, but they are seen and operated by very few, whereas an infantry brigade, a comparatively low-cost entity, is very visible.

No wonder civilians think we don't know anything about money. For most organizations, money is the driving force, the primary purpose for the establishment's existence. As self-evident as this fact may seem, it is worth stressing. A former military professional who goes to work for a manufacturing company is likely to assume that the product is all-important. Equating the product with the mission that he is accustomed to placing at the top of his priority list, he will naturally become fixed on the various aspects of production. But he has missed the point. The real purpose of the company is not to make a product but to make money. Even experienced civilian managers can get fooled by this one, especially in an era like the 1980s, when buyouts and takeovers were endemic. Successful companies with good products were taken over and, to the astonishment of traditional managers, closed and the assets sold off. Why? Someone thought more money could be made that way.

Organizations outside the world of commerce are not so closely tied to money as a reason for existence, but it is a determining factor in their lives nevertheless. Teachers don't go on strike for an increase in the finger paint allowance; they strike for more pay. When a clergyman meets with his church elders, the biggest topic of conversation is . . . guess what.

Former military people moving into the civilian world sometimes mistake this concern for a preoccupation with the dollar. But if we refuse to acknowledge the legitimate place of money in the workplace, we risk being seen as the classic stereotype of a military careerist, blissfully unconcerned with where the money is coming from or how much is spent.

Learn to look at your organization the same way the boss does, which will usually have a lot to do with profit, savings, or cost-effectiveness. Becoming profit conscious is one of the best ways to establish yourself as someone with a solid grip on reality. That's why they call it the "bottom line."

RELATIONS WITH YOUR SERVICE

After being retired for a while we develop a variety of attitudes toward our former service. At one extreme is the person who cuts all ties and becomes 100 percent civilian, acting as though a major chunk of life had never existed. At the other end is the unhappy soul who is so lost in his new situation that he clings desperately to yesterday, hoping that shutting out the present will somehow make things better. In between are the rest of us who gradually learn to appreciate the advantages of our new status but enjoy keeping in touch with the military profession and maintaining old friendships.

The first extreme will not directly affect how you live your life after retirement. You will collect retirement pay and be eligible for the same benefits regardless of your attitude. But turning one's back on the past is an impoverishing experience. Most studies of midlife note that an important part of successful transition from one phase of life to another requires a healthy attitude not only toward the future but to the past and present. Our personal history is deeply embedded in us, and to deny it is not natural.

For some people, the last few years of active duty may not have been the best. Too much time in a less than interesting job or the slow realization that the best part of our career was over and that it was time to retire may have caused the most recent memories to be less than ideal. We may have faced retirement with resentment and bitterness and convinced ourselves that we were glad to get away from those SOBs and get started on our own life.

The trouble with this thinking is that it doesn't go away when we end our association with the service. The resentment and anger are directed at different objects—family, job, or ourselves—and lead to problems. People with this attitude can become hypercritical of the military, not realizing that they are condemning something that was very close to them for most of their adult lives and by extension criticizing themselves.

The past cannot be denied. Anyone who retires from the armed forces after a full career has stored up an enormous amount of experience and memories. And most of this experience is worth remembering fondly. No one survives a career filled with danger, challenge, and competition without gaining a great deal of character and a large store of achievement and recognition. These are the parts to remember because they are what made you who you are. If you can accept this view of your past career, you will probably find that after a while you will look forward to the chance to meet old friends, visit places that were once important to you, and maybe even feel a little smug when some young person on active duty says, "Were you *really* there when. . . ?" That feeling is much better than one of bitterness and rejection of a past that can't be changed.

Living in the past can be an equally sterile alternative. Everyone has to face the future sooner or later. By its very nature, transition demands movement from one place in life to another. The train is moving whether or not you are aboard. The retiree who haunts the bar at the club and bores everyone in sight with stories of the "old days" is a pathetic character. This is not the person you once dreamed of being.

It's inevitable that there will be a few twinges of pain after you have been out for a year or so. You will probably discover that the professional knowledge you were so proud of is quickly becoming dated, that there are new faces, new slang, and new points of view. Someone living in the past can be devastated by this experience. When your whole life is built around an attempt to stop time and preserve what used to be, a confrontation with the harsh reality of the present is a depressing experience. Anyone who has ever attended a class reunion is familiar with the "eternal alum," whose best days were in high school or college. Having done nothing worth remembering since then, he insists on reliving old times ad nauseam. He is usually someone to be avoided.

One of the main purposes of this book is to present retirement as a process of transition from one phase of life to another. That journey is one that has to be completed by all of us. We accomplish nothing by blowing up the bridge behind us or by refusing to step across when it is time to move on. A much better alternative is to adapt, and an even better one is to make a new contribution to our service and nation.

A CONTINUING CONTRIBUTION

You don't have to keep your old fatigues in the hall closet or practice celestial navigation on the front lawn to continue your contribution to the nation's defense. Now that you are retired there are other people on active duty who are perfectly capable of taking care of their end of the job. What you *can* do is to put your experience and prestige to work supporting the establishment into which you put so much time and effort. As most military retirees discover, the civilian world owns a wealth of ignorance and misinformation about the armed forces. Cities distant from military installations have almost no contact with the uniformed services. With the end of the draft, the experience of military service once shared by most American families is now much more limited; the general public's knowledge of defense matters is confined to what appears in the mass media. Military towns are not much better. Aside from the small portion of the population that has frequent contact with military organizations or service members, community life is surprisingly insulated from the uniformed populace, sometimes intentionally so.

Retired military people have a marvelous opportunity to improve public awareness of defense issues and to help bridge the gap between military and civilian communities. Veterans' and civic organizations are always eager to listen to someone with personal experience of the armed forces, especially in areas where contact with the military is limited. Business groups, chambers of commerce, and even academics are more interested in hearing what you have to say than you would imagine. Volunteering to speak at a luncheon or talking to a high school class is also fun. It is a fine way to improve our own knowledge of how the "others" think and an excellent opportunity to make new friends (and job contacts, too).

Political activity is another way to make your voice heard. Professional military people pride themselves on being aloof from politics, and though that is a commendable attitude for those still in uniform, it is a good habit to change once you are retired. There is no law or regulation that gives you an excuse for remaining a bystander in the political process. The constituents who shout the loudest are usually the ones who get the most attention from politicians; the famous "silent majority" might have had strong feelings, but their silence did little to achieve their goals. Congress and state governments have been known to come up with some frightening legislative proposals affecting the armed forces, particularly in the areas of retirement and medical benefits. Often, the only defense against the more extreme forms of legislative nonsense has been an active, vocal community of military people mobilized by the various military retirement organizations.

ROCKS AND SHOALS IN THE FIRST YEARS

By this time it should be apparent that you will face psychological and emotional challenges in the first year of retirement from the armed forces. The process of change and adjustment begins when the decision to retire is first made and continues through all of the rest of life, but its impact is felt most acutely in the first year or two. More changes are being made in a short time and more difficult decisions are required. If a person is going to have psychological problems, this is the time they are most likely to occur.

Sociologist Naomi Golan suggests that most complications that can arise during a life transition process can be divided into four categories: inability to separate from the past, inability to make decisions, difficulty in carrying out decisions, and difficulty in weathering the period of adjustment.

Golan also points out the difference between *difficulties* and *problems*. Difficulties are defined as the normal rough spots in life that can eventually be overcome. Problems indicate a more serious situation, probably requiring outside assistance. The line between the two can vary among individuals—an aspect of change that is only a difficulty to one person can be a source of serious problems to another. A difficulty allowed to go unresolved can eventually turn into a problem. An unexpected change in life such as divorce or illness can add a dimension to transition issues that makes even the smallest obstacles hard to overcome.

It may be hard for someone who is doing well at the transition process to imagine why anyone would not do the simple things required for his or her own welfare, but it happens. Every retiree knows of a former colleague or friend who has not been handling the experience very well. His or her name comes up in conversation, and when someone asks, "Whatever happened to. . . ?" we are shocked and saddened to hear stories of divorce, hospitalization, alcoholism, or that most ominous statement of all, "I don't know. ____ just dropped out of sight."

The most tragic thing about personal problems after retirement is that most of them could have been prevented or solved if someone had seen what was happening and taken action. As a group, military people are physically and psychologically sounder than most of the population. Nevertheless, a certain number of us fall by the wayside during the transition process. People who have survived combat, hazardous duty, great stress, and prolonged hardship in their service careers wither away and die within a few years after retirement. Why?

Storms at sea are a powerful natural force that man, with all his technology, cannot prevent, but an experienced seaman learns how to recognize their approach and when to take evasive action or rig for heavy weather. Weather forecasts give warning of dangerous conditions, records of old storm tracks provide additional information, and to the trained eye, the look of the sky and the motion of the sea trigger an intuitive alarm inside the brain. There is no way to make the storm go away. We can't avoid it completely except by never venturing out of port. So we learn how to recognize the danger signals and do the best we can to ride it out.

The next few pages are a rough chart of the storm tracks and warning signs of trouble in the retirement process. Like a weather forecast, they can never be totally certain or completely predictable and accurate. An understanding of how these potential problems occur and some options for dealing with them can, however, make the difference between a hopeful future and a life of unhappiness. This book is not meant to be do-it-yourself psychoanalysis, nor is it a substitute for the support and professional help sometimes needed to solve serious problems. But if any of the conditions described touch a nerve, it may mean that something is not quite right in your life or the life of someone close to you. It might be worth looking into.

Psychological Problems

Some joker once summed up the psychological dictionary by saying that neurotics build castles in the air, psychotics live in the castles, and psychiatrists collect rent. If only it were so simple. Human psychology is so complex and contradictory that even the experts can't agree about what causes mental disorders, let alone how to cure them. Fortunately for us, the range of problems likely to emerge as a result of retirement from the armed forces is fairly limited, and really serious situations are rare enough to be readily apparent. We are more likely to be affected by the beginning signs of trouble than anything else and, with knowledge and perhaps outside help, need never be emotionally or psychologically crippled.

Depression is the most common illness. No one knows for sure, but most psychologists believe that a significant percentage of the population suffers from severe depression at some time and that some are afflicted with it all the time. Depression is not unhappiness. It is a potentially incapacitating condition that can be fatal. The condition is described by one psychologist as follows:

Psychological characteristics of depression include abject and painful sadness, withdrawal of interest and inhibition of activity, and a pervasive pessimism with diminished self-esteem and a gloomy evaluation of the present and the future. Depressed persons often experience difficulty in making decisions, and their thought processes, speech, and movements are significantly slowed down. Physical symptoms include loss of appetite, weight loss, severe fatigue, sleeplessness, constipation, and/or diarrhea. In addition, a considerable rise in anxiety and tension often occurs. . . . Strong self-accusation and feelings of guilt regarding past transgressions may be felt. (Naomi Golan, *Passing through Transition*)

A long, frustrating job search, discontent with your new lifestyle, and financial problems can create conditions to cause some degree of depression. The dangerous part is that a depressed person has progressively less ability to cope with the situations that bring on the illness. Someone who is deeply depressed at not finding work may give up and spend the day immobilized in front of the TV set rather than working on a job search, his dilemma deepening every day until it becomes desperate.

Mild depression is an experience shared by everyone at one time or another and is usually cured by the common-sense approach that is natural to healthy people: we get out and do something about the problem, we talk to family and friends, and after a while it goes away. Serious depression, which doctors call clinical depression, will not go away by itself. One's condition in this situation cannot be evaluated with a drugstore kit or a quiz from a pop psychology magazine. *If there is any doubt in your mind* about the seriousness of the condition, get help while you can. At the worst, an unnecessary call for help can cause a little inconvenience. Failure to take action can bring much more serious consequences.

Stress would seem to be an unlikely problem in the retirement process. A successful military career is filled with stress of all kinds. In training courses we intentionally induce stress day after day so we can teach our people how to do the job under pressure. We look upon it casually as one of the facts of daily life and sometimes even intentionally create it in our environment because that's the way we like it.

In retirement, stress is another animal altogether. Now we are constantly confronted with situations new to us. Frustration at not being able to control our own destiny, the annoyance of having to learn work skills all over again, and uncertainty about our true place in a new world can combine to cause dangerous levels of stress. And it will not be the familiar kind that we used to relish. Instead, it will be the yell at the kids, kick the dog, snarl at the boss brand of stress that brings with it a sensation of helplessness, resentment, and anger. It will probably go away as the rules of the civilian game become familiar and the uncertainties are ironed out. But if it gets worse, it can be a signal to call time out and give thought to what is going wrong. None of us retired so that we could kill ourselves in a new career or a different social situation. Stress, like depression, is a normal part of everyday life when it is at the level of a passing annoyance. When it goes beyond that and begins to affect the way you live, look for outside help.

Anxiety is another area that can get out of control if we are not careful. Feelings of anxiety begin bothering us about the time we take the first concrete step toward a retirement decision, increase as retirement approaches, and lessen as we adapt to our new situation. Change, uncertainty, and fear combine to create an uncomfortable level of anxiety, and as these factors fade, so does the feeling. It is when the feeling doesn't go away that we should begin looking into its possible causes. Normal people worry when they are waiting to hear about the results of a job interview. They feel a bit of fear about moving to a new town without the familiar backstop of the military service to ease the sense of strangeness. The change from normal to unhealthy occurs when the anxiety becomes a permanent unfixed feeling, focusing on nothing in particular and everything in general. Professionals call this "free-floating anxiety," and without treatment it can be incapacitating, extending into all facets of life and causing its victims to live in permanent, irrational fear. If this sensation seems familiar to you, talk it over with someone.

Beyond depression, stress, and anxiety, psychological problems move into the territory best handled by therapists. There isn't any way to look into the mirror and coolly decide that you are a schizophrenic, a manic depressive, or a victim of any other abnormal condition. The rule of thumb is the same that you would use for any other physical concern. If things don't feel right, or if it hurts when it shouldn't, check it out. Psychological problems, especially in challenging situations like the retirement process, are nothing to be ashamed of.

Alcohol and Drugs

According to navy alcohol rehabilitation experts, the average life span of someone who retires with an active drinking problem is twenty-four to thirty-six months. That, no pun intended, is a sobering statistic. Alcohol abuse is one of the nation's most serious health problems, affecting as many as one in three families. The extra strains imposed by retirement are enough to challenge a healthy person. Someone impaired by alcohol or drugs is behind the power curve from the very start and as the stresses build up will become a candidate for serious life-threatening problems.

It's no secret that some people on active duty have long-standing alcohol problems. Despite the services' active substance abuse prevention and rehabilitation programs, not all victims of this disease are discovered. Commanders are sometimes reluctant to confront a senior officer or enlisted service member who is within a year or two of retirement and has a fine career behind him. The problem continues unchecked until retirement, then accelerates until the individual either gets help or is destroyed by the disease.

Progression of the disease is often slowed by the structure and discipline of active-duty life. When retirement takes away that structure and adds the burden of changing a career and adjusting to new living conditions, a situation is created that can speed up the progress of the condition and intensify its effects. Isolation, fear of the future, and the physical debilitation caused by alcohol abuse act together to crush the victim under a burden that eventually becomes impossible to escape without assistance. The planning, decision making, and action required to make the transition from active service to retirement become progressively more difficult for a problem drinker, and as his life begins to come apart, other serious handicaps such as depression and constant anxiety take their toll.

Less visible but perhaps even more dangerous is a problem that does not begin to show until after retirement. The experts disagree on what exactly causes the onset of alcoholic behavior after years of normal social drinking, but they have observed that a crisis in life or a period of great emotional upheaval often causes people with a predisposition to the disease to slip over the line from social to unhealthy drinking. The retiree at the club bar every day may not be a problem drinker at first, but if the habit continues and the causes for his behavior are not addressed, there is a good chance he will become one.

Not everyone who is a heavy drinker is an alcoholic. There are people who can put the stuff away year after year and never seem the worse for it. But they, too, sometimes turn that corner and a bad habit becomes a killing disability. Retirement from the armed forces should be a time to use all the skill and knowledge you have absorbed over the years to move forward into a new and full life. Alcohol abuse can make that future disappear before your eyes. Drinking more than usual to ease the stress and occasional frustration of the transition process or to "take the edge off" a bad day is not necessarily anything to be alarmed about in the short term, but if it becomes habitual, maybe you have something to worry about.

If a person thinks he has a drinking problem, he probably does. All the uniformed services and the VA have an array of alcohol awareness and rehabilitation programs. Getting in touch with the people who can help is not always the easiest thing to do, but it can make the difference between a hopeful future and none at all.

All the bad things about alcohol abuse are equally true of drugs, only more so because drug abuse almost always involves breaking state and federal laws. Getting in trouble with the authorities can not only land you in jail; under certain circumstances it can cost all of those hard-won benefits. Although drug abuse is not as common as alcoholism among the retired community, it does exist. The problem often begins with overuse of a legal medication prescribed for tension, stress, or one of the other side effects of the retirement process. Most doctors are very careful about the quantity of medication and the length of time it can be used, but there are exceptions. Addiction to tranquilizers can occur without the doctor or the victim realizing it. It can be more life-threatening than alcohol. Unpredictable reactions and psychological effects can be bizarre and dangerous.

This is a grim picture, but it is not an exaggeration. Anyone retiring with a chronic, worsening medical problem can expect it to get worse. Alcoholism and drug abuse are no exceptions.

Divorce

At any social event where military retirees gather, the chances are fairly good that at some time you will hear something like: "I used to think I hated it when _____ was away, but now seeing him (or her) at home all the time is driving us both crazy!" The statement is usually not made with real anger. Couples who are having serious problems seldom discuss them so openly. But the joking remark often accurately describes a situation that is anything but funny. Military retirement can be a double whammy for marriage problems. The experience of change places an extra strain on shaky relationships, and it occurs during midlife, when even the most stable people have been known to behave in very odd ways.

A certain amount of change in marriage roles is an inevitable by-product of military retirement. Until now your spouse was often required by the conditions of service life to be relegated to second place behind the ever-present "needs of the service." Career plans and personal ambitions may have been put on hold because of frequent moves, well-loved homes were given up again and again (always just at the time when the lawn finally started to look good), and frequent separations led to a roller-coaster life split between single-parent responsibility and loyal follower of the head of household. Over the years these challenges are bound to create strain in even the best marriages. Only those with a truly saintly disposition can be expected to get through the hectic years of marriage to someone in uniform without developing a few resentments and agenda items of their own.

Retirement, with its implicit promise of change, can bring old discontents and unfulfilled promises to the surface. The retiree, engrossed in the business of adjusting to a new world, starting a new job, and accepting an unfamiliar role, can easily become so self-absorbed that the needs of a spouse take a back seat . . . again. And that can mean trouble. It is a new game now, and having dutifully paid dues for a long while, a spouse may decide that it's time for a new set of rules. You can't shift blame to the service anymore or use promotion requirements as an excuse to have your own way. You will have to listen and compromise.

Like other crisis situations in life, marriage problems can be hard to solve without outside help. Professional or pastoral counseling offers the opportunity for both partners to work out their issues in the presence of an uninterested third party, a referee who is trained to identify causes of disagreement and offer possible solutions. If you have not been successful at including your spouse in retirement plans, counseling may offer a chance to correct mistakes and demonstrate your own willingness to change. The experience can also point out new directions in life that make the effort worth attempting.

Marriage counseling and our best efforts sometimes are not enough. Divorce, like war and drought, happens to the best people at the worst times, and when it does we learn to live with it. After retirement the differences between two people may appear so great that without the bond of a shared military career there is nothing left to hold the marriage together. Divorce becomes the only way out, and we are suddenly in the middle of yet another new and difficult experience.

The emotional aspects of divorce are too deep and complex to be covered here. The books suggested in the bibliography can offer insights into the dynamics of marriage and divorce and are worth reading for someone who feels that his or her marriage may be in trouble. Books cannot take the place of professional or pastoral counseling, and nothing can substitute for a commitment—by both partners—to work harder at the marriage.

There are, however, some practical aspects of the situation that are important to military retirees and will have to be taken into account in almost any divorce. Foremost of these is the question of retirement pay. In many states this is considered property, which goes into the pot to be divided, regardless of financial need or remarriage of a spouse. Division of retirement pay as property does *not* preclude the award of additional alimony. In theory (and occasionally in practice) this can mean that a retiree can lose up to half of his or her retirement pay in a property settlement and more as alimony or child support. The law that permits this (PL 97–252, Former Military Spouse Protection Act) is sex-neutral. Applicability of this and other laws dealing with the effect of divorce on rights and benefits will vary with the length of the marriage, the date the divorce became final, and other considerations. The retired affairs section of each service personnel headquarters can tell you how the law relates to your particular situation.

Problems on the Job

By the time you have been working in a postretirement job for a year, you should have a fairly good idea of how you feel about it. Not everyone settles into the ideal job immediately. Some are not sure what field is most attractive, others get a job opportunity in an unexpected field, and still others go to work because it is necessary and expected. Once your feet are on the ground and the period of major transition is over, that first job may not seem so attractive. Experience in the civilian job world may also suggest that there are other, better alternatives. This is not unusual. An informal survey by the author showed that well over half of a group of retirees changed jobs or career goals within the first few years after leaving the service.

A more difficult problem is discontent caused by other aspects of the job. After a difficult job search, you may have been grateful finally to be offered a well-paying, prestigious position, only to realize after a year or so that you hate everything about it. Dubious ethical practices, office infighting, and a nasty boss can cause disenchantment and the growing feeling of What am I doing here? At the same time, family and old friends from the service are impressed by the job you are in and the great salary you are earning. There is more money available than there ever was in the service. The company gives you a credit card and an expense account much more generous than anything the military ever offered, and you seem to be in line for a promotion.

But you hate the job. Dashing in and out of airports and staying at decent hotels was fun for a while, and the growing bank account still gives you a pleasant feeling. Lately, though, during one of those interminable meetings, you find your thoughts wandering back to the indescribable pleasure of a hot cup of coffee after a long, cold midwatch, or the special excitement of walking out to the flight line on a clear, crisp morning, and you think, Is this the way it's going to be for the rest of my life?

Maybe the time has come to take a hard look at your priorities. Prolonged misery should not be one of the rewards of military retirement. If it is becoming a way of life for you something is wrong. It is either the job or you, and one of those (or both) has to change. Either way there will be a price to pay. Leaving the job means another job search and all the frustration that goes with it. Quitting may also cause personal hardship. If you have become accustomed to a higher standard of living, it may not be easy to go back to a more austere budget. Staying on and accepting the conditions at work will exact a price from you in terms of inner satisfaction, self-respect, and possibly even health if the situation is bad enough.

The worst course of action when you are in this dilemma is to do nothing. Inaction will only lead to steadily increasing strain until something gives way. Being fired, encountering marriage problems, or being perpetually dissatisfied with life will eventually force you to take action. Why wait until then? Life was meant to be lived, not endured. Decide what your goals in life are; talk about them with your spouse, with friends, and if necessary with professional counselors. And then do something about it. The excitement and challenge of a life well lived are among the great satisfactions in the world. Don't let your chance slip away. There are a lot of jobs in the world, but there is only one of you.

TURNING THE CORNER

It might seem at this point that much of the information about the retirement process has focused on challenges, difficulties, and potential problems. In fact, most people going through the experience will encounter few if any of the extreme aspects of transition from military to civilian life. We will work our way through it with the same competence and good humor that we learned in uniform. We will learn the rules, overcome the obstacles, and build good, happy lives. And when we are the old retired character in that Sunday night conversation back in chapter 1, and someone who is about to retire asks us, "What's it *really* like?" we will smile wisely and say, "It was a piece of cake."

9

RETROSPECTIVE

♦

In his mid-seventies, the great historian Samuel Eliot Morison was doing research for his book *The European Discovery of America*. Not content to pore over old manuscripts and reconstruct explorers' voyages in the quiet of his study, Morison went out into the field to see for himself the places described by Magellan and Columbus. On foot, by ship, and in small aircraft, he studied some of the most wild and remote places in the world, always with the delight and enthusiasm of a young man. Flying through the Strait of Magellan and over notorious Cape Horn, Morison saw these places not as desolate spots at the end of the world but as new territory that he would love to sail in his own boat, if only he were younger. "Oh," he wrote wistfully, "to be forty again!"

In a society that sometimes seems obsessed with the need to extend youth to the point of the absurd, Morison's outlook is refreshing. A man who was still writing and working through the last years of an active life, he saw his forties as a time for finding new worlds to conquer. He knew that we do not continue to grow and broaden our perspectives by sitting back and counting the traffic. The idea of drawing back from a challenge and conceding new experiences to the young probably never crossed his mind. He was too busy using every day to learn more about himself and the world he lived in.

After retirement from the armed forces we have the opportunity to live our lives in a way that many people will never be able to achieve. Once the transition from a military career to a new place in the civilian world has been completed, we are at a point of high ground in our lives. While the process was going on, we seemed to be faced with an endless series of new, difficult, and sometimes frightening decisions and changes. But now, having weathered it all, we can look back and realize that we are different from the person who sat down one day not so long ago and, with mixed feelings of sadness and anticipation, wrote out a request for retirement.

That realization does not necessarily come as a sudden "Gee, I'm different now." But if we pause occasionally, as we all should, to look back and take stock of where we are, it becomes apparent that we see the world with an altered outlook. That discovery should not be surprising. Everyone, even the most confident and phlegmatic of us, has crossed one of the watersheds of adult life. The passage may have been as well organized as the best military operation we ever planned or it may have been as rough as a North Sea winter, but we have made it. Added to the experience of an active military career is another dimension, the achievement of change and growth. If that description seems an exaggeration, think about it for a while. Better yet, compare it with what has happened to your civilian friends over the last two years or so. You will see minimal changes in most of them. Except for those who have been forced to cope with change or the bold few who have struck out in a new direction, they seldom experience a sweeping transformation like you did with your military retirement.

BALANCE AND CONSOLIDATION

Our lives take some unexpected directions in the first years after retirement. Issues that seem to be the most important things in life one year are resolved and forgotten the next. Time deals with some things in its own way with or without our intervention. The theme that unites the common experience of retirees who have been through the process is adjustment to change and a shift of focus from coping with the external world to answering questions about our internal selves.

You have arrived at a milestone in life, which, unlike those preceding it, allows time to pause for breath. Time is less critical than it used to be. Our situation in relation to family matters, work, priorities, and other conditions of life is becoming more settled and predictable. There are fewer urgent matters to be dealt with for the simple reason that many of the burning questions of life have been answered by the passage of time. The answers were not always the ones we wanted to hear, but we are learning to accept them. You know now that you are not going to be chairman of the JCS, and you probably won't become a millionaire, but the nagging questions about surviving after retirement, finding a place to live, and getting the kids through college are (or soon will be) behind you. You can look ahead to making more decisions that relate directly to your own happiness and fulfillment, while facing less pressing demands from the rest of the world. The balance between the "must do" for others and the "should do" for yourself has tipped in your favor.

This situation and how it affects you can be described in a number of ways. What you have just read is one of many. Richard Bolles's book *The Three Boxes of Life* describes another. In examining what he calls life/work planning, Bolles looks at life in terms of three "boxes"—education, work, and retirement—and examines the weight given to work, learning, and play while we are in each box. The normal expectation of society is that in each box one activity dominates our lives at the expense of the other two; during the work period of life, education and leisure take a back seat. After retirement, learning and work are less "normal" to society. Bolles's approach to dealing constructively with planning one's life is to work toward a more even balance between activity in *each* of the boxes, and most of his book is devoted to a plan of how to do that.

Military retirees do not fit neatly into any of the three boxes Bolles identifies because of our early retirement age and postretirement work life. Still, his approach is useful as a way of organizing our priorities to strike a better balance between our version of the last two boxes. For us "Bolles Mark II" boxes might be work/retirement and retirement/work, followed by final retirement.

A third approach to thinking about your situation is described by Gail Sheehy in *Pathfinders*. This book, written a few years after her best-selling *Passages,* is based on interviews with dozens of "pathfinders" who have made successful transitions through life. Sheehy sees the issue as a search for well-being, which she defines as "an accumulated attitude, a sustained background tone of equanimity behind the more intense contrasts of daily events, behind even little periods of unhappiness." Sheehy's interviews and the conclusions she draws from them are extensive and worth reading. They restate in a very personal way most of the alternatives that confront a person after retirement.

Like Bolles's boxes, they lead to conclusions valid for those in the phase of life when the turmoil of military retirement has ended and a time of consolidation has begun.

These conclusions are as follows: We are entering a time when personal fulfillment (or as Sheehy defines it, well-being) is assuming a larger role in life. We should strive to balance the various life activities—work, leisure, and learning—throughout our lives rather than following society's expectations. Once the retirement process is complete, we are at neither a pinnacle nor a plateau. We are at a way station for consolidation and beginning the journey into the future.

There are no check-off lists for the future, and a full life doesn't always require development of a master plan. At the same time, arrival at an apparently settled stage of life does not signal the satisfaction of all our goals. Instead, it prompts reexamination of where we have been and raises the question of where we now wish to go. When we ignore this question or refuse to pay attention to it, we stand a good chance of becoming fixed in a rigid, stubborn attitude that denies the existence of the need for a new outlook on our lives. In other words, we get in a rut. Every study and book written on change in later life makes it clear that the alternative to growth and change is stagnation and unhappiness.

Psychologists and philosophers have long recognized the importance of confronting and understanding the differences between the needs of early and later life. Individual experience confirms this principle in action. We have all known older people who are healthy and financially secure yet who drift through lives that have become empty of purpose. Having finished the business of raising a family and establishing a career, they have nothing left to attract their energy. What they thought was their life's direction has come to a dead end, and there is nothing new to replace it.

But why should we worry about new directions and change? What's wrong with just going along day by day without burdening ourselves with thoughts of change and direction? Nothing, really, except that giving a purpose and an aim to our later lives makes them better. In his essay *The Stages of Life,* psychologist Carl Jung concluded, after a lifetime of studying human nature, that "a directed life is in general better, richer and healthier than an aimless one, and that it is better to go forwards with the stream of time than backwards against it."

The suggestions offered in his chapter present some possible ways of going forward with the stream of time. At this point in your life you may not feel the desire to take any action or to bother too much about the future. There's nothing wrong with that. It never hurts, though, to check out a new idea.

POSSIBILITIES: EMPTY NESTS AND FULL LIVES

For those who have decided not to stagnate, the prospects are exciting. Once you have become even a little interested in the possibility of a more interesting future beyond the "normal" work years, a variety of choices unfold. One of the benefits of our society is that more options are available to more people today than ever before in history. Older people can go back to school, learn new skills, and take part in community and social activities that would have been either improper or inaccessible a few decades ago. And as the population of the United States steadily becomes older in the next few years, horizons will continue to broaden.

There are also some very practical reasons for staying away from that ol' rockin' chair. Staying active not only enriches your life, it may actually prolong it. Medical research has proved that there is a powerful link between mental and physical health. Both of these facets of well-being are dependent on keeping active, involved, and engaged in life. A recent survey of retirees from a large midwestern company showed that those who took early retirement because they wanted to "take it easy" developed a much higher rate of illness than those who began second careers and remained active. In another study, nursing-home patients, all over the age of eighty and in poor physical condition, were put on a supervised weight-training program. After a few months of pumping iron, almost all of these octogenarians not only showed improved health, they actually gained back muscle structure they had lost years before. It doesn't seem to make much difference *what* you do; what's important is that you do *something.*

The possibilities that follow are by no means exhaustive. Rather, they are a jumping-off point to suggest new paths worth exploring. By the time each of us reaches the age and the place in life at which they become a subject for thought, we may have changed. But willingness to explore new vistas will always provide the means to find them.

Work

Some people never retire. The end of a second career becomes another transition to new work of a different kind. The big difference is that this final career can be devoted almost exclusively to self-fulfillment. Your job expectations change because there is less pressure to satisfy an employer and more incentive to find a job setting that satisfies you. And that doesn't have to be lofty. A recent study showed that an increasing number of people in the sixty-to-eighty age bracket were taking part-time jobs as grocery baggers and fast food workers, not because they needed the money but because of the satisfaction gained from being a part of life rather than an onlooker. People who work late in life seem to enjoy better health for a longer time. Physical and social activity, according to the experts, is excellent at preventing disease.

The type of work you can do becomes more limited with age, but not as much as you might think. Comparatively few jobs these days are physically demanding, and you don't want one of those anyway. People whose intellectual powers have been their main resource find that with age their job role can be brought into harmony with the tools that age and experience have given them. Many are forced by mandatory retirement or a loss of stamina to give up managerial or supervisory positions. Yet the experience and perspective gained over the years make them an ideal choice for part-time consulting work, which is less demanding but perhaps even more satisfying than the old job. Teaching, in all its varied forms, is a profession that cries out for the experience and judgment of maturity. Rediscovered job needs can make skills you once thought obsolete in high demand. When the navy began recommissioning battleships, the personnel experts were compelled to go to the retired lists to find gunners' mates who could instruct others on the care and feeding of sixteen-inch guns.

Job satisfaction comes easier when the need to compete and advance is removed. A retired senior noncommissioned officer, who had recently retired from his second career as a manager, took a job as a grocery bagger "just to get out of the house" and said he loved the job because other employees were constantly asking him for advice. The only drawback he reported was that salesmen often mistook him for the store manager.

Family

The empty-nest phase of family life has been the subject of much weighty study and hand wringing by psychologists and social scientists. They warn of the effects of loss, the problems that arise when a married couple must live without the buffer of children, and a collection of other potential problems long enough to scare anyone. Apparently they never got around to surveying the couples in their fifties and beyond who are traveling, going to school, working at jobs they like, and generally enjoying life in blissful ignorance of what the experts say.

The time when children are grown can be one of the most pleasant of all periods in a family's life. Husband and wife have more time for each other and for their individual interests. Relationships with children can be close enough to be warm but distant enough to give everyone needed breathing space. It can even be a good time for families with problems. The perspective given by separation offers a chance to see old disagreements in a different light, and time itself can heal all but the deepest domestic wounds. As you and your children get older they will probably think you are becoming wiser, whether you are or not. The new role of counselor and adviser can be very satisfying, especially since you usually won't have to pick up the check. And if your relationship with your children is a good one, they may be able to advise *you* now and then.

Community Involvement

After a successful military career and a few years in the civilian world, service retirees possess a blend of civic skills and experience too valuable to be wasted. There is always a need for organizational and leadership talent at all levels of the community. Volunteer service organizations in most areas are chronically short of help. The ability to walk into a new situation, roll up your sleeves, and get the job done is almost second nature to career service people; when you get involved in community and volunteer work you will find that it is not a universal talent. Few institutions teach hands-on leadership as well as the armed forces do.

The American Association of Retired Persons (AARP) is an organization that has steadily increased in both power and size. It is now a significant force in community, state, and national politics. In addition to offering a broad range of benefits and assistance to its members the AARP is in the vanguard of most legislation and government policy relating to older and retired people. Membership is open to anyone who is 50 or older. You should join as soon as you hit "the big five-oh." The modest membership fee will be a worthwhile investment.

People sometimes discover new interests and unexpected talents by working in the volunteer arena. Involvement in advocacy projects like day care centers and improved parks for children has been known to fire a renewed sense of purpose in life and can become the starting point for an unexpected career in local politics.

Most important is the pride and deep personal satisfaction that come with helping others and making a contribution beyond satisfying one's own personal happiness. It's a feeling you had about the special relationship you had with your service, and maybe you have not really recaptured it since retirement. Being an active, helping part of the community keeps you in touch with life outside yourself and satisfies the fundamental urge to leave something good in the world to mark your passage. As Gail Sheehy wrote in *Pathfinders,* "Involvement may not be noisy or dramatic or even public, but it connects the individual to his or her neighborhood or culture at more than the level of 'Dear

Occupant.' As much as does helping a friend in trouble or despair, [community] purpose makes a person feel good. It is a friendship for the world."

Learning and Creating

Conventional wisdom used to dictate that after a certain age learning ability decreased too much to make education worthwhile. Social expectations reinforced this belief. To many people, the idea of their parents going back to school was a little embarrassing, especially if the old folks enjoyed the experience. Grade B movies and TV sitcoms did their part to discourage older people from thinking about continuing education by making the experience look as ridiculous as possible.

While all this was going on, tens of thousands of people over forty were going back to school, getting degrees, and confounding the psychologists by consistently scoring higher on tests than their younger classmates. Taking their example from the bumblebee, they ignored the calculations and flew anyway. Today, gray hair is a common sight on campuses, and many schools offer free or cut-rate tuition to people over a certain age. There is less reason not to go back to school than there ever was.

The Elderhostel organization is one example of a program that is designed specifically for older people interested in broadening their knowledge of the world and themselves. In cooperation with a number of colleges and universities, the program offers a catalog of short courses on campuses all over the nation. Costs are moderate ($200 to $300 a week, including lodging and meals) for the courses, which are conducted during summer vacations and other school holidays. Similar programs on a smaller scale exist all over the nation. Their value is not only in the educational experience they offer but also in the intellectual stimulation they give. This is an important benefit. It is an established fact that mental fitness, like physical fitness, must be maintained by exercise. Creative people like Samuel Eliot Morison, Helen Santmeyer, and Albert Einstein were vital and intellectually adept in their later years because they never stopped thinking and learning. Age may get to your legs and dim your vision, but a well-exercised mind keeps right on churning out ideas.

The greatest intellectual achievements sometimes come in the second half of life. Between the two world wars, Winston Churchill was thought to be "finished," and he spent years out of government, seemingly in self-imposed exile. Yet during that temporary retirement he wrote historical and biographical works that have become classics. And after World War II, when he was again voted out of office, Churchill completed the six-volume history of the war and, later, the four-volume *History of the English-Speaking Peoples.*

One reason for the continued creativity and accomplishment of people like Churchill seems to be an unquenchable thirst for knowledge and an ability to maintain an almost childlike curiosity about the world around them. Heinrich Schliemann, the amateur archaeologist who discovered Troy, was a businessman until middle age. Then, driven by a lifelong fascination with the ancient world, he retired from commerce and set out on an intellectual adventure that was to occupy the rest of his life.

Not everyone has to dig up old cities or write books to stay creatively active. Most of us have a dream that has been gathering dust for years because the time was never right. It could be learning to make pottery, rebuilding antique furniture, or researching and writing a family history. The creative act does not always have to have cosmic significance. The process of creating is fulfilling enough. It is an affirmation that we are alive and connected with the world outside ourselves.

THE LONG ROAD

There are goals beyond change and growth. At various times in our lives all of us feel the need for a philosophy of life. We seldom state the question in such formal terms, but there is something in everyone that demands that what we do have meaning. The question of meaning and purpose surfaces again and again, expressing itself in the rebellious questioning of everything in youth and in the somber late-night thoughts of middle age. Some find their answers easily and quickly; others remain searchers throughout their lives.

In its own way, each of the issues discussed in this book is one expression of that search for meaning and purpose. Retirement from a military service is a turning point in life, not only because it brings upheaval and change but also because it raises again that most fundamental question of life: Who am I and where am I bound?

We do not answer that question by going off to Tibet to seek enlightenment or by sitting on top of a mountain waiting for a message. The answer comes in the way we choose to live our lives. The values that we make our own in the ordinary day-to-day business of living define us better than any manifesto. Career military people, whether they are on active duty, newly retired, or years from their last day in uniform, have a special source of satisfaction when they look back on the high points of their life in the service. We possess a wealth of achievements and contributions and at its core the knowledge that our time in uniform had a meaning. We are bashful patriots who like to pretend that our service was nothing more than an ordinary job, but the principles we lived by during the greater part of our adult lives were no ordinary principles and our dedication no ordinary dedication.

All through the transition from military career to civilian life there will be good reasons given to abandon that value system and replace it with one that is more "useful" or "realistic." It will be easy to mistake expedience for adaptation and self-deception for compromise. But before discarding a set of ethics we know and are proud of, we must carefully examine what is to replace it. When the days of active service are behind us and our daily contact with the men and women with whom we served is ended, new and conflicting demands on our values will challenge us. Our old values will be questioned by representatives of a society that often sees the armed forces only in stereotype. Principles may be tested on the job by a philosophy that measures no other value but the bottom line. At those times we owe it to ourselves and to our colleagues still in uniform to remember that the oath we all swore was more than a bloodless legal agreement; it was a promise to ourselves and to the future.

Appendix A
SAMPLE LETTER TO A RECRUITER

(Your Letterhead)

Date

Recruiter's Address

Dear Mr. Smith:

I am beginning a job search, and it was suggested that I get in touch with you.

My objective is a position in electronics systems integration in an aerospace-oriented company. I consider my greatest strength to be in defense-related avionics and have a total of five years' experience as a project manager in that field. I also have three years' experience in defense contract preparation, review, and evaluation and hold an MSEE from the University of Illinois.

My present salary is $42,000 plus benefits. I would anticipate a position with a total financial package in approximately the same range.

My geographic preference is for the West Coast or the Southwest.

If one of your clients is seeking someone with my background, experience, and qualifications, please give me a call. I would also like the opportunity to meet with you and discuss any positions that may be available.

Sincerely,

Attachment: (Your résumé)

(*Note:* Information on salary and geographic preference is optional.)

Appendix B

SAMPLE LETTER IN RESPONSE TO
AN ADVERTISEMENT

(Your Letterhead)

Date

Address (from ad)

Dear _____

I am writing in response to your advertisement in the June 30 *New York Times* for a precision machining quality assurance supervisor. I am enthusiastic about the opportunity to work in the quality assurance field and believe that I possess the qualifications you require. In my 12 years' experience in precision machining and supervision I have

—*Supervised* an engine repair and inspection shop and was responsible for all quality assurance.

—*Certified* as a laser surface measurement technician and supervised the training and qualification of other technicians.

—*Managed and Supervised* a computer-based quality assurance documentation system.

—*Developed* a new in-process precision engine balance checking system.

I am very interested in this opportunity and look forward to discussing my qualifications with you in more detail.

Sincerely,

(Note: Qualifications in the letter should all refer to those described in the ad. If you do not have all the qualifications sought by the advertiser, *do not* mention the ones you lack.)

Appendix C
SUGGESTED RECORDS FOR A JOB SEARCH

The following is a typical list of records that should be kept to monitor the progress of your job search. They will also help you evaluate which methods are working best for you.

Format and layout are matters of individual preference. Don't get so wrapped up in record keeping that it becomes a chore or an end in itself. The object is to get a job, not pass an administrative inspection.

1. *Telephone log:* To record all job-search-related incoming and outgoing calls. Include a space to note the city called and length of the call.*

2. *Expense record:* Save receipts and sales slips for all job-search-related expenses. Record amount and dates. Log trip expenses and mileage.*

3. *Replies to ads:* Use a looseleaf binder with clear plastic inserts to save ads. File copies of response letters and replies.

4. *Networking log:* Create a form to track all networking activity, including:

  Name of contact
  Source of contact
  Contact's organization and title
  Date of initial contact

*Possible tax-deductible items.

Date of follow-up
Remarks

5. *Job decision matrix:* Create a form to include job decision categories. These should include as a minimum:

Salary
Other compensation
Advancement potential
Location
Organization's reputation/standing
Job satisfaction potential

Use a grading system to evaluate these and any other categories you choose. The system may be a simple upcheck or downcheck, a one to five, or a one to ten system. If one factor is more important than others (e.g., location), weight it accordingly. Don't make the system too complicated or sophisticated. If you do, it will be too much trouble to use and you will not benefit from it.

6. *Recruiter/agency list:* List all recruiters and agencies contacted.* Include dates and responses.

7. *Market/broadcast letter record:* List all organizations for each mailing and the date of the mailing.* Group responses to each mailing to check effectiveness of your letter and your targeting.

8. *Interview notes:* Save your notes on all interviews to help in analyzing your strong and weak points. Include a follow-up checkoff to ensure that you remember to send thank you notes.

Appendix D
SAMPLE RÉSUMÉ

Your Address
(Centered)

Telephone number

**JOB
OBJECTIVE:** *Personnel Director/Human Resources Manager* in a financial services or financial management organization requiring an individual with experience in personnel security and vocational testing and training program development.

EXPERIENCE:
Personnel
Security:

Security Manager, Smith Air Force Base. Managed all phases of a personnel security and screening system for 2,000 military and 600 civilian personnel. Supervised a security office employing 12 technical and 55 security/administrative personnel.

Installed and Managed a prototype computer-based screening and documentation system without assistance from outside contractors. Saved $250,000 in contractor costs.

Reorganized security clearance documentation system to reduce duplication. Won annual cost-reduction award.

Established new vendor security system, which reduced pilferage by 25% in one year.

Personnel Management:

Head, Personnel Directorate at Military Airlift Command Headquarters. Developed personnel assignment standards, directed personnel planning at a major headquarters consisting of 270 officers, 1,300 enlisted personnel, and 77 civilian employees. Managed a $900,000 budget.

Introduced a streamlined check-in and orientation system; which reduced processing time for new personnel from two weeks to one week. Resulted in annual savings of 1,000 man/days.

Instituted individual recognition and incentive program for civilian personnel. Commended in writing by commanding general.

Vocational Testing, Training:

Deputy Director of an air force technical school training an average of 80 students per year. Devised testing methods and standards, developed training plans, and supervised instructors. Conducted and analyzed vocational/aptitude testing for all incoming students.

Converted old "pencil and paper" testing system to ADP-compatible system and adapted on-site computers to run system at no additional cost. Promoted to major.

Directed and Supervised complete revision of school curriculum to take advantage of new programmed instruction methods. Reduced instructor requirements from 24 to 18.

EDUCATION: B.A. Psychology, Michigan State University. Dean's list.

Management graduate degree equivalent (10-month mid-level course in residence), Industrial College of the Armed Forces.

Earned 18 hours graduate-level credit in personnel management through evening school classes, Boston University. Average 3.5 on 4.0 grading system.

Completed 3-month Department of Defense security managers course. Top 5% of class of 50.

PERSONAL: Chairman, United Fund drive, Peoria Illinois, 1986. "Young Man of the Year," Wichita, Kansas, Chamber of Commerce, 1984. Married, 2 children. Completed service in U.S. Air Force in rank of lieutenant colonel.

Notes on Sample Résumé

• Major headings, job titles, and lead verb of achievement subparagraphs should be in bold lettering.
• If the experience supporting your job objective is continuous with no breaks for nonrelevant assignments, use dates with each job paragraph.
• Include grade point average or class standing only if it is above a "B" average.
• Do not include number of years served in armed forces. This is an age tip-off.
• Try for two to three examples of achievement per job. Do not include experience that is not significant to job objective.

• Job objective may be more or less specific than the example, but experience *must* support the objective.

• The résumé should be no longer than two pages.

• For some technical or systems-oriented jobs, major headings titled EQUIPMENT QUALIFICATIONS, CERTIFICATIONS, LICENSES should be used.

SELECT BIBLIOGRAPHY

Chapter 1

Bolles, Richard N. *Where Do I Go from Here with the Rest of My Life.* Berkeley: Ten Speed Press, 1974.

Bowman, Thomas F. *Finding Your Best Place to Live in America.* New York: Red Lion, 1982.

Boyer, Richard. *Places Rated Almanac.* New York: Rand McNally, 1989.

Ford, Norman G. *The 50 Healthiest Places to Live and Retire in the United States.* New York: Ballantine, 1991.

Gross, Andrea. *Shifting Gears; Finding a New Strategy for Midlife.* New York: Crown, 1991.

Non Commissioned Officers Association of the USA (NCOA). *Analysis of Government Benefits and Personal Affairs Inventory.* P.O. Box 33610, San Antonio, Tex. 78265.

Retired Officers Associations, The. *Help Your Surviving Spouse—Now!* The Retired Officers Association, 201 N. Washington St., Alexandria, Va. 22314.

———. *SBP Made Easy.* 1993.

Sheehy, Gail. *Passages.* New York: Bantam, 1981.

USAA Foundation. *Leaving the Military: Your Guide to Separation and Retirement.* USAA Publication #508. USAA Foundation (to order, telephone 1-800-531-6131). 1993.

Government Publications

Bureau of Naval Personnel. *Navy Guide for Retired Personnel and Their Families* (NAVPERS 15891G).

Department of the Air Force. *Retirement Processing Package* (AFR-35-7).

Department of the Army. *Handbook on Retirement Services for Army Personnel and Their Families* (DA-Pam-600-5).

Department of Defense. *The CHAMPUS Handbook.*

Department of Labor. *Transition Assistance Program.*

Chapter 2

American Council on Education. *Guide to Evaluation of Educational Experience in the Armed Forces.* Riverside, N.J.: McMillan, 1989.

Banford, Janet. *The Consumer Reports Money Book.* Yonkers, N.Y.: Consumer Reports, 1992.

Bly, Robert W., and Gary Blake. *Out on Your Own.* New York: Wiley, 1986.

Cort-Van Arsdale, Diana, and Phyllis Newman. *Transitions; A Woman's Guide to Successful Retirement.* New York: Harper-Collins, 1991.

Golan, Naomi. *Passing through Transitions.* New York: Free Press, 1981.

Quinn, Jane Bryant. *Making the Most of Your Money.* New York: Simon and Schuster, 1991.

Retired Officers Associations, The. *Planning for Military Retirement.* 201 N. Washington St., Alexandria, Va. 22314-2529, 1994.

Schlacter, Gail Ann. *Financial Aid for Veterans, Military Personnel and Their Families.* San Carlos, Calif.: Reference Service Press, 1990.

Uniformed Services Almanac, Inc. *The Retired Military Almanac.* P.O. Box 76, Washington, D.C. 20044. Annual.

Government Pamphlets

Department of Defense. *Once a Veteran: The Transition to Civilian Life* (DOD PA 5G). Washington, D.C., 1992.

Federal Benefits for Veterans and Dependents. Washington D.C.: U.S. Government Printing Office, 1993.

Chapter 3

Barrett, James, and Geoffrey Williams. *Test Your Own Job Aptitude.* New York: Penguin, 1992.

Bolles, Richard. *The Three Boxes of Life.* Berkeley: Ten Speed Press, 1981.

Budahn, P. J. *Drawdown Survival Guide.* Annapolis, Md.: Naval Institute Press, 1993.

Caple, John. *The Right Work: Finding It and Making It Right.* New York: Dodd, Mead, 1987.

Gale, Barry. *Discover What You're Good At: The National Career Aptitude System and Career Directory.* New York: Simon and Schuster, 1990.

Hopke, William E., ed. *The Encyclopedia of Careers and Vocational Guidance.* Chicago: J. G. Ferguson, 1993.

Hyatt, Carole. *Shifting Gears: How to Master Career Change and Find the Work That's Right for You.* New York: Simon and Schuster, 1990.

National Forum Foundation. *Guide for Occupational Exploration.* Circle Pines, Minn.: AGS Publishers, 1984.

Nyman, Keith. *Reentry: Turning Your Military Experience into Civilian.* Mechanicsburg, Pa.: Stackpole, 1990.

Schein, Edgar H. *Career Anchors: Discovering Your Real Values.* San Diego, Calif.: University Associates, 1985.

Government Documents

Department of Labor. *Dictionary of Occupational Titles.* Washington, D.C.: U.S. Government Printing Office, 1991.

Chapter 4

Brabec, Barbara. *Homemade Money: The Ultimate Guide to Success in Homebased Business.* Crozet, Va.: Betterway Publications, 1989.

Creedy, Richard F. *Steps to Professional Independence.* New York: Madison, 1988.

Feingold, Norman. *Making It on Your Own*. Washington, D.C.: Acropolis, 1981.

Fine, Janet. *Opportunities in Teaching Careers*. Chicago: VGM Career Horizons, 1989.

Foster, Dennis F. *The Complete Franchise Book*. Rocklin, Calif.: Prima Publishers, 1988.

Hammer, Hy. *The Civil Service Handbook*. New York: Arco, 1988.

Jessup, Claudia. *The Woman's Guide to Starting a Business*. New York: H. Holt, 1991.

Johnston, J. Phillips. *Success in Small Business is a Laughing Matter*. Wake Forest, N.C.: Meridional Publications, 1982.

Mancuso, Joseph. *Have You Got What It Takes? How to Tell if YOU Should Start Your Own Business*. Englewood Cliffs, N.J.: Prentice-Hall, 1981.

Potter, Beverly A. *Maverick Career Strategies*. New York: American Management Association, 1984.

Sullivan, Nick. *Computer Power for Your Small Business*. New York: American Management Association, 1991.

Tepper, Ron. *Become a Top Consultant*. New York: Wiley, 1985.

Whittesley, Marietta. *Freelance Forever: Successful Self-Employment*. New York: Avon, 1985.

Periodicals

Consultants News. Kennedy and Kennedy, Inc., Templeton Road, Fitzwilliam, N.H. 93447. Monthly.

Consulting Opportunities Journal. 1629 K St., Suite 520, Washington, D.C., 20006.

Government Publications

Department of Defense Dependent Schools (DODDS). *Employment Opportunities for Education Overseas*. Alexandria, Va.: 1987.

Small Business Administration, Office of Business Development. *Starting and Managing a Small Business of Your Own*. Washington, D.C., 1981.

Chapter 5

Bolles, Richard. *What Color is Your Parachute?* Berkeley: Ten Speed Press, 1994. Updated periodically.

Connor, Richard A., and Jeffrey P. Davidson. *Marketing Your Consulting and Professional Services.* New York: Wiley, 1990.

Henderson, David G. *Job Search: Marketing Your Military Experience in the 1990's.* Mechanicsburg, Pa.: Stackpole, 1990.

Jackson, Tom. *Guerilla Tactics in the Job Market.* New York: Bantam, 1991.

Kennedy and Kennedy, Inc., *The Directory of Executive Recruiters.* Kennedy and Kennedy. Templeton Rd., Fitzwilliam, N.H.: Updated annually.

Retired Officers Association, The. *Marketing Yourself for a Second Career.* The Retired Officers Association, 201 N. Washington St., Alexandria, Va. 22314-2529, 1993.

Standard and Poor's Corporation. *Standard and Poor's Register of Corporations, Directors and Executives.* New York. Updated periodically.

Vogel, Stephen E. *Directory of Employment Opportunities in the Federal Government.* New York: Arco, 1985.

Wood, Orrin G. *Your Hidden Assets.* Homewood, Ill.: Dow Jones Irwin, 1982.

Periodicals

National Ad Search. Published by National Ad Search, Inc., 2328 W. Daphne Rd., Milwaukee, Wis. 53209.

National Business Employment Weekly. Published by the *Wall Street Journal,* Dow Jones, Inc., 420 Lexington Ave., New York, N.Y. 10170.

Chapter 6

Bixler, Susan. *The Professional Image: The Total Program for Marketing Yourself Visually.* New York: Putnam, 1984.

Fitzpatrick, William G. *Does Your Resume Wear Combat Boots?* Charlottesville, Va.: Blue Jeans Press, 1990.

Freedman, Howard S. *How to Get a Headhunter to Call.* New York: Wiley, 1986.

Hizer, David, and Arthur Rosenberg. *The Resume Handbook.* Boston: Bob Adams, 1990.

Ilich, John, and Barbara Davis. *Successful Negotiating Strategies for Women.* Reading, Mass.: Addison-Wesley, 1981.

Molloy, John W. *The New Dress for Success Book.* New York: Warner, 1988.

Petras, Kathryn, and Ross Petras. *The Over 40 Job Guide.* New York: Simon and Schuster/Poseidon, 1993.

Studner, Peter K. *Super Job Search: The Complete Manual for Job Seekers and Career Changers.* Los Angeles: Jemeniar, 1991.

Wendelton, Kate. *Through the Brick Wall: How to Job-Hunt in a Tight Market.* New York: Villard, 1992.

Chapter 7

Bingham, Mindy, and Sandy Stryker. *More Choices: A Strategic Planning Guide for Mixing Career and Family.* Santa Barbara, Calif.: Advocacy Press, 1987.

Bradford, Leland P., and Martha I. Bradford. *Retirement: Coping with Emotional Upheaval.* Chicago: Nelson-Hall, 1979.

Curran, Dolores. *Stress and the Healthy Family.* Oak Grove, Minn.: Winston Press, 1985.

————. *Traits of a Healthy Family.* Oak Grove, Minn.: Winston Press, 1983.

Jones, Rochelle. *The Big Switch: New Lives and New Careers After 40.* New York: McGraw-Hill, 1980.

Lauer, Robert H. *Watersheds: Living with Life's Unpredictable Crises.* Boston: Little, Brown, 1988.

Powell, Barbara. *Alone, Alive and Well.* Emmaus, Pa.: Rodale Press, 1985.

Vickers, Ray. *The Dow Jones Irwin Guide to Retirement.* Homewood, Ill.: Dow Jones-Irwin, 1989.

Chapter 8

Bell, Robert. *You Can Win at Office Politics.* New York: New York Times Books, 1984.

Hatton, Hap, and Laura Talbot. *Helpful Hints for Hard Times: How to Live It Up While Cutting Down.* New York: Facts on File, 1983.

Lareau, William. *Conduct Expected: The Unwritten Rules for a Successful Business Career.* Piscataway, N.J.: New Century, 1985.

Waitley, Dennis, and Reni L. Witt. *The Joy of Working.* New York: Dodd, Mead, 1985.

Chapter 9

Cooper, Cary L., and Derek P. Torrington. *After Forty: The Time for Achievement?* New York: Wiley, 1981.

Ellison, Jerome. *Life's Second Half: The Pleasures of Aging.* Greenwich, Conn.: Adair, 1978.

Epictetus. *The Enchiridion.* New York: Bobbs-Merrill, 1955.

Jung, Carl. *Modern Man in Search of a Soul.* New York: Harvest/ HBJ, 1933.

LeShan, Eda. *Oh to Be 50 Again!* New York: New York Times Books, 1986.

———. *The Wonderful Crisis of Middle Age.* New York: Warner, 1973.

Marcus Aurelius. *Meditations.* In *The Outline of Knowledge,* vol. 13. New York: Richards, 1924.

Sheehy, Gail. *Pathfinders.* New York: William Morrow, 1981.

Turk, Ruth. *You're Getting Older, So What?* Independence, Mo.: Herald, 1976.

INDEX

ABOUT THE AUTHOR

K. C. Jacobsen retired as a captain from the U.S. Navy in 1986 after twenty-six years of military service. Since then he has conducted seminars in job search and career transitioning for private industry, worked as a corporate outplacement counselor, and served as a consultant to Virginia's attorney general. He also regularly writes articles on defense-related issues for newspapers and national magazines.

During his naval career Jacobsen served as the commanding officer of the frigate *Valdez* and earned several personal decorations, including the Bronze Star and four Navy Commendation Medals with Combat "V." A 1960 graduate of the University of Louisville, he holds a master's degree in international affairs from George Washington University, attended the Naval War College, and has lectured widely on national security affairs.

Captain Jacobsen is the reviser and editor of the eleventh edition of the Naval Institute's *Watch Officer's Guide* and has written articles for the U.S. Naval Institute *Proceedings*. A native of Brooklyn, New York, he now resides in Louisville, Kentucky.

The **Naval Institute Press** is the book-publishing arm of the U.S. Naval Institute, a private, nonprofit society for sea service professionals and others who share an interest in naval and maritime affairs. Established in 1873 at the U.S. Naval Academy in Annapolis, Maryland, where its offices remain, today the Naval Institute has more than 100,000 members worldwide.

Members of the Naval Institute receive the influential monthly magazine *Proceedings* and discounts on fine nautical prints, ship and aircraft photos, and subscriptions to the bimonthly *Naval History* magazine. They also have access to the transcripts of the Institute's Oral History Program and get discounted admission to any of the Institute-sponsored seminars offered around the country.

The Naval Institute's book-publishing program, begun in 1898 with basic guides to naval practices, has broadened its scope in recent years to include books of more general interest. Now the Naval Institute Press publishes more than seventy titles each year, ranging from how-to books on boating and navigation to battle histories, biographies, ship and aircraft guides, and novels. Institute members receive discounts on the Press's nearly 400 books in print.

Full-time students are eligible for special half-price membership rates. Life memberships are also available.

For a free catalog describing Naval Institute Press books currently available, and for further information about U.S. Naval Institute membership, please write to:

Membership & Communications Department
U.S. Naval Institute
118 Maryland Avenue
Annapolis, Maryland 21402-5035

Or call, toll-free, (800) 233-USNI.